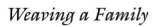

Weaving a Family

Weaving a Family

Untangling Race and Adoption

Barbara Katz Rothman

Beacon Press
Boston

Beacon Press books
are published under the auspices of
the Unitarian Universalist Association of Congregations.

08 07 06 05 8 7 6 5 4 3 2 1

This book is printed on acid-free paper that meets the uncoated paper
ANSI/NISO specifications for permanence as revised in 1992.

Text design by Patricia Duque Campos
Composition by Wilsted & Taylor Publishing Services

LIBRARY OF CONGRESS CATALOGING-IN-PUBLICATION DATA
Rothman, Barbara Katz.
     Weaving a family : untangling race and adoption /
Barbara Katz Rothman.— 1st ed.
        p. cm.
     Includes bibliographical references and index.
     ISBN 0-8070-2828-2 (cloth : alk. paper)
     1. Interracial adoption—United States. 2. Interracial
adoption—United States—Case studies. I. Title.

        HV875.64.R68 2005
        362.734′089′00973—dc22   2004021448

To Cassie, Alexandra, Victoria,
Samantha, and Kaylee, with love

Contents

Preface
A Word on Theory, Method, Language
(and Source Notes)[1]

This book is written in the vernacular. It relies heavily on spoken English. For a sociologist writing in the early part of the twenty-first century, this is an unusual choice of language. "You write well," my colleagues tell me, as my professors used to — and it's not always a compliment. If things are too easy to read, they don't always sound serious.

Different languages are suited to different tasks. Academic language obscures feelings and heightens (if obfuscates) intellectual content. The vernacular obscures the theoretical and intellectual substrate and displays emotive content.

It would be a mistake to read academic language and think it is devoid of values, feelings, or experience. It is no less a mistake to read the vernacular and think it is devoid of theory and research.

The language I've chosen is ordinary, everyday English, and that language is a rich and nuanced one. My word choices are deliberate, reflecting my values and politics. I'm writing about raising children, and about race. We have so many words to use for each of these ideas, each so fraught. I am choosing to use the word "mothering" rather than "parenting" to refer to this intimate, nurturing work of childrearing, which is done by both men and women[2]—and more on that later. As to race: I've thought long and hard about what to call "black" and "white" people, and settled on just this: deliberately not capitalized. I'm going to be talking about "race" and "ethnicity." Black and white are not ethnicities, or cultural categories, the way African-American or Irish-American or Haitian-American or Korean-American or even Midwestern-American might be. And race, as a way of categorizing people, doesn't deserve the formal recognition that a capitalized title would give it. So for now, between the time we have acknowledged that race doesn't exist as a biological category, and the time I hope for, when it ceases to exist as a meaningful social category, I'll settle for "black and white."

But it's not only language that makes this book look different from most sociological work: this is also a personal book, one that grows out of and is informed by my life. Some sociologists call such work "autoethnography,"[3] to distinguish it from simple memoir. In memoir, the driving force is the story: you want to tell your life. In autoethnography, your life is data.

This is closer to the latter, but not quite. What I am doing here is pretty much what I do in the classroom. The driving force is neither the story nor my life as data. In writing this book, I have a number of concepts I want to get across. I search for examples, and draw from whatever is available to me. That includes my life.

On the other hand, my life is also what gives me some of my ideas: concepts develop out of living. Experience congeals into an idea. Then when I go to express the idea, I draw upon my life. I'm not searching my life for interesting scenes and seeing how I can fit them into a book, the way I would if I were doing memoir. I'm wrestling with ideas, ideas that have often come to me in the course of living my life. I use my writing to try to explain these ideas, introduce them to others.

Inevitably, then, in this book I'll slide back and forth between memoir and sociology, treading recklessly close to what my colleague Juan Battle calls "me-search" rather than research. "What theory are you using?" one of my graduate students asked me at a party when I described this project. She's doing a dissertation: she listed the theorists that seemed appropriate. I stammered answers—we're at a party, not an exam. I sipped my wine. Hell, I thought, I'm not using theory here, I'm using practice. But practice is, for all of us, grounded in theory, in ideology, in ways of thinking about the world. I'm a sociologist: I'm more a sociologist than I am a Jew. It's my way of thinking, my stance in the world. So this is a book about sociology and motherhood and race and adoption, my attempt to weave it all together.

Weaving is my metaphor here. We weave our way in the world, moving around the obstacles, wandering on and off our paths, weaving our way along. We weave things that seem disparate together: ideas, theories, stories. We weave people together into families and communities, creating the web, the fabric of life. And—my source for this metaphor—we weave hair, white fingers learning to braid and plait and grease and comb a black child's hair—and in doing that, maybe more than in any single other act, we work to weave a black child into a white family, and weave that child into the black community.

I
Personal Strands

I
Family, Obviously

This book is about how we weave a family, how we weave ourselves into the world through familial ties.

Mostly, that's the kind of thing people don't even notice. We just do it. We take our kids off to grandma's, drive six hours to wherever our sister lives with a quart of cranberry sauce for Thanksgiving, stop everything and do a bedside vigil when a mother-in-law is dying, wrap endless piles of gifts for our nieces and nephews for birthdays and Christmas or Chanukah or whatever potlatch we celebrate.

The ice-cream truck rings and the little children swarm to the street and cluster at the truck with their assigned grownup. Two kids and a woman with dusty jeans come out of one house, one kid and a guy with a dishtowel out of another, three and a woman with her hair tied back with a flowered scarf out of the third house down, a really little one carried by a woman with her shirt buttoned wrong out of the house next door.

Mostly we "read" these clusters as families. Or not. That woman with her hair tied back—she's black and the three kids are all blonde, their straight, wispy hair flying from matching ponytail holders. Oh, that one's a nanny. A quick glance at them and we think we've "got" the story. And we probably do.

Victoria and I come out. She's about five years old. When the ice-cream guy turns to me I give her a look, her last chance to change her mind yet again, and then I order the weirdest, bluest thing he has, preferably with a bubblegum nose. He hands it to me, takes my two dollars, gives me my quarter back, and turns to Victoria: And what do you want? She looks at me, shakes her head and says, "I hate when that happens."

What happened was that we were not seen as a family. That wasn't actually my block I described—I don't think you could find three blonde kids on my block, in this decade. And my ice cream guy knows us. But that is the story of our lives together. We don't look like a family. I'm white, and Victoria is black. So we've learned, over the years, the little tricks we need, to make you see us as a family. I learned to stand behind her with my hand clearly on her shoulder when we rang the violin teacher's door. "Hello, I'm Barbara and this is my daughter Victoria," I say before the teacher can so much as open her mouth. And put her foot in it. I call Victoria "my daughter" like a newlywed on a fifties sitcom said "my husband." Often. With a big smile. Straight at you.

Victoria and I "do" family, "present" as family, the way that a transsexual does gender, presents as female. We're just doing what "normal" people do, but we *know* we're doing it.

I think of Agnes, a transsexual that Harold Garfinkel interviewed.[1] Garfinkel was an ethnomethodologist, developing an approach to sociology that tries to "unpack" how people get through everyday life. Part of how we do it is to explain ourselves to ourselves, construct narrative, make a coherent story— as I am doing in this book, making sense out of my life as a mother. Ethnomethodology, in this close look at the everyday, shows how we do ordinary things, how we make things seem natural. Agnes did it with gender: she presented herself as a woman. But she did it with a man's body, and so for her it was a real accomplishment. But when you stop to think about what it is Agnes had to do—how she had to use her hands, angle her head, move her legs and eyebrows, how she had to *present* as a woman, you realize that's what women do too. Gender, Garfinkel was showing through Agnes's account, is a social accomplishment. It is an accomplishment for women doing "woman" as a performance, and it is for men doing "man," just as it is for those who are border-crossing. Garfinkel showed us that Agnes took the most taken-for-granted actions of daily life and made them obvious.

For those who are doing what they are expected to do, or-dinary girls and women doing the expected gender stuff, the accomplishment is hidden, naturalized. Even we don't realize what we're doing most of the time. That doesn't mean we're not doing it. That doesn't mean that we can't recognize the things we do if you call them to our attention. It just means we don't have to think about it.

So it is with family. If you are an ordinary family, an expected family—a mama bear, papa bear and the little bear cubs born to your type of family—you don't think about presenting yourself. It just seems obvious. You don't think about how you construct the family, weave the relationships between the various parts, and present the seemingly solid fabric of your lives to the world.

But if you're a family like mine, a family that mixes race in unexpected ways, it's not obvious. If you're a family in which the mother's in a wheelchair that the kid is helping to push, you're going to have to make clear that you're a mother and her child. If you're a family that does different things with gender—two mothers or two fathers—then you're going to be called upon to account for yourselves. If you look old enough to be your kid's grandmother, or young enough to be her sister, you're going to have to explain yourself. If you're not ordinary, you have to show just how ordinary a family you indeed are. That "ordinariness" is an accomplishment. You're going to be aware of what most people take for granted.

I've been raising kids for so long. More than half my life, and I'm not young. They're widely spaced, my kids—fifteen years between the youngest and the oldest—so here I am, three decades into motherhood, and I still have a kid, a child at home. And I'm a sociologist. So what with one thing and another, I've had time to think about it. And it's striking how much of what was ordinary, unquestioned, not really thought about with the first two, my white kids, had to be constructed more overtly, tenderly and lovingly and strategically, with the third, my black kid.

I've had other moments of marginality—we all do now and again. I brought Daniel with me to share the celebration when I was elected president of one of my professional associations. He was about twenty at the time. And I overheard a bit of gossip about what a young husband I had. I had to (or felt I had to) clarify that one. I can still remember this odd moment from my teens: I was with a boyfriend, and a kid came over and asked if I was his brother. I must have done the white girl hair-flip thing,[2] something to show I was a girl. I got pushed around in a wheelchair for a little while once, with a badly broken ankle, and saw how totally dismissed I was as any kind of real person—mother, worker, anything. Irving Kenneth Zola, the person who established "disability studies" within sociology, called me the day I got home from the hospital, and said, "Barbara, this is carrying participant observation altogether too far!" But actually it wasn't; it was just far enough. I learned what I needed to know.

Years ago, before I had adopted, I was at some meeting somewhere when a little black toddler darted out and was reaching up to pull on a tablecloth. I dashed over to keep him from pulling the table over on himself, and scanned the room. A white woman was right there in front of me, but she didn't register—until she scooped up the baby, smiled at me, and said: "It's OK, it wasn't obvious."

I've used her line a million times since, and thank her for it.

When things are not what people expect, it's not obvious. And so you have to think about how to make obvious who you are, who you are with, what you are doing.

If you think about your life, there will undoubtedly be those little moments, sometimes comical and sometimes not, when you too were just a bit off-center and got a fresh glimpse of how the world works, because you had to *make* it work. If you step just an inch off "ordinary" family—the inch that adoption moves you, or the extra inch that an "obvious," transracial adoption gives you—you get a fresh angle on family.

Adoption is probably interesting enough in and of itself. As is race. As is motherhood. But what is so interesting to me is the way that putting these things together shows you ordinary, taken-for-granted, obvious stuff in American life.

We have race, and ethnicity, and community and family, and the nation and the global economy—but we mostly don't see them. We don't see ourselves establishing our place in the family, the world, the communities in the in-between levels. Take a kid from a Chinese orphanage and put it in a middle-class "Euro-descent" American home, and a lot of what parenthood is about in America is put into sharp relief. Take an African American kid and put it in a white home, and the same thing happens: you can see how race and family are put together in America. They're put together—race constructs family and family constructs race—when a black woman is raising a black child and when a white woman is raising a white child, but it's almost invisible. It's that water-to-a-fish thing. But move across that race line in your mothering, and the relationship between motherhood and race jumps right out at you.

Each person has a place in families and friendship groups and communities and ethnic groups and races and nationalities and the global economy. We have our place in those social systems when we are part of "ordinary All-American families" and when we are not. When we are not, we become very aware of how we fit ourselves in. We notice that we are *doing* what other people think they are just *being*.

Fitting in, finding your place, belonging: these are important to everybody. They're crucial to kids. No kid wants to stick out, to "not belong." I love *Sesame Street*; they did many, many good things. But they did screw up on one. There's this song they sing:

> *Three of these things belong together*
> *Three of these things are kind of the same*
> *Can you guess which one of these doesn't belong here?*
> *Now it's time to play our game, time to play our game!*

In reading the literature of transracial adoption and of mixed-race families, and just plain hanging out with people who grew up on Sesame Street, I've heard more complaints about that song! All those little kids, identifying with the one that "doesn't belong." They tried to make it better, the *Sesame Street* people being far from stupid. When they sang about kids, they never said "doesn't belong," but "is doing his own thing." That's not what the now-grown kids I've been reading and listening to remember; they remember that the odd one out doesn't "belong."

We belong. Our kids by birth and by adoption belong. They belong to us, they belong right where they are, however they got there. Our families belong. We belong to the larger families and the communities we're in—however we got there.

But it's not obvious.

2
Our Story

I profit from American racism. More than almost anybody I know, I am a beneficiary: I have Victoria.

I am one of the white Americans who has adopted a black baby. Fifteen years ago Victoria came into my life, a perfect, healthy, beautiful baby with world-class dimples.

That makes us part of what is called "transracial adoption," the placement of black children into white homes. In theory, a lot of other things might be thought of as transracial adoptions: the Chinese girls being brought to America, the Korean adoptions of some years back, maybe the kids being brought up from Central and South America to North American and European homes. Or, in a better theory, *nothing* could be considered transracial adoption because race is a useless, meaningless category, biologically speaking. But we don't speak biologically, or accurately, very often. We recognize race as a very, very important social category, and no racial distinction is as important in America as the one we know as the "color line" between black and white. So, while much of what I write about transracial adoption in this book applies to all of these border-crossing families, much is also specifically about black/white families. And similarly, much is specifically about adoption, because that's where my experience comes from, but much is also about nonadoptive border-crossing families, however they are formed and whatever borders they transgress.

Transracial adoption is a good example of what *Ms. Magazine* used to call "mid-revolutionary mores." It's the way we have to act in a world that hasn't gotten it right yet, but is moving in that direction. In a more overtly racist system, in a no-holds-barred racist system, there wouldn't be any transracial adoption; the color line would be hard and fast, and the state wouldn't be doing adoptions like ours. In a completely nonracist system, the concept wouldn't make sense because we wouldn't think of people as grouped into races.

In our system we have enough racism to recognize race, to categorize babies and adopting families by race, but enough of an attempt to overcome our racism to place children in homes across the race line. It's an awkward moment that's lasted almost fifty years now.

We also have enough racism so that it is black babies and children that disproportionately are up for adoption, and white families that disproportionately have the wherewithal to adopt —and enough racism that it is hard to imagine the circumstances in which a black family would/could adopt a white baby. And so here we are.

I came to the decision to adopt out of my work as well as out of my personal life. I had given birth to my first two children, aged fifteen and eight by the time Victoria arrived. My early decision to have home births and my subsequent interest in midwifery brought me to my dissertation and my first book; my work in that area brought me to my work on prenatal diagnosis and genetic counseling, the subject of my second book. And that work, which was more or less on reproductive technology,

had me on a lot of reporters' and television producers' rolodexes
when the "Baby M" surrogacy case arose in the late 1980s. In that
case, a woman hired as a surrogate, a "rented womb," found herself unable to go through with the contract once the baby was
born. She tried to keep the baby; the state sent police after her,
took the child, and turned it over to the contracting father.

I found myself part of the media circus. Arguing against surrogacy, arguing that every woman is the mother of the child
in her belly unless and until she chooses otherwise, I found myself arguing alongside a sometimes strange assortment of colleagues. Priests and religious leaders of other denominations
were on my side, while, bizarrely (to me anyway), some feminists sat on the other side, talking about women's rights to enter into contracts, and the necessity to hold them to those
contracts. The TV people particularly liked to have two people labeled as "Feminists" (literally labeled, the white caption
beneath our names when we first spoke) arguing against each
other. Hoping for a cat fight? Just enjoying anything that would
heighten controversy and so, hopefully, raise ratings?

I found little common ground with the priests and other religious people talking about "women's natural spheres" and
"maternal instincts" and what an awful thing "choice" had now
led us to. I had more in common, much more, with the feminist
opposition. They had their own problems in these debates,
stuck on their side of the argument with the brokers, the guys
making money off of the deals. One of the feminist women on
the "other side" and I invented a game we'd play: I'd get a point
when the awful man on her side said something that made us
cringe; she'd get the point when the awful man on my side did.
We racked up points pretty quickly.

Besides the religious leaders, the other people on my side
time after time in television studios, chatting over stale coffee
in green rooms, were adoption advocates. I came to appreciate

having them on my side, being on theirs. The problem, they assured the public and me, was not a shortage of babies for adoption; it was a shortage of the kind of babies people like the Sterns, the hiring couple in the Baby M case, were willing to adopt. Forcing people to adopt babies and children they don't want is hardly the answer, but making that clarification did shift the question a bit, made us realize that hiring surrogates wasn't just about becoming parents, but about getting the "right kind" of child.

The unadoptable children included black children, and in the late 1980s—when so-called crack babies and what were called "boarder babies," babies left in hospitals awaiting some kind of placement—were in the nightly news alongside so-called surrogate mothers, it also included newborn black babies. The media liked to portray crack, street cocaine, as the enemy, destroying families and the lives of young people. The hard edge of Reaganomics, the large-scale structural forces operating at all levels—from the leaking of solid jobs to underpaying international corporations, to the underfunding of city schools—those forces went largely undiscussed on the nightly news. The highly photogenic baby left in the newborn nursery at a city hospital made a better news story.

Whatever the cause, wherever one lays the blame, for a brief while there in the late 1980s the unplaced and seemingly unplaceable, unadoptable children going into American foster care included newborn black babies. That is not always the case, a point I'll come back to later, but it did seem to be true at that particular moment in time. There were, at least for a few years there, more newborn black babies available for adoption than there were black families applying to adopt. And yes, there's something to be said about who applies and why and what happens to would-be adopters.

But to make a long story short, I started with great skepticism: Prove it, I said to one adoption advocate backstage. Prove to me that there really are more black babies than homes, prove the need is there. And he did. I was convinced that, yes, there were black babies available for adoption, babies who were headed into foster care.

My first two kids, Daniel and Leah, were growing up, and I could see the end of my active parenting years approaching, all too quickly. Hesch, my husband, and I hadn't planned on having any more children. Like many couples of our generation, we first thought "just one," and then "went for the second." We didn't have fertility problems, and though our kids were widely spaced, allowing for completing a doctorate and landing a tenure-track job, we had the prototypical "planned family." We even, by luck of the draw, had the idealized pattern of older boy and younger girl. By dint of will we refused the dog and the suburbs. We had a complete, lovely family. And we loved it. We loved raising our kids, being an active child-rearing couple. But we knew all about world overpopulation, and besides, kids are expensive and time-consuming, and we shouldn't just be doing this for the fun of it. The idea that there might be a good reason to have another child was enormously appealing.

When Hesch and I first began this process of adoption, with our first tentative steps of interviews, still checking around to be sure that there really were more babies than available black homes, thinking about what this decision would mean for our life as a family, Leah was the same age Daniel had been when Leah was conceived. We came to feel ready, then more than ready, then eager.

The hesitation was that we did not want to enter into a competitive situation with black women and families looking to adopt. A colleague told me how, over a decade before, she had been denied the opportunity to adopt—as a single, African American, professional woman, she was turned down, while at that same time white families in entirely white communities were being given black babies. I'm a sociologist; it may not have been "my area," but I'd read, paid some attention to the transracial adoption debates of the 1970s, knew something about the racism that ran through the institution of adoption. I did not want to participate in a racist system. We had to find an agency that had African American social workers actively involved in policy on its staff, that was known to be making outreach efforts into the black community, and that would regard my family as what it should be: a last resort, preferable to foster care. I was strongly holding the position Randall Kennedy now calls *moderate race matching:* "a policy of preferring same-race adoptions as long as they can be arranged without excessive delay."[1] That's the middle position between "strong race matching," in which babies are only placed "within race," and being "color-blind," doing no race matching at all.

Kennedy disagrees with me. He characterizes me perfectly, and disagrees with me totally:

> Even many adopters and adoptees who have together created loving multiracial families nonetheless believe that, all other things being equal, same-race adoption is preferable to interracial adoption. They are wrong. While less misdirected than strong race matching, moderate race matching is still grievously mistaken.[2]

If you take a hard-line color-blind approach, then babies should just be randomly assigned, first-come, first-served, never race-matched. Given the current demographics of adoption, that would result in some black families ending up with white babies; more white families with black; some families accidentally "matched." You make that one statement, that "race should not matter in adoption," and you've resolved all the ethical dilemmas. Kennedy doesn't actually go that far. He makes room for the "race preferences" of adopters. Some don't: Richard R.

Banks, cited by Kennedy, suggested in a *Yale Law Review* article in 1998 that adoption agencies should "decline to accommodate adopters' racial preferences."[3] Hawley Fogg-Davis, in a book called *The Ethics of Transracial Adoption,* calls white adopters' preference for white babies racist.[4] Whether people you've identified as racist should be encouraged to adopt black children is highly debatable. Some space for allowing people not to enter into an adoption they don't want seems only fair to the *child.* Kennedy says Banks has pushed a "good idea—racial nondiscrimination—past its right and prudent boundaries," but defends racial preference, not based on the needs of the child, but the rights of the adopters. He calls for an "ambit of privacy" within which people may form intimate relations, the "breathing room" lawmakers have left for "*private* racial discrimination."[5] Neither he nor Fogg-Davis seems to feel that birth mothers are entitled to the same private space, or perhaps they feel that placing a baby for adoption is *not* entering into an intimate relationship, but rather abandoning one. More on that later.

On the other hand, if you take the opposite position to being color-blind, a hard-line race-matching position, you're on tricky terrain. Are you doing that because you are a racist? Do you think that, as the people who passed antimiscegenation laws and other eugenic policies held, the races should not mix? Charges of racism fly—both ways, white against black, black against white—when people talk about race matching. Alternatively, you can take that position not in response to race, but in response to *racism,* claiming, as the National Association of Black Social Workers famously did, that the history and existence of white racism require race matching for black babies. Their position[6] is that the children themselves need the support and socialization only a black family in America can provide, and that the black community needs to maintain and sustain its children and families.

But hard-line policies, even if they are absolutely correct on a policy level, can leave you in a difficult position. Or more to the point, in this case, they sometimes leave some poor little baby in a difficult position: put into foster care because a race-matched family is not available. And that, I feel, as do so many others, cannot be right either. So back to moderate race matching.

Participating in, or even just being supportive of transracial adoption thus inevitably puts one in an impossible situation. There may well be an absolute necessity to sometimes place black babies and children with white families in order that they have families at all. There is an absolute necessity to step in and help the families so formed, a situation not unique to adoption. White people raising black children in America, whether they've given birth to them or adopted them, need some help, support, assistance from the black community. But if you place that child, if you help the family formed by transracial adoption, are you then implicitly supporting the formation of such families? Are you acting in such a way as to encourage the removal of black children from the black community? The adoptive family and particularly the child need support, but all of what got that child into that situation needs to be stopped.

Transracial adoption is a band-aid solution where far more radical solutions are immediately needed.

There is a story we tell in medical sociology that is useful here as well. A man is walking alongside a stream when a dead fish floats by. He reaches in with a stick and flips it out, so that the rotting fish doesn't pollute downstream. A moment later, another fish floats by and again he flips it out. Within minutes, he is standing there pulling out dead fish as fast as he can. He is almost too busy to stop, look up, and wonder, "What the hell is going on up there?"

The moral of the story is that we have to refocus upstream.

Some versions of the story have drowning people floating by and the rescuer doing artificial respiration on one after another, without time to stop and see who is pushing them in. Sometimes the story, like the one I told, is about industrial pollution, about the factory up at the top of the stream that systematically produces dead fish. But always, as much as the work needs to be done downstream, the problem basically needs to be solved upstream.

There are several streams that feed into transracial adoption, each of which is deeply problematic at its source. Adoption itself is one: Why is there *ever* a child being placed for adoption? Adoption solves, in a wonderful and satisfying way, the problem of infertility for so many people that we tend to forget that adoption itself is a problem and not just a solution. I once led a student reading group on adoption. Half a dozen graduate students, touched one way or another by adoption, wanted to explore the issue together, as sociologists. We read widely, bringing in books and articles to share with each other. One evening a man brought in a table of international adoption statistics. Sweden—not Utopia, but a place with good social services, readily available contraception as well as abortion, decent services for single mothers, along with all mothers and children— Sweden had twelve domestic, nonfamily adoptions that year. Twelve Swedish women found themselves in a situation where placing their babies out for adoption was their best option. Twelve. When you take away most of the social forces operating upstream that put women in that awful position, you are left largely with personal idiosyncrasy, personal reasons. Twelve.

The United States is bigger than Sweden; if we had the kinds of social supports the Swedish have, we would still have more than twelve babies available. But we would never, ever have anywhere near the number of babies we currently have placed "voluntarily" for adoption, and we would never, ever have enough to solve the problem of infertility. Adoption is the result of some very bad things going on upstream, policies that push women into giving birth to babies that they then cannot raise.

Racism is of course the other feeder stream: more women of color find themselves in just that situation, placed there willingly or very much against their will. Some, like Victoria's birth mother, make careful adoption plans and lovingly place their babies in waiting arms; some have their children wrenched away by a deeply neglectful state that then accuses the mothers of neglect. A lot of what adoption is about is poverty: a lack of access to contraception and abortion, a lack of access to the resources to raise children. And a lot of what poverty is about in America is racism. It's not just that people of color are more likely to be poor. It's also that poor people of color lack the resources to overcome racial discrimination, find themselves powerless before the state. Race and poverty play out together to push/pull black children out of black homes.[7] Race plus class plus gender are not just additive; they multiply each other. And so it is children of color, specifically the children of black women, who are pushed out, pulled out, of their mothers' arms. And given the ways that racism and sexism in America portray black men, it is their sons who are most likely to be left without families. Both black and white families show a gender preference for girls in adoption, and especially in the adoption of African American children. One of the biggest surprises of my life was that the child the agency found for me was a girl; having said we wanted whatever baby they needed us for, I had assumed we'd be getting a boy.

Racism, combined with, *multiplied by*, poverty creates a stream of children needing homes. As much as the black community stands with open arms, absorbing as many of those babies and children as it can, the same poverty that pushes all those babies and children into the adoption stream ensures that there won't be enough black homes to take them all.

A similar process is operating globally, with the children of greatest poverty being disproportionately the darker children of the world. Whenever we see families formed by an adoption that crosses any color line, it is almost always children of darker skin going to lighter-skinned parents. Color preferences play out internationally: White Americans and Europeans turn far more readily to the Eastern European countries for transnational adoption, secondarily to the Asian countries and Latin American countries, and virtually not at all to the countries of Africa.

In a better world, adoption would all but disappear, leaving us infertility as a problem that still needed to be addressed on its own terms. And in a better world, race too would almost cease to exist; race as a system of power and domination would collapse. Ethnicity, community based on heritage, would or could continue, but race, with all of its history of horror, would disappear. What would that mean for adoption?

I sent my children to a Quaker school for their elementary-school years. I share the values that Quakers have tried to bring to education, their respect for each and every child as a person. My middle child, Leah, was eight when Victoria arrived. I brought the baby to school to meet Leah's third-grade class. It was, as private schools tend to be, a largely white class, but being a Quaker school with the Quaker commitment to diversity, it was not entirely white. The class sat around in a circle on the floor, for morning meeting, and the baby and I joined them. The children asked a million questions: they asked about babies—there aren't that many new brothers and sisters by the time you get to third grade. What does she *do* all day? Can she understand *anything*? And they asked questions about adoption: Is there a big room with a lot of babies? Who picks? The questions went on for about half an hour. The question they never asked, these bright, interested children, was "How come they gave a black kid to a white family?"

In that little, almost Utopian social world of a Quaker elementary school, in those early years before the rest of America forces itself upon them, that third-grade class did not recognize race. I am not suggesting that children are "color-blind" until the big bad racist society gets to them. Very little children do see difference. And these older, more sophisticated kids knew all about color, and history. Martin Luther King's portrait was far more likely to be on the wall than George Washington's. But they did not understand race as a currently operating system, race as a way of dividing people up against each other. Maybe I'm kidding myself—maybe if Debra Van Ausdale and Joe R. Feagin, authors of *The First R: How Children Learn Race and Racism,* went into that school, they'd find the same early racism they found in their observations of a preschool. As they point out, "Children think race but believe that they should not."[8]

So maybe I'm hopelessly naïve, but I think it didn't occur to these third graders to match for race in adoption. There were mixed-race families in their class, mixed-race families among their teachers, and mixed-race friendships all around them. Why would you divide up the babies by race?

But this world we live in is clearly not such a Utopian world. It was fairly a miracle, what they pulled off for those few years for kids in that school. As a parent, and as a prospective parent of a black child, I knew I could offer such a Utopian vision as reality for at best a decade, give the kid ten years of celebrating diversity without understanding and experiencing racism.

That first decade is about psychology—nurturing and love and building a strong foundation. The clichés are close to true when the children are little enough: all you need is love; race doesn't have to matter. It requires a lot of hothousing, keeping kids away from television, living in a genuinely mixed-race neighborhood, having friends who are black and friends who are white, putting the kids in schools that maintain a real mix of kids and teachers and administrators and custodial staff. It's a fantasy world you can try to create for children, and if you succeed, they think that race and sex discrimination are only things of the past. But you can hothouse kids for just so long.

In that second decade—the one we're now in the middle of in Victoria's life and the life of my family—the rest of the world needs to be dealt with, and race as a system enters our lives more and more.

My last book was on genetics, moving out from prenatal testing and reproductive technologies to look at the human genome project and the way that it was shaping and being shaped by our thinking.[9] As part of that project, and of course as my children's mother, I've spent years thinking intensively about genetics, biology, culture—thinking about who and what we are, thinking about identity. I found myself fascinated by the way genes shape our bodies, and how we use those shapes to construct community. That is what race is about, certainly, the obvious example. But it is not always about race. For that project, I read a lot about dwarves and dwarfism. A single errant gene, a random mutation, and people are born with that distinctive body shape. It is a body shape associated with childhood, even babyhood: the large head, small limbs—in a way, rather endearing. But it is a shape not generally associated with adult sexual development, and so presents a sometimes comic juxtaposition with beards or breasts, or other signs of adulthood and sexuality. Probably not an easy body to live with, surely a tough adolescence: growing up without growing *up*. That gene constructs a shared experience; that experience becomes the basis for constructing a community, a people connected across time and space, a tribe in diaspora.[10] Dwarves form a community—formally, in organizations like Little People of America, and informally, in networks and relationships, in the connection any given dwarf feels to the historic treatment of dwarf people.

If my daughter Victoria's skin and hair and bones mark her as African, if the genes that shape her body mark her place in the race scheme of America, how different is that from the way achondroplastic dwarfism genes mark people's membership in the world? I knew, when I offered to raise Victoria, that I would be raising a child in one world for another, that there are separate worlds of black and white in America—and that however my life tries to straddle and spread and blur the line, the line does exist here, and it is a line she has to cross. That crossing is what Heather Dalmage calls "tripping on the color line,"[11] tripping as in stumbling, and tripping as in playing, fantasizing, enjoying. Race can be a barrier between worlds, but it can also be a bridge. I will never be a black mama, but when the African American parents meet to discuss issues of concern to them at my child's school, don't I have to be there? I am part of that community through my child, just as Victoria is connected to a Jewish ethnic community that we think of as white. She has a right to cook chicken soup just like her mother, grandmother, and great-grandmother; old-fashioned Jewish chicken soup with *kneidlach* are her soul food too. But she cannot grow up to be a Jewish woman in the taken-for-granted way Leah could, any more than I can be a black mama. As long as there is a color line in America, we'll be straddling those worlds, and white families will have to raise their black children for worlds their mothers and fathers can never fully enter.

Families will always find themselves made up of all kinds of people. Hearing people will be raising deaf children, and deaf people hearing children; straight parents will be raising gay children, and gay parents straight children; big people raising little ones, and little ones raising big ones. And what of race? One way or another, by birth or by adoption, by accident or by design, as long as a color line exists, families will find themselves straddling it.

Victoria and I, a child and her mother, are at the bottom of a long strange funnel. There is the Eastern European anti-Semitism that brought my great-grandparents to New York, where the confrontation with American racism bleached out their Semitic race and made my family white. Victoria got to where she is via the slave trade to the American South, and the Great Migration to the Northeast. These larger historical streams landed us in Brooklyn—ensconced in a predominantly Caribbean neighborhood.

Ours is one story. But there are lots of families like mine. By adoption and by birth, in marriages and outside of them, there are, all over America—for reasons good and awful, out of love and despair, out of the good and the bad, the beautiful and the ugly, for all reasons and no reasons—there are mothers and daughters like Victoria and me, white mamas and their black children.

We greet the ice-cream truck, sign up for violin lessons, make holiday dinners and birthday parties, hug and squabble, do homework, do the dishes, and do hair: we weave together a family.

II
Motherhood, Adoption, and Race

3
Unraveling the Pieces

For years I had a raggedy index card thumbtacked over my desk, on which I'd typed a quote from Albert Einstein: "Everything should be made as simple as possible. But no simpler."

The wisdom of that came home for me again when I organized a panel at the annual sociology meeting on working with the media. The journalist I invited, from one of the major city newspapers, explained—patiently, as she no doubt had done a million times before—that her job was to make things clear. If we wanted to work with her, as so many sociologists really think they do, we had to find ways of make our work clear, simplifying our academic work.

My colleague from the Department of Sociology at Georgia State University, Behrooz Ghamari-Tabrizi, was there. His job, he explained—and ours as sociologists—was to make simple things complicated. What we had to do was take something that looked pretty straightforward, pretty obvious, and show just how nonobvious it was, how many things went into creating the obvious reality before us.

He's right. It doesn't make sociologists wildly popular on

TV. Or at parties. But yes, that's what we do: we complicate the obvious. We unravel the strands, look for hidden structures, see how things are constructed, how they are put together to seem so obvious.

Few things seem as obvious as family, as motherhood particularly. Its rooting in the body, in biology, naturalizes family, makes it such an obvious given. What else could be as obvious a connection between people as motherhood? Well, maybe race. There too you can see the connections, see who's related to whom, and who is not.

Adoptions challenge the natural order; adoptions across race lines do so all the more. So one thing we can look at is how people "renaturalize" adoption, make different families "normal," including families across race. And that is indeed part of my project here—the part I'll get to later, when I look at the stories told about families that cross the color line, especially about white families that raise black children.

But that involves starting with ideas about motherhood, about children and their place in families, about race. Those things are not simple. They occur in complicated contexts, parts of larger stories. And so first I need to look at these things themselves.

What is motherhood? What does it mean now, today, in America? It's a lot about choice these days, choices women make to become mothers, and then the consequences of those choices for their lives. "Choice" is a market term, a consumer idea. Motherhood itself, I'll be showing, is increasingly placed within a consumerist frame.

And adoption: what is that? It's about children, right? But adoption has been used historically to connect grown men, to establish dynasties. Adoption now is a word we use not just for children and babies, but—way over at the other extreme—for embryos. We have now a host of new technologies of procreation, an alphabet soup of baby making from IVF (in vitro fertilization), which now seems simple, through to GIFT (gamete interfallopian transfer) and ZIFT (zygote interfallopian transfer) and yes, ET, embryo transfer. These are the technologies many people try out before they consider adoption, changing both the way we think about babies and the way we think about adoption.

Race too is being affected by those new technologies, as genetic science reinvents race, erace-ing and redrawing the race lines, and as other technologies—of communication, of transportation—make the world smaller. American ideas about race stem from the very earliest contacts between European explorers and the people they came upon, and they change as an overnight flight now brings a baby from China to America, as American kids watch European kids copying American black style, as big-city schools claim dozens of language communities among their students. Race just isn't so black-and-white anymore.

Before I can talk about what it means to be a mother who adopts across race, I have to "unpack" each of these: motherhood, adoption, and race.

4
Motherhood in the Marketplace

I once read somewhere that the United States doesn't have a culture; it has an economy. The values of the market are the dominant values, and they affect everything. Everything.

I'm not exactly immune to this myself; we are all complicit, all shoppers, all consumers, and all shaped by that experience. When I find myself in some interesting foreign city and I've seen the various museums and tasted the street food on offer, I wander the shopping sections. I buy so much when I travel—next year's Chanukah presents, shoes, tourist junk, local artifacts. And when I do this, I find myself feeling kind of guilty about it, feeling as if I really ought to be in another museum or something, not *shopping*. I find myself repeating over and over in my head like a little mantra, "this is harmless, I'm not hurting anyone."

There probably is nothing inherently wrong with shopping, even shopping for things you don't really need. I suppose I should be thinking more carefully about where those things came from, whose underpaid labor I am exploiting, what natural resources of the earth I am despoiling. But if I shop responsibly, if I am an informed, conscientious shopper, then, well, this is harmless, not hurting anyone, and I probably should relax.

And what is it I'm shopping for? Not just when traveling, but generally in life, what is it I want to buy? Pretty things, lovely things. I value beauty. There really is no reason why a doorknob shouldn't be well designed. In our two short days in Berlin, I dragged Hesch and Victoria off to the Bauhaus museum to pay my respects to furniture and salt shakers and other things that I've had in my house—or at least had in their cheaper knock-off versions. I really do enjoy design, am interested in it, do go to design museums. I read about that, I *care,* really I do.

But I'm irritated with various friends (and I can name at least six of you over the past year, so don't take this too personally!) who are redoing kitchens or, god forbid, whole houses, talking about the enormous pressure they're feeling when each and every decision *counts* somehow. Each little purchase, they're telling me, each faucet, switch, light fixture, is a separate decision, reflecting your taste, a reflection of *you.* To be lost in the aesthetics of a hinge—*genug,* I think, *genug.* Yiddish for "enough." A good thing gone too far.

Some of the objects in my house are beautiful in and of themselves. Not too many, actually—it's an old house, but not well maintained. All the original detail was long gone before I got here. A few lovely things are left: an old, carved oak door I stripped, using borrowed dental tools to get paint out of crevices. It would have taken less time to carve a new one. And I own beautiful, really beautiful dishes: Dutch pottery, Zaalberg. Each dish is a thing of beauty, each individual.

But I can't think of many things that I own that are themselves really lovely. Most of the reason I own and love an object is a story it evokes in my mind. I pick up a bowl to put the broccoli in and think of Kit. I take a pencil from a jar and think of

Leah in second grade, cutting felt scraps. I mash the potatoes with the masher Annemiek gave me before I left Holland. I boil the potatoes in a pot my sister gave me. Even the art, chosen as art, becomes stories. The only real, serious piece of art I own is the drawing that Ken Nishi did of an old woman weighed down by a bundle of firewood. She looks like my grandmother, the one who had polio as a child, weighed down by her body. Ken was the husband of Suki, Setsuko Matsunaga Nishi, my first sociology teacher.

And so it goes, an inventory of my life in my objects, my things. I think about moving to smaller space and losing not these things, but the stories and thoughts and memories each contains. Would I ever, ever think of Mrs. Herman, my junior high teacher if I didn't have the mushroom-decorated porcelain bowl she gave me as a wedding present? Probably, sometimes. But not tonight, I wouldn't have thought of her tonight if I hadn't put the salad in that bowl.

There are two kinds of value then in objects, as I understand it. One is intrinsic beauty or function. I chose the new portable mixer because the cord is retractable, and it fits in the bowl from the old countertop one. The old one, ah, a flea-market find of my mother's. But after twenty years it gave me shocks, and I had to throw it away. I lucked out, found one in a secondhand store just exactly like it, and so it gave me shocks too. Bad design— forty, fifty years, and that mixer just dies. I kept the mixer's old bowls; they're stainless steel and beautiful. And the birthday cakes I have made in them. . . . So yeah, one value lies in intrinsic beauty and function, and the other in what the object evokes. That's the priceless part, the way that no teapot ever will replace your grandmother's, no wedding ring ever replace yours.

But actually, you can replace those things. I broke my great-grandmother's bread bowl. Twenty years ago, it must be now, I was holding it, it slipped, shattered. I did not shed tears. I would not permit myself to cry over an object, a thing. But I was so sad. Hesch bought me a new bread bowl; it's the same size, a bit heavier. When I tried to picture it just now, as I was writing, I had to run downstairs and look: couldn't be sure which bowl was in my mind, this one or my great-grandmother's. That's how thoroughly this one replaced that one: I use it and think of my great-grandmother and of Hesch, searching to replace her bowl.

Things are replaceable. It's people that are not. You cannot get another one.

When Daniel was a little child, I explained a bit of family history, that my father had died and my mother had remarried, that Grandpa Red had not always been my father. Daniel was shocked: "You can DO that?!" The idea of replacing a person was so bizarre. And, of course, you can't. You can have a second husband, a stepfather, but that doesn't replace the original.

Babies, though, are often held to be another story. Women whose babies have died have been offered as comfort, "You can have another one." It's not comforting. You can have another one, but it will never, ever be the same one. Babies are not fungible, not for their mothers. When a baby dies, it can never be replaced.[1] And adoptive mothers can have much that same experience: when an adoption falls through, that baby is indeed lost to that mother, lost forever, and not replaced by the next one. A woman who has traveled halfway around the world holding the picture of her promised baby won't accept just any baby, but wants that one, *her* baby.[2]

Children are priceless. And yet we know they are costly. We know that getting and maintaining children is about as expensive as anything in this society. A child costs more than a car, less than a house. There really are price tags here. If you just get easily pregnant the old-fashioned way, there are still the costs of pregnancy care, birth attendants. One adoptive mother, rightly offended when asked how much the baby cost, replied, "Less than a Cesarean section." But if you can't get pregnant, there are often serious costs: reproductive technologies, adoption—these are big-ticket items.

This is a tension we live with. Viviana Zelizer expressed it perfectly in the title of her book *Pricing the Priceless Child*.[3] She talked about the sentimentalization of children, their priceless-ness, and the necessity of putting price tags on them. A kid is killed in a car accident and we sue. A dollar value is assigned. An infertile woman or a man without a woman wants someone to get pregnant, grow them a baby. A dollar value is assigned. And the costs are not the same for all babies. A minister at the Anti-och Bible Church is trying to raise money for a billboard that will show a white baby, a Latino baby, and a black baby, and next to each the fee charged by adoption "facilitators," of thirty-five thousand, ten thousand, and four thousand dollars, respec-tively. "I raise thoroughbred racehorses. I sell them by supply and demand. I'm not going to let people sell children by sup-ply and demand."[4]

Mostly it's not quite that blatant. The dollar signs are usually hidden, the message more subtle. But when it comes to the fore, you realize it is everywhere. Working on issues around reproductive technology, and especially surrogacy was what made me really start to think about the ways capitalism shapes motherhood.[5]

When I first began writing about that, I did not even have a vocabulary available to me. I struggled for a word to describe what was happening to fetuses and to babies, and came up with "commodification."[6] A copyeditor rejected it: not a word, not acceptable. I insisted, as have others, and it is a word that now sails right through copyediting (but not yet, sorry to say, through my spell checker).

Women under capitalism, I have argued, have found that the babies they grow are commodities, and the only real question being asked is: "*Whose* commodity?" To whom does the baby belong, who has rights of ownership? In struggling to (re)claim their own babies and their own bodies, women have drawn upon the same language of ownership, the "rights talk" that makes so much sense in America. In this country, we are all supposed to have equal rights. Think back to the images of the civil rights movement: picture those black students seated at a Woolworth's counter. They had a *right* to be served. They had a dollar in hand and a right to buy. In truth, at that moment in American history, a bigger problem for the blacks of the American South was their poverty: how many of them didn't have the dollar? Economic inequality is, for most Americans, just the way things are, not really fixable. But having the dollar and not being served—that's *wrong*! They had a *right* to service. That's what is meant by saying we have a focus on individual rights rather than social justice in America.

This is the ideology, the way of thinking, that feminism also drew upon, focusing on individual rights rather than larger questions of social justice. "Rights" thinking permeates everything about motherhood in America. You can see this, painfully clearly, when we talk about adoption, and phrase our questions and concerns mostly in terms of rights—who has a right to the baby, who has rights to access information about the baby and the birth mother, who has a right to adopt at all.

But the language of rights is also used by those of us active in the home birth movement, the midwifery movement, the women's health movement. On issues as varied as abortion, adoption, home birth, surrogacy, breastfeeding, sterilization, and more, we have invoked rights, and by implication, ownership. A woman has, we declared, a right to do as she wills with her body. That was the argument the feminist on the "other side" of the surrogacy debates was making. It is her baby she produces with that body, and she has rights over that baby as well. Feminists of all stripes, on an enormous range of issues, have defended these rights, rights that are repeatedly threatened, under constant attack, until perhaps a callous has built up over the argument. We cannot hear, we cannot afford to hear, the limitations, the potential threats of the rights and ownership of language itself.

But what does it mean to own a body when that body itself is disvalued? What does it mean to have a baby of one's own, when "own" is defined by others? What does it mean to have a right to services, when those services are fundamentally human relationships? These are the questions that have troubled me. I've looked at the *production* in r*eproduction,* and so my focus has been on women as producers, the proletariat in family relations. Sometimes women own and control their labor, sometimes not.

But there's another side to this I hadn't thought about enough: the consumption end. Last year the editors of a new book on motherhood, *Consuming Motherhood,* invited me to write a commentary for their book.[7] Twenty-five years and more of scholarly, feminist, critical work on motherhood, even thinking long and hard about motherhood under capitalism, did not fully prepare me for the insights of critical scholarly work on consumption.

Most of the energy in the sociology of the economy has been focused, as I have been, on the production end, like the work of Marx. But there's also been a continuing body of work looking at consumption. Over a hundred years ago Georg Simmel did an article on fashion.[8] Fashion, he argued, was very much an urban product: it is in cities that we need ways to signal to others who we are, what our values are. In cities we stand alone rather than embedded in community and family, and so we need to mark, to "decorate" ourselves, to declare ourselves. And fashion is the perfect way to do it, allowing us to follow social norms while expressing personal taste and values. It's that funny thing we become so aware of with teenagers and fashion: they imitate others in order to distinguish themselves.

Whether it is our bodies, our homes, our cars—or our children—that we are decorating, we are consuming in order to distinguish ourselves, to mark and so to make ourselves. This is work that Bourdieu developed in *Distinction*.[9] We become our own project: "The consumer is someone engaged in a 'culture project,' the purpose of which is to complete the self."[10]

So where do babies fit in? On the one hand, mothers produce babies. On the other hand, mothers "consume" babies: we use babies as objects to produce ourselves as mothers. The baby is like an accessory, the very important object we have to add to our homes to complete ourselves and our families.

The family itself has shifted from a unit of production in society to a unit of consumption: we don't *make* things as a family, but we *buy* things as a family.[11] And in buying things, we make, display, distinguish ourselves as family. Family as we now understand it, family as haven, that place where we are valued for our own selves and not our labor, is itself a product of our economy. This is a point that Eli Zaretsky made in a wonderful little book called *Capitalism, the Family and Personal Life*.[12] He noted that as work became more and more alienating, it got separated from who we "really" are. Personal life became the quest for personal fulfillment, and that search for personal meaning most often takes place in the family. For women, this has been complicated by our being responsible for so much of that plain and simple work that goes on to make the family a haven.[13] Havens, I have noticed, still need their floors washed, their toilets cleaned, and clean linens put on their beds. Warm and cozy family dinners after hard days at the office require vegetables to be peeled, garbage taken out, tables set, dishes washed.

And havens involve a fair amount of emotional labor as well, the active nurturing, loving attention, heading off arguments, resolving sibling and spousal fights, and all of that. That too has traditionally been the province of women-as-mothers. So for us, the family has been both a unit of production and a unit of consumption, and—oddly enough—consumption has been one of our big products. Think about getting ready for a family holiday: think about the shopping! Think about celebrating a birthday, a wedding, a new baby: think about the shopping! That shopping that we do *as mothers* is part of what creates us as mothers.

We may or may not have to confront an overt marketplace when we get our babies. It's interesting that in English we usually say "get" pregnant and "have" a baby, but I've noticed my Dutch and German friends, in speaking English, say that someone "got" a baby when talking about giving birth to one.[14] Americans typically use "got" for a baby by adoption: They got the baby from China, from a private adoption, from the state system.

But part of getting or having a baby is shopping for it—and Oh! the ambiguity in *that* statement! It means both shopping *for* and shopping *on behalf of* the baby. Some of us may get pregnant easily and not have to buy the baby, but we buy the things—cribs and cradles and blankets and clothes and toys—and so create a home for the baby, and that is how we create the kind of baby we're having.

Here's an embarrassing little moment from my life: I was on the subway once, on my way home from work, and there was a family seated on the opposite bench. They had a little baby, all wrapped in white: white "stretchy," white hat, white blanket. Leah was less than a year old. I thought: How pretty that looks, and I have everything but the stretchy! I got out at my stop and bought one. That was back in the day when all my children were white. I honestly don't know even now how much the creamy pink whiteness of the baby was part of the package I admired.

And a friend of mine who adopted older children, later in her life, past the point where most of her friends had "had" their babies, said that when the kids came, and she first went into a department store, she felt a wonderful thrill of entitlement, legitimacy, as she entered the children's department. She was there to shop for her own children: she belonged there!

In our shopping, we are creating ourselves as mothers, our households as families, our children as the kind of children we want to have: pretty, well taken care of, lavished upon. That is, obviously, largely a class-based project. My great-aunt Eleanor once gave Daniel a toy that, she assured him and me, he would learn *nothing* from! It was *not* an educational toy. She realized that all the toys she'd given her children, and probably all the toys I was likely to give mine, were part of the project of creating a smart, educated kid. This one was just for fun, not part of the grand middle-class child-rearing project.[15] But it too was purchased, consumed to create a particular kind of childhood moment.

So one way of thinking about motherhood is as a grand shopping expedition. From birth services and practitioners through infant clothes and lactation consultation to candy and junk food, from the cloth versus disposable diaper issue through Barbie Dolls on to shopping for the right schools—nursery through college—mothering can be understood as a series of consumer choices.[16]

And mothers do this at the same time that we're all too aware of the consumerist tide that is threatening to swallow our children. We walk them through stores where we are carefully reading tiny print on the back of boxes, and they are grabbing at cartoon characters drawn large on the front of sugary junk food. We are pushing books and sports; someone is selling television and video games. One of the first and classic works of this "consumption studies" approach to parenting found that mothers see the television as a "corruption of the child by an external force acting against its own welfare." I read that, and—excuse me while I turn down the sound of my kid watching MTV—but, well, yeah.

Victoria and I spent some time watching DVDs of the old *Howdy Doody Show,* the kids' TV of the 1950s that I grew up on. And so I watched Buffalo Bob sell "Wonder Bread," which "grows strong bodies twelve ways, boys and girls, just tell your mother to look for the red, yellow, and blue balloons!" and Twinkies: "Just have your mother look in the store near the check-out counter for the familiar 'hostess' lady on the wrapper" (a nice set of clues not requiring literacy of me as a kid in the grocery store). Watching this now as a middle-aged woman, remembering how much I just loved Howdy Doody time, I do feel a bit, oh, corrupted? Used? Duped?

That was me the child being turned into the consumer that I the mother now am, facing my child and the next wave of consumerism. Consumerist motherhood requires a double vision, an ability to keep an eye on two things at once: one is the needs of the baby and what needs to be purchased to meet those needs, and the other is the way the world sees the woman herself as the mother/producer of the baby. So babies are dressed and "styled" to represent a particular type of mother(ing), to identify the competence and style and taste of the mother, much the way her own dress or her home furnishings identify her. In that context the child's development as an independent consumer threatens the mother's identity.

Two highly gendered examples come to mind: girls and Barbies, and boys and guns. In the awful Barbie battle,[17] the mother (her possible feminist credentials, her sense of the kind of person she is) is threatened by the child as a Barbie-owner. I am not—she feels, I feel, probably most of us feel—the kind of mother whose kid plays with Barbies. And yet. Apparently I am, apparently most of us are. Just as my own mother found herself to be the kind of mother who lets her kids eat Wonder Bread and Twinkies!

There is pretty much no way to become a mother in America without entering through the door of consumerism. It's most obvious when looking at adoption, but it's just as true, if somewhat more subtle, when we look at women as consumers, purchasers of pregnancy and birth services.

This is, in a way, where I came in. This was the door through which I entered motherhood originally: as a young woman wanting a home birth at a time when it was pretty well unheard-of. I got my home birth, and I also found my intellectual work for the next decade or so, and probably my political, intellectual, and moral grounding, in midwifery.

We had a home birth and midwifery movement in the United States in the 1970s and onward. My first child, Daniel, was born in 1974; a year later Ina May Gaskin had published *Spiritual Midwifery,*[18] which became the bible of that movement.

In the early days of a social movement, people often draw upon the academy for justifying arguments. Scholarship and academic work are used to buttress social movements, to provide the intellectual scaffolding on which to build a movement. We— those of us seeking to change the way birth was practiced in the United States—drew upon available scholarship to show that change was necessary. We used anthropology to show how much better other societies organized themselves around birth;[19] psychology to look at how the social management of birth affects women, children, and families; history[20] to look at how birth had grown the way it had;[21] and my own discipline of sociology to look at the structural concerns, the way that birth is institutionalized. We drew upon the available literature, and we went on to do new research, research stimulated by the concerns raised by the midwifery and home birth movement. One of the products of many a social movement, probably a more predictable product than social change, is research. And so it was with the home birth and midwifery movement in the US: home births are still only a tiny fraction of all births; midwives attend a just slightly higher fraction; births are more highly medicalized than we could have imagined in our worst nightmares. But do we ever have a lot of good research and books!

Later on in a social movement, the academy comes to have a very different role. Rather than being used to support the movement, scholarship develops to evaluate, analyze, and critique the movement itself. The changes brought by the movement become the new institutions to be studied. And it may well come to pass that new social movements grow out of that new understanding, that new activists draw upon that scholarship to create yet newer social movements.

You know you are getting old when your work moves from the former to the latter, from the work being used to buttress a social movement to the work that is analyzed by the scholars constructing the current wave of the movement. And that has been the case with me of late. My earliest work, my dissertation and first book, on the home birth movement in the United States[22]—and other pieces of my earlier work that were part of the home birth movement, and more generally the childbirth movement, and even more generally the women's health movement—are now ripe for analysis. Newer scholars, with ideas and approaches never thought of in the early days of the movement, including the lens of consumer studies, are now taking an appropriate critical stance towards the little we did, and the very great deal we did not accomplish.

It seemed important, for example, at a certain point in the

women's health movement, to adopt the language of consumers and providers, rather than patients and doctors. We were, I can assure you, no longer patient. The roles of both patient and doctor had become so embedded in a particular paternalistic, gendered scheme that the vocabulary itself had to go. "Consumer," believe it or not, was a role with more dignity, more power, than that of "patient." Now why is that? It has, presumably, a great deal to do with the development of capitalism. But if your focus is on improving the position of women receiving services—and sometimes we meant quite literally "off our backs," up from the flat-out, legs-in-stirrups, lithotomy position—then the reason *why* "consumer" seems better than "patient" doesn't really come up. You grope around for a different model, a better way of thinking about a woman seeking assistance in her birth or in her abortion, with her breastfeeding or with her contraception, and you use what is available.

In a capitalist system, in a fully consumerist world, consumption and the language of consumers is not just an idea, it is the tool that comes to hand.

Women who are looking for a better way to have a baby, who are exploring home birth options, find themselves both borrowing and simultaneously disavowing the language of the market.[23] When you try to choose a better place and way to give birth, you do end up talking about "shopping around." When you choose one type of practitioner over another, you are indeed comparing services in a marketplace. And, as the anthropologist of midwifery, Robbie Davis-Floyd,[24] and I have discussed endlessly, with each other and with midwives, when midwives offer their services, paid or unpaid, they inevitably, for good or ill, become part of the marketplace of services.

It is hard not to laugh at the "plethora of paid services surrounding home birth" these days, something Klassen has pointed out in a study of home birth.[25] It struck me first with breastfeeding—the first time I spoke at a lactation conference and saw a huge room full of marketers selling special pumps, pillows, nipple creams, breastfeeding teddy bears, every imaginable and some unimaginable objects one could insert between a breast and a baby. The claim that breastfeeding was simple, direct, separate from the marketplace of baby formula became laughable as I saw the array of goods and services that had grown to surround, prop up, intervene in breastfeeding.[26] And so too with home birth. I myself own a nice collection of midwifery and home birth tee shirts!

But Klassen, observing this commercialization, does not dismiss the politics, the values, the morality of the issues these women are confronting. Those of us who are involved in the home birth movement, and most especially the midwives, are not just talking about a better birth as an alternative consumer experience. We are trying to find a way of talking about meaning in life, in our bodies, in our experiences, and a way to bring that meaning to birth.

Klassen saw this call to spirituality, this religious aspect in home birth mothers. I've always presented myself as spiritually tone-deaf, always defended the right to not think of birth in spiritual terms. I'm known at midwifery meetings for easing my way out the back of the room, off to have coffee with a few like-minded friends when the spirituality stuff gets too heavy, when the meditation sessions start, the earth goddesses get invoked too often. But while I know absolutely that it is not the only reason women want home births, and for some of us not the reason at all, the spiritual and/or the religious is indeed a driving force for many, and maybe most, women in choosing home birth.

Of course, in this world, the spiritual itself enters into the marketplace, and goddess necklaces, blessing rites, all kinds of goods and services come to be for sale. (Buffalo Bob would be okay with that—after selling Wonder Bread, he reminded the children each Saturday morning that tomorrow they should go to the Sunday school or church of their choice, to practice their freedom of religion.)

People don't want everything commercialized, don't like seeing every human relationship and value and experience up for sale, but we don't really know how to stop it. Reject the local hospital that gives you glossy brochures and shows a nicely decorated "birthing room"—with a bait-and-switch policy involving a 25 percent Cesarean section rate—and you still have to "purchase the services" of a midwife for a home birth.

And so it goes with all of the birth-related services, part of the medical mainstream or out of it. Lactation consultants, doulas,[27] even the sonographers[28] are trying to help women, trying to reach out as women to women, with respect and sometimes even awe. Yet each works within a larger system, and ultimately faces corruption by that system.

Sonography is the newest of these birth services, a field like so many others that started out as largely male, but was turned over to women as it became more routine. Sonography is used in the medical setting as a possible prelude to further testing and eventual selective abortion, though that's rarely discussed. You do it to "check that the baby's OK," without a lot of talk about what happens if it is not. It is that checking on the products of conception, that evaluation, that most strikingly brings a consumerist approach to pregnancy.

But sonography is also offered these days outside of the medical setting, just for the fun and for the pictures.[29] In both kinds of settings, medical and commercial, the sonographer strives to be professional, to offer a high level of technical skill, the only thing for which she will be valued in the marketplace. And yet she also offers her human skills, her highly gendered skills of understanding, relating, mediating between the machinery and the woman.[30] In the case of the sonographer, she ends up placing herself between the woman and her own body, the very stance the midwives try so hard to avoid, creating, with the active participation of the willing woman, the fetal commodity.

Pictures are sold, even little videotapes, to share with the family. Resistance is hard: One woman, for example, said, "I think we'll forget the picture. It looks like a deep-sea animal." But the technician responded, "Can you see that? The foot. Little toes." And as the woman and her husband peered into the screen, the technician continued, "tickling" the toes on the screen, "It's so cute."[31] Who can resist?

The sonographer, in her eagerness to show the baby, to (re)present the baby to the mother, participates in the erasure of the mother's own body. To make the fetus visible, the mother becomes invisible, even to herself. She turns away from her own body, away from her lived experience of the fetus, and watches it on the screen. The erasure of inconvenient mothers and the glorification of much-wanted fetuses/babies are very much the ongoing story of contemporary motherhood, with ever more sophisticated technologies being used to reify the ancient concept of the woman as vessel.

Sonographers participate in this erasure with their technology, but adoptive parents do it as well, with their stories, and even with their technologies. In international adoptions, a photo of the baby serves much the same function as the sonogram does, making the baby real, but also obscuring the mother. One adoptive mother on an e-mail list[32] wrote that receiving the photograph was like watching her child being born on the fax machine.

It is not only the availability and almost-whiteness of the children that draws Americans to international adoption; it is also the almost complete erasure of the mother. The children ap-

pear to come from orphanages, not mothers. Barbara Yngvesson did a study of a "roots" trip, a journey back to the land
of origin for international adoptees and their parents.[33] She
studied a trip to Chile by Swedish adoptive parents and their
children. Yngvesson quotes a Swedish social worker who rec-
ognizes a tension inherent in such a journey: a roots journey to
the country is one thing; a journey to the mother would be
something else again. Background and country and decoration
are all fine—they are the sanitized "ethnicity" we find so charming. But the reality of a grieving mother, a woman who birthed
and bled and lost, is far more than most adoptive parents want.
Some, perhaps particularly the lesbian mothers who are drawn
to Chinese adoption because it rescues girls qua girls, have
particular reason to feel vulnerable. They know that whatever
power an American birth mother might have could be used to
threaten their already threatened families, and so prefer the
anonymity of the Chinese adoptions.[34] And some adoptive
families do actually seek out birth mothers. But most do not,
and adoptions that promise anonymity are marketed for their
reassurance to adopters.

In that way, by denying the mother herself, many adoptive
parents participate in this erasure of mothers and simultaneous
commodification of children. Adoptive parents, and I myself
am one, bristle and feel genuine anger and revulsion when people ask about the costs of adoption, implying the cost/worth
of the child. But only a comparative few of us have taken that
position to its logical conclusion and opened adoptions up, acknowledging and even celebrating the complicated tangle of relationships among the child, the birth mother, the adoptive
parents, the other children of both sets of parents, the extended
family on all sides. Rather than thinking of the child as a person
in a web of relationships, with families by birth and by adoption, we make the child into an isolated "object," a property that

belongs to someone. Adoption thus becomes mired in the language of rights, and the rights of adoptive parents trump entirely those of birth parents.

For most parents, by birth or by adoption, the image of the child as a product and a commodity is indelible, and ownership inevitable.

What I find so depressing, so distressing, is that there seems to be no way to think *beyond* consumerism. I can consume differently, but almost whatever I do as a mother becomes just one more cog in the consumer wheel. In a capitalist, consumerist system, motherhood and its defenses, its reinterpretations, the very battles of motherhood, will take this form. This is a level of analysis that could not have been done twenty-five years ago, when we were struggling to find alternatives to the medicalization of motherhood and found consumption a useful tool. And it was, and continues to be a useful tool.

Now *that* is the other, less depressing side of this problem of commodification. In helping me work on my piece for her book, Janelle Taylor clarified for me that "commodification is not always or only about the *de*valuation of people, it can also sometimes be about creating/asserting/claiming *value* for people." [35] That is the work that mothers do when their children are devalued. They, *we*, turn the power of consumption around, to claim and proclaim the value of our children.

Danielle Wozniak studied how foster mothers stand up for the value of their children. One foster mother recounted a story of buying glasses for a teenaged girl. The eye doctor pointed to the cheap, ugly, unfashionable glasses and said:

> "These are all we have for state children." I said, "What do you have for normal children? We don't have state children. We have children." [36]

She and other foster mothers are consuming—in this case, spending her own money—on behalf of the children to mark them as valued, loved. I saw something similar in my own family: My mother never, ever said a word to me when Daniel or Leah was dressed in tattered clothes, some old hand-me-down thing we had around the house. But it bothered her no end if Victoria wasn't dressed nicely. She was thinking about how she might look to the outside world: the child was not to be seen as a charity case.

The world of international adoption offers some interesting insights into how we all create the "kind" of baby we have. Unlike the adoption of identifiably black children by identifiably white families, in most cases of international adoption the children are perhaps less valued, but not racially disvalued. They are most often what I once heard called "a discreet shade of off-white," not white perhaps, but most assuredly not black. The ability to "tame" race into "culture" or "ethnicity" speaks primarily to the "whitening" of Asian Americans that students of whiteness have observed.[37] It is that almost-whiteness that makes Asian children, first the Korean cohort and now the Chinese, so appealing for American would-be adopters—unlike children from Africa. Or Brooklyn. Americans and Europeans go to Asia and South America and bring home babies that they will turn into middle-class American and European children.

In her work on Americans going to China to adopt the girls that the one-child family policy has made "redundant," Ann Anagnost describes the way families use the Internet to "meet" each other, to learn from each other, and to jointly construct their families as "normal."[38] Part of the project is to incorporate the "differentness" that the child's racial/ethnic/national identity marks on her body. She describes the ways people shop for things—from Asian-featured dolls to "anything with pandas on it"—as a way to capture ethnicity or culture with consumer goods. I think back to myself on that train, admiring that baby swathed in white, when I was more simply just a white mother with white kids. I didn't have to think about the ways buying white baby clothes and blankets might have contributed to the construction of a perfect baby as white: a bundle of pink and white glory. But when the baby is "raced," the construction and management of race through shopping become more obvious.

A baby or child is removed from its country of origin, an act that one of my graduate students at the City University of New York, Hosu Kim,[39] has pointed out to me is a form of forced migration, and the parents/purchasers work on turning that act into something cute. Something vaguely identified as "culture" or "ethnicity" displaces race and class, Anagnost claims. That may work for Asian children brought to the United States—but not for our own black children. Can you picture the motif white parents could use for their African American babies that would be the equivalent of pandas for Chinese babies? Watermelons, anyone? You could turn to Africa and kente cloth, but anything that would mark *American* black would be automatically offensive. But we, like the international adopters, have plenty to purchase: Black Barbie, books about one hundred great African Americans. We're not able to turn the baby's identity into something cute to observers, but we try to make the world look more hospitable for the baby.

Any time the outside world disvalues or threatens to disvalue the child, the mother has the job of displaying its value, showing its worth. In a study of mothers of disabled children, Landsman showed that mothers use consumption as a conscious strategy. They "normalize" their children as much as possible with the objects and accessories of normal childhood.[40] Picture the little boy in a wheelchair wearing the most stylish sneakers, the sports logos on his clothes, and picture the teddy bear tucked into the incubator. What these mothers are doing is using consumption while at the same time utterly rejecting the idea of the child as a commodity, let alone a flawed commodity. Perhaps the most poignant example of this is in the work of Linda Layne on motherhood and mourning.[41] Mothers of babies who have died "curate" the few items of babyhood they have, the few toys or pieces of clothing, to create enough of a person out of their lost baby so that others can share in the mourning. In each case, the foster child being fitted for eyeglasses, the disabled child, and the child who has died, consumption is used to claim value for a profoundly disvalued child.

In the human struggle to create meaning, to live meaningful lives, we all use the tools we have to hand. The battle is to use those tools and not be used by them. That is the action, the struggle, the work that we see performed by mothers. As foster mothers, as adoptive mothers of racially disvalued children, as mothers of the various "rejects" of the consumer hierarchy, and even as the ordinary mothers of ordinary children in their most ordinary moments, mothers use consumerist language and practices to fight for their children. And it is those same tools that midwives use to fight for mothers. We speak the language of consumption, but we aim to achieve meaning and value.

We fight the good fight from within and from without, as part of the market, when as consumers, as cogs in that wheel, we try to turn it to a different purpose. My dear friend and colleague Eileen Moran reminds me that in a market economy, even the critics point to the gaps between the ideology of fair and open markets and the reality we face, to "show how the fix is in." In other words, they buy into the ideology of the market to show how its reality does not even live up to that standard. Similarly, Eileen reminds me, if we were living in the Middle

Ages, our critiques of the establishment would most likely be offered in religious terms, accepting at some level the religious perspective while critiquing it. "But does it matter?" she asks, ever the pragmatist and activist. "It's still resistance." Of course there is no place of purity, no "outside" in which to stand; yet, to accept the religious point of view, or to accept the market point of view, does damage even while we argue against it. It is the loss of language itself that troubles and saddens me: the inability to get outside of the system even in our thoughts. If I feel that birth is something more, more than a service offered or purchased, more than a moment of consumption or production, how am I supposed to talk about that? Whether as a woman who has given birth, or as a woman who has adopted, how can I talk about the births of my children without falling into the language of consumption? Use the language of religion? That works for most of the women that Klassen[42] interviewed, but it does not satisfy my needs to move outside of that system of oppression as well. How can I speak of that which I value?

The language of consumption itself cheapens the language of value, reducing it to cost. In this language, a value is a bargain! And so I, perhaps given to a rather dour view of the world anyway, come back to the depressing part. We each take that which we hold sacred, and try to hold it out of the marketplace. Mothers do it with their babies; I find I am tempted to do it with some abstracted, romanticized, sentimentalized idea of motherhood. Midwives often want to do it with birth. Yet we all are functioning within a system that takes the language out of our mouths, turns it around, and pushes us further into the world of consumerism. Midwifery becomes yet another service, a purchasable commodity—a better birth, a better baby, a better midwife, a better mother, all there to be purchased in whole or in part. Adoption becomes an exercise in thoughtful comparative shopping.

I recently spent a lot of time in Germany, a sabbatical semester during which I was talking about genetics, bioethics, and related things with German students. A Jew in Germany, thinking about motherhood, I was immersed in the way other systems, nonconsumerist systems, have tried to use motherhood in the service of evil. Nationalism, racism, patriarchy—those are not systems that do well by mothers either.

The relationships between human beings are something I value. They are something I think we ought to value—as individuals, as societies, as a world community. Motherhood is a, and maybe *the,* prime relationship, primary in the lifespan of the person being mothered, primary in establishing our understandings of what it is to be connected with another human being. If motherhood is or can be a force for good in the world, one of the ways that we can learn and teach the interconnectedness of our lives, then how can we understand motherhood outside of the systems, often systems of evil, in which we live?

What can we use to weave a family?

5
Adoption in the Age of Genetics

The very word *adoption* is problematic: one adopts pets, highways, textbooks, political platforms, and, yes, children. And plenty of people have objected to these other uses of the word "adoption," mostly claiming that it trivializes the concept. It feels wrong to use this same word for my relationship with my cat, let alone my decision to use a particular textbook in a class I teach, or some business's decision to sponsor highway clean-up campaigns. But what all of the uses of the word, used in this broad way, imply is taking something foreign, other, and making it one's own.

Adoption, as I adopted Victoria, is taking a child and making that child one's own. And yet we also, in contemporary society, routinely distinguish between a child "by adoption" and a child "of one's own." The fact of being adopted is forever in the present tense—I *am* an adoptive parent; she *is* an adopted child—and so the otherness, the foreignness of the child and the parent are continually reinforced in our language and in our thinking. The language doesn't accept me as her mother the way it legitimizes me as Leah's mother. Leah, a grown woman, will always be my *child,* but that takes no qualifier: not my "born child" or "birth child," but just *my child.* I've seen *obituaries* that report people as the "adopted" children of their parents; the language of adoption just never lets go.

What is it that makes that child "other"? Wherein lies the consistent, abiding foreignness of the adopted child to the adoptive family? It is certainly not how we feel; like every adoptive mother I've ever talked to, I feel no less the mother of my child by adoption than my children by birth.

Much has been written about this otherness from the side of the adoptees. They are the people living the Freudian family romance: the dream that there is, somewhere else, a better, truer, more real set of parents, people who could really understand us. Like most dreams, it has its dark side. Coming out of the "sealed records" era,[1] the drama of the search not only captured the imagination of many adoptees but also inspired talk shows, movies, novels, and magazine articles. Adoptees who didn't want to search, who didn't claim feelings of "genealogical bewilderment"[2] were accused of being in denial. In the reading group I once ran on adoption, one graduate student shared the story of being "found" by her birth mother. A strange woman came up to her when she was in her early adulthood, and told her that she was her birth mother, told her an awful tale of being forced to give her up, of all the years of longing and looking. The student said, "I felt so sorry for this poor woman who lost her baby." But no, she didn't feel like the baby this woman had lost.

The contemporary drama of the search is only the most recent manifestation of a longstanding public interest in adoption stories. Marianne Novy recently edited a book on adoption in literature, and identified "three mythic stories that European and American cultures have typically used to imagine adoption: the disastrous adoption and discovery, as in *Oedipus,* the happy discovery as in *Winter's Tale,* and the happy adoption as in the novels (*Silas Marner, Oliver Twist, Anne of Green Gables* and more recently, *The Bean Trees*)."[3]

What all three myths assume, she points out, is that a child has only one set of parents—something that she, as an adopted woman herself, can see is an overly simplistic story.

From the highest of literature to the lowest of the talk shows, the major portrayals of adoption do seem to qualify as one or another of these three mythic tales. And real life is indeed a lot more complicated.

The stories of adoption from the point of view of adoptees are often coming of age stories, finding oneself. Read in light of the "family romance," the search is part of ordinary coming of age: many of us spend some time in late adolescence and early adulthood thinking about our parents. It is primarily women who search, and the search is primarily for birth mothers. It seems to me much like what I did when, as a nonadopted adolescent, I tried to understand what my mother's life had been like when she had me. We want to know when and where we entered, what the back story was.

My focus in this chapter is less on the adoptees' perspective, and more on that of the adopters. Our understanding of this relationship is probably best summed up for me in two book titles: *Shared Fate*[4] and *Perspectives on a Grafted Tree*.[5] Once we have adopted, once we have made a child ours, like any parent's, our future lies there, with that child—that becomes our fate. And it is less like a transplanting and more like a grafting: the attachment is as solid as any branch.

But here I am speaking almost psychologically, speaking about the bonds, attachments, feelings we have as family. This is family through the eyes of those who do it, who weave it together: traditionally a mother's-eye view of family, even when expressed by loving fathers.

Adoption also has a political legal history that is more from a traditional father's view. One of the earlier ways of understanding adoption was that the child belonged to someone else: adoption was primarily about moving the allegiance of, and responsibility for, the child from one family or community to another. The adoption was a transfer. It was often done politically; adoptions, like marriages, were arranged to accomplish some purpose outside of the family. When I was in Japan, talking to several feminist groups, women's health activists, midwives, women dealing with infertility issues, all assured me that adoption was simply not acceptable to the Japanese. Few Japanese men, they told me, would ever agree to raise a child not "their own." And then, on a walk off to do some touristing, I found Osaka Castle, and the history of the ruler who "adopted many sons" because he had no children and needed them. Adoption wasn't about loving families, but about strategic alignments.

But we would no more do that in America today than we'd do arranged marriages. Adoption, like any form of creating family—marriage being the other example of a purely legal, non-birth creation of family—is supposed to be, ideally, based on choice, not on individual need. As choice has become so powerful in our imaginations, the language of "needing to get married" begins to sound quaint. In adoption as we practice it, a lot of the focus is on choice—but the choice of the adopters is, if we are honest with ourselves, the only real one. As Rickie Solinger has so forcefully shown in *Beggars and Choosers: How the Politics of Choice Shapes Adoption, Abortion, and Welfare in the United States,*[6] "choice" rarely defines the situation of the birth mothers, and obviously choice is not the experience of the adopted baby. "Need," the other piece of the equation, comes into play for those actors.

Those of us who adopt, and the culture of adoption that supports us, like to think that birth mothers act out of choice, that—especially in contemporary, more open adoptions—we are the "chosen people" of those birth mothers. It begs the whole question of what "choice" means, where individual agency comes into play. It's hard to imagine a woman who "chose" to place her child for adoption in the same way I "chose" to adopt: out of no need but her own desire to do so. True enough, once pregnant, once well on the way to a motherhood that she does not want, adoption may be only one of a woman's options, and any given adoptive family only one of her choices. But even under these most ideal of circumstances (not faced with a strong desire for sons in a country with a one-child-only policy, not faced with war and famine and heartbreak of all kinds), it's hard to imagine a woman choosing to become a birth mother without the circumstances pushing hard in that direction.

Birth mothers *need* to place their babies; babies *need* families. Infertile women/couples may be said to "need" children, but it is a lot closer to a choice, a choosing, for them. It is when need meets choice that adoption can happen: the needs of the birth mother and the needs of the baby lead them to accept the choice of the adopters.

Motherhood is defined as a problem for birth mothers, a problem that needs to be solved. It's not acceptable for the woman to think of herself as possessing a precious resource, having hold of something enormously valuable. If she's carrying a healthy white baby, she most certainly does have hold of something of economic value. But any woman who expresses it that way, who talks about selling this baby, is demonized. It's not her baby, it's her problem. And besides, we say, you can't "own" a baby.

Contemporary, highly individualized American society has encouraged us to see the child as a unique, almost disconnected person, not belonging to anyone. Even fetuses are presented as separate: the ultrasound imagery we have made omnipresent shows us a fetus without the maternal body surrounding it, a self-contained, free-floating fetus. Babies, we say, "arrive," as if from outside, "entering the world." Mothers themselves, biological mothers who have just given birth to those babies, are said to "greet" and "bond with" them, as if the babies landed from Mars.

This way of thinking about fetuses and newborns might make adoption easier and more palatable as a concept; the waiting arms can be other than those of the woman who has borne the child. Babies can arrive, enter the world, and be "brought home from the hospital" without our really thinking very hard of how they got there in the first place, of the women who mothered them through their first nine months. Sandra Patton, in *Birth Marks,*[7] says, "Adoptees cannot help but be aware of the role of the state in constructing who we are when the story of our beginnings typically involves elements like *the home study* and *being picked up at the agency rather than coming home from the hospital.*" It is an amazing naturalization of the hospital as where babies come from—one institution (the agency) substituting for another (the hospital), with the mother erased.

But with this dismissal of the nurturance of pregnancy comes the increasing significance of the individuality and uniqueness of the fetus/baby/child. And, in this era of genetic ideology, that uniqueness is said to come from its unique genetic structure. No two people are alike, we are repeatedly told, with the exception of identical twins; our genetic composition makes us unique. But that genetic composition itself comes from somewhere, and in this lies the tension between the individual and the larger social world. The individual is both altogether unique and altogether constructed of his or her (genetic) parents. In this ideology, nurturance—of pregnancy, of infancy, of childhood—is the nurturance of that unique, inherent, and inherited nature. While the "free-floating fetus" makes adoption an easier concept in American society, the fetus as product of a seed, genetic material unfolding, developing, makes adoption a more difficult concept. You can never, after all, rewrite that genetic encyclopedia that we are, those genetic instructions that are part of the ideology. Birth certificates can be rewritten, but the code book not.

And it can happen *before* the birth: it is now possible to "adopt" an embryo, to transplant an embryo from one woman to another, or to create an embryo in vitro out of the ovum of one woman and place it in the body of another. It is very telling that the word "adoption" is used in this context: it is the genetic material and very little else—the surrounding cytoplasm, still far too small to be seen by the naked eye—that is being "adopted." Note that we never speak of a transplanted kidney or heart as "adopted." That biological material becomes part of the "host," though of course it remains genetically distinct. A transplanted embryo, on the other hand, is understood as adopted, because the child that grows remains, in contemporary ideology, always other, always foreign. The transfer can never be completed. It does not, in our current talk, grow to be entirely one's own baby in one's own body, but remains adopted, someone *else's* child nurtured as if one's own.

If the nurturance of pregnancy, the growth of a human baby from a blastocyst, does not make a child one's own, then how can other, later nurturance offered to a born baby or child ever make that child one's own? This negation of the significance of nurturance, its relegation to the background as genetics is foregrounded, thus shapes the understanding of adoption.

It is important to distinguish the science of genetics from its function as an ideology for our time. The scientists inform us that genes do not determine much of anything about us. Rather, genes are one factor in a multifactorial process; genes interact with other genes and with the environment, and complex processes cannot be reduced to simple discussions of genes for diseases, characteristics, types. But while the more responsible scientists issue statements about the dangers of oversimplification, the public mind is more taken by statements like that of James Watson, that "our fate lies not in the stars but in our genes." Genes as determinative, genes as *fate*, capture the public imagination.

Seeing fate this way—inborn, inbred, predetermined—has profound implications for parenting in general, and for adoption specifically. All parents are helpless bystanders as the child's fate plays out. We can nurture, supervise, protect, but are essentially powerless. We do not create our children, we oversee them. This is true of all parents in this ideology. The child is what it is, and the parent cannot change that.

In adoption, what is different is a deep sense of the unknown and perhaps unknowable: if the child is the product of its genes, and the sources of those genes are not known, then the child is essentially unknown. In reality, of course, we are all unknown and unknowable. Which genes are inherited and which not; which genes are being passed along a family silently, not showing consequences until the right (or wrong) combination of genes and environment arises; which new genes have mutated and appeared for the first time—these are the genetic unknowables. Give birth to a child and you still will not know the genetic fate that child has been given.

But we are not talking about genetic science; we are talking about genetic ideology, the popular belief system that has grown up with, alongside, out of, and underpinning the genetic science. A significant piece of that has been the selling of new reproductive technologies, from in vitro fertilization to the fancier technologies that attempt to insert a single sperm of an otherwise infertile man into a harvested egg—all technologies that are risky to the health of women, all technologies designed to maintain genetic ties between parent and child. In that belief system, which sees only the child of one's own genes as one's own child, the child of unknown genes will be the foreign and unknown/unknowable child.

That is the sense, then, in which adoption is impossible to complete: one can never make the child one's own, because it will always be the product of foreign seed. So, no matter what I *feel,* I will always be spoken of as the *adoptive* mother of Victoria, she will always be called my *adopted* child.

I don't think it's really possible to characterize an age you're living through. But if I did, I'd have to agree that we are living in the information age, that information is a defining concept for twenty-first-century Americans. In so many arenas of our lives, we feel that we need information. We define responsible behavior as "informed" behavior; we value knowing what we're doing, what we're getting into, making informed decisions and by so doing controlling ourselves, our lives and our destinies.

The values of the market, of good consumer behavior, are increasingly influential, pervade more and more of our lives. Being informed, making careful decisions, thinking through the consequences—that's how we're supposed to shop. You shouldn't buy a car because something about it just appeals to you. You should get all the information you can—on that model, that make of car, and even, radio ads now tell me, the history of the particular used car you're looking at.

Is it making you uncomfortable to have a discussion of buying a used car while addressing issues of adoption? It's making me crazy. It is totally inappropriate. And yet. It is the model that we have to draw on, the idea of responsible behavior that we know, and it does influence adoption.

In the heyday of the eugenics movement in America, back in

the 1920s and 1930s, there were "better baby" exhibits at county fairs, just as there were contests for the best pigs and cows, judged on breeding and not just beauty, an explicit statement that there were "blue ribbon" babies—and, by definition, runners-up, also-rans, and losers. Pink (never brown), plump, smiling babies were brought to the fair—just to show off, of course, not to market. But if you were, say, in the "market" for a baby, what are the characteristics you'd be looking for? What in the baby's history? What in its genes?

We no longer are nearly as explicit about our eugenics as we were, but one would be hard put to argue that Americans think in any less eugenic ways, that we worry less about our genes, place less value on good stock, good genes. Our genetic science is far, far more sophisticated than it was in the pre–World War II era, and so is our language, but I think our values have changed less than we might think. With new tools, with new science, things just play out a bit differently than county fairs.

We live in the information age, as embodied in the tools we're using. I'm writing this on a computer, the iconic tool of the information age. I e-mail copies of it to friends and colleagues for comment, to myself for storage, then to my editor, and eventually the version you are reading may be printed out in a book that you may well have bought over the Internet, or that may be presented on your screen. The computer as an information tool gives us metaphors for understanding our world. When the clock was first invented, it was the dominant tool of its time, and provided metaphors for understanding the world. God, people came to imagine, was the Master Watchmaker, the Being who made the clocklike universe. The machine—its gears and cranks and springs and pumps—became the metaphor for the world outside and the metaphor for the world inside, the way of thinking of the body.

The body-as-machine is certainly still there in our imaginations, and language of plumbing, of wear, of parts, of stress, moves back and forth seamlessly between our machines and our bodies. And we hook our bodies up to machines, circulating our blood through machines, working on artificial heart pumps, using breathing machines from the iron lung to the smallest portable respirator. Walk into any intensive care unit, and it is impossible *not* to think of the body-as-machine.

The computer as information-machine, the place where hardware meets software, now holds the dominant place in our imagination once held by the clock. The kind of machine we are is a computer-run machine, an information system with its too, too weak flesh for hardware, and its genes for operating systems.

Genetics then is not just a branch of science, it is also an ideology for our time, a way of thinking about ourselves, our bodies, our families, our lives. Inevitably the lens that genetics is, its way of seeing the world, is going to influence the way that we think about adoption. Through the genetic lens, what people are, essentially—in our essence—is our genes. Our genes produce us, construct our bodies, and the locus of action, the source of our essential being, is thought to lie in those genes.

The deep logic of genetics, the frame or prism of understanding that genetics gives us, is that genes are causes. As Evelyn Fox Keller, philosopher of science, summarizes the logic of genetic thinking: "Genes are the primary agents of life; they are the fundamental units of biological analysis; they cause the development of biological traits; and the ultimate goal of biological science is the understanding of how they act."[8] If genes are the cause, the active force, the predictor of traits, then to read genes is to predict traits.

But geneticists often cannot predict traits, and so they have introduced a useful distinction, noting the difference between genotype and phenotype. The genotype is the genetic reading. The phenotype is how it actually played out, the being before you. Environment can then be understood as that which muddies the waters, that which interferes between the genotype and the phenotype. Geneticists themselves are very aware of the significance of the environment, from the environment of the rest of the cell outside of the gene-laden nucleus, to the environment of the rest of the body, to the environment that lies outside of the body. What we are is the product of the interactions of genes with each other and with the environment. But in popular thinking, in the dominant ideology of genetic determinism, genes are seen as the real, the ultimate causes, environment as a variety of contributing, or even complicating, factors.

Genetics—as an ideology, a way of thinking more than a science—puts all of the essence of life, all of its energy, majesty, and power, into the nucleus of the cell. The old-fashioned word for that essential bit, that source of life, was the "seed." In the history of Western society, that seed was something that men had, and women were part of the environment: the place where the seeds of men grew into babies, the children of men.

In the current version, both men and women have "seeds," have a genetic essence which they pass on to their children. Their children are the embodiment of the genes of the parents and this genetic connection comes to define parenthood. The word "gene," it is interesting to note, long preceded the current biological understanding of genetics. "Gene" was the name given to an unknown force that transmits qualities from parent to child, whether among people or among pea plants. What is now called genes are stretches of DNA that code for the production of specific proteins.

And that is what DNA does. That famous double helix, that intertwining spiral staircase whose image shows up all over, is a code to produce proteins. (Dim the lights, turn on Power Point, and here we go!) There are four molecules that make up DNA:

adenine, thymine, cytosine, and guanine, usually identified only as A, T, C, and G. Each molecule is in the form of a disc, called a "base," and the rungs of the ladder that connect the two spirals are made when two molecular discs form what are called "base pairs." Adenine pairs with thymine; cytosine pairs with guanine. The human genome is made up of these base pairs, about three billion of them arranged on twenty-three pairs of chromosomes. Segments of DNA, ranging from as few as several thousand to as many as several hundred thousand base pairs, "code" for the production of a specific protein; these segments are the genes. Proteins themselves are made up of amino acids in a particular sequence: three base pairs translates into one amino acid.

Try putting the science of it together with the popular discourse, the facts with the ideology, and the disconnect is pretty clear. It is one thing to understand how faulty coding can produce a missing or changed protein, and how that might cause a disease. So a genetic disease like sickle cell anemia or cystic fibrosis makes some sense. But we talk about genes for talents, for interests, even for occupations: an article recently described someone as having a concentration of economist genes, because his parents and uncles were all economists. Try to imagine the forces of evolution working to create the DNA sequence that codes for a protein that produces an economist. This is *not* what the scientists have in mind.

The facts of genetic science may not support the cultural image of genetics, but the ideology, genetics as ideology, is very much part of our time, and it does have consequences for our understanding of adoption.

In one interesting way, the ideology of genetics and genetic determinism becomes freeing for adoptive parents: the responsibility for passing on "bad genes" is removed. If all kinds of behavior and characteristics are seen as genetic, then not having produced the genes that go into the child frees the parent from responsibility. Is the child depressed, smart, hyperactive, mathematical, addicted, bulimic, absent-minded, musical? Whatever the characteristic, good or bad, desirable or not, it simply is what it is, and the parents do not get the blame or the credit. Now I wouldn't know this from personal experience, because no child of mine has ever had or been a problem in any way (and if you have any question or doubts, feel free to contact my mother, who will vouch for this completely), but just conduct a little thought experiment: Say one of my kids did have some kind of problem. Just try to imagine that. If it's one of the children by birth, then clearly Hesch and I screwed up somewhere: in our child-rearing practices (thank you, Drs. Freud and Spock) or in the genes we passed on. But if it is the child by adoption, well then, what noble people we are to be taking care of this problem our little adopted child has.

This may in fact be one understudied reason for the well-known fact that parents are more likely to make use of stigmatized mental health services for adopted children: the parents can be free of the stigma. If a child "of one's own" is in need of mental health services, counseling, therapy, drugs, that says something about oneself. If an adopted child has such needs, then it can be read as an undesirable characteristic inherited by the child from its family of origin, something with which adoptive parents must cope. In this ideology, the adoptive parents switch from causative agents of their child's misery or problem to innocent victims of bad genes passed on, and perhaps martyrs for dealing with it at all.

This is one of the points of connection between genetic determinism writ small, or micro-eugenics (eugenics at the level of the individual) and genetic determinism writ large, or macro-eugenics (at the level of population). Adoption does not occur randomly across race and class lines. Adoption most often means moving a child up from its point of origin to a family higher in the social and economic hierarchy. Poorer women and families are put in the position of relinquishing children; wealthier women and families take those children in, take them on. The history of eugenics makes clear its connection between socioeconomic status and genetic status: better genes rose to the top. The very fact of placement, the factors that would lead to placement, were themselves often seen as proof or indication of bad genes, inferior genetic stock. Adoption was discouraged by this very belief that children available for adoption were likely to have a history of mental illness or instability in their families and thus in their genes. Historians of adoption[9] have discussed this, but so too have novelists and filmmakers. I remember watching the movie *The Bad Seed* on television as a kid; the mother of the evil, evil child discovers that she herself was adopted, taken from an evil, evil mother.[10] The bad seed skipped her generation but flowered in her daughter. Her father, the grandfather of the evil kid, is the poor, duped martyr who thought love would overcome bad seeds. (Sorry if I gave away the ending.) Stories like that are deeply woven into our cultural lore; they shape the way we think about adoption.[11]

These eugenic ideas were in disfavor in the post–World War II era, but they have never entirely left American society, resurfacing periodically, especially in discussions of race, but also underlying discussions of class. American culture continues to maintain and produce sometimes vague notions and sometimes elaborately footnoted, badly researched books about the genetic, racial, and class-stratified basis of intelligence—as well as mental illness, and perhaps personality characteristics, too. (See *The Bell Curve*[12] if there's still a copy around; otherwise a similar book should be published any minute—they come as regularly as biblical locust plagues.)

Racial stereotypes cut many different ways, and that too has consequences for adoption. The image of the smart Asians undoubtedly influences both the decisions of Americans to adopt from Asia and feelings about those Asian children brought among us. Characteristics that are on the one hand explained with reference to culture (hard-working, studious, model immigrants) are at the same time racialized, or perhaps we should say geneticized, and seen as inbred in the baby, as independent of upbringing or cultural influence. Negative imagery too slides from culture to genes, from "culture of poverty" explanations to "genetic predispositions" for what are far better understood as cultural outcomes: crime, school failure, teenage pregnancy, and the like.

There is a well-known hierarchy in adoption, a ranking of adoptability—or more crudely even a ranking of cost, dramatized in the aforementioned billboard—that reflects the socioeconomic structure: white babies of middle-class college-educated women are the most costly; babies of poor women of color the least, with the nuances of race and class played out in the middle. This market reflects eugenic values.

While macro-eugenics plays out in race and international marketing of babies for adoption, micro-eugenics is increasingly coming into play. By micro-eugenics I mean a eugenics of the individual, a valuing or disvaluing of specific characteristics believed to be genetic. Micro-eugenics was first seen in American life in the marketing of prenatal diagnostic technologies. By means of amniocentesis and a host of interrelated technologies, fetuses have been tested for genetic disorders or characteristics widely considered undesirable.[13] Down syndrome and neural tube defects are the most common conditions for which testing is done, but a host of other conditions are also being tested for, including Tay-Sachs disease, sickle cell anemia, cystic fibrosis, and literally hundreds of others.

It should come as no surprise—and yet, somehow it did surprise me—that genetic screening for newborns would be used
as a form of pre-adoption screening, just as prenatal screening is
used to avoid the birth of a baby with an undesirable genetic
condition. In prenatal diagnosis, abortion is the only real option; if a fetus is found to have a condition such that the potential mother decides its life would be too burdensome—for the
potential baby itself, actually, not necessarily for the family
alone—the mother can decide not to continue the pregnancy,
not to make a baby at all.

In pre-adoption screening, the issues are quite different: a
baby exists. The testing is done after birth, on a baby someone
is deciding to adopt or not. The question of "burden" shifts entirely to the potential adoptive family: Are they willing to take
on this particular baby, with its projected problems? Newborn-
screening programs have existed for quite a while and been
widely accepted in the United States. PKU screening presented
a paradigm case. PKU, or phenylketonuria, is a disorder in
which a baby cannot metabolize certain proteins. Without a
special diet and treatment instituted immediately, mental retar-
dation and physical disorders result. With treatment, normal development is possible. Mandated in almost all states, PKU
screening was thus a case in which perceived benefits (diet and
treatment preventing damage) were perceived to far outweigh
risks (stigma and potential psychological or financial harm), and
it opened the way for other newborn screening.

Now let us do a little thought experiment. The PKU diet and
therapy program is not easy; it is psychologically demanding for
child and family. Babies are screened. If a baby has screened positive and has the PKU enzyme-deficiency disorder, might it not
make that baby harder to place for adoption?

Other screening tests are available. Might not potential
adoptive parents want to avail themselves of such screening be-

fore making a commitment to a particular adoptable baby? The ethics, as well as the legal and social ramifications, of this testing have been explored particularly by Janet Farrell Smith.[14] It seems that "increasing numbers of prospective adopters consulted medical geneticists for a physical or genetic testing examination that was done privately, independently of adoption agency screening procedures," with the results used for adoption decisions by the prospective parents. Just as one would take a car off to one's own mechanic before purchasing, some potential adopters take the baby in for testing before final papers are signed. In a thoughtful and wide-ranging panel discussion on the ethics of genetic testing in adoption, led by Farrell-Smith, a number of issues arose. One, of course, was the parity with prenatal testing: if parents by birth can test for and avoid a particular condition, then surely adoptive parents have equal rights, don't they?

Trying to think this through, one participant in the discussion, Leonard Glantz, compared this kind of testing with kicking the tires of a used car, or in the more comparable metaphor I've just offered, taking a used car to one's own mechanic before buying it. Might this car have a nonobvious but potentially expensive problem with its transmission? Shouldn't you know this before you purchase it? Might this child similarly have a problem that is nonobvious but potentially expensive (emotionally, physically, and financially), a problem that could be diagnosed/predicted from genetic testing? And should one not know that before making the commitment to adoption, or have the right to sue for wrongful adoption if the information was not disclosed?

At first blush, "wrongful adoption" is a horrible concept: it's a legal case in which adoptive parents sue the agency or agent who placed their child with them for adoption. The thrust of the argument is that if they, the parents, had known what the agent or agency knew, they would never have taken the child, landing us squarely back in used-car salesmanship territory. If you knew the transmission was faulty, you'd never have bought the car. If the seller knew and didn't tell you—they put one over on you, and you should be able to get your money back.

Undoing an adoption because of concealed information is not a new thing, and has a troubling history with regard to race. In some states it was the case that an adoption could be reversed or set aside if the child turned out to be the "wrong" race. The fear of passing is deeply rooted in American racism, and there was concern that a baby could appear to be white but really be black, could darken with age. Remember that we have had laws in many states that forbid marriage between blacks and whites. So Missouri and Kentucky had laws[15] that said that if within five years the child "prove(d) to be a member of a race the members of which are prohibited from marriage with members of the race to which the parents by adoption belong" (Kentucky) or "reveals traits of ethnological ancestry different from those of the adoptive parents and of which the adoptive parents had no knowledge or information prior to the adoption" (Missouri) the adoption could be canceled. And presumably if the agency lied about race, a case could brought.

The trope of the white woman who gives birth to a baby who darkens over time, revealing either the woman's true race and her passing, or her liaison with a black lover, shows up regularly in American fiction. And probably occasionally in American fact.[16] The same is true of adoption: it can happen that a baby looks white at first and looks "not white" later on. When race matching is so profoundly significant, all kinds of awful scenarios open up.

In more recent times, wrongful adoption cases have been about concealed medical rather than racial history. Sometimes the concern is the treatment of the child in the period before the adoptive parents took him/her, including pregnancy-related behavior. Sometimes the concern is with genetic disease, or conditions thought to be genetic that show up in the child and that adoptive parents claim the agency knew existed in the child's biological family history.

Such suits are not limited to adoption: there are also wrongful birth suits, in which the parents claim that had they known what the doctors knew or should have known, what the doctors had an obligation to find out, they never would have gone ahead with the pregnancy.

Who would bring such a suit? It sounds monstrous, parents suing because they have the children they have, whether by birth or by adoption. On the other hand—and there always, always is another hand—consider this situation. A young woman goes to the doctor saying she's planning on getting pregnant. He prescribes folic acid and tells her to stop drinking wine, stuff like that. He takes a cursory history. She gets pregnant, gives birth, and the baby starts to get sick, sicker, is dying. It has, say, Tay-Sachs disease. It turns out the woman has a cousin who died of Tay-Sachs. Her husband had a baby brother who died young, and nobody ever told him anything about it. The woman and her husband are stupid, I suppose; they should have asked some questions. But people have a right to be stupid about a lot of things. The doctor? He has no such right to be stupid. He should have asked a few questions, and he would have found this out, would have suggested she get screened for Tay-Sachs, and she wouldn't be the mother of a dying baby right now.

The legal issues get all tangled up in the very fact of the baby's life. Can the baby sue? For what? Existence? It's not as if *that* baby could have been born without Tay-Sachs. The suit the baby could bring would be for "wrongful life," which is both an intellectual conundrum and a moral one.

But the mother, she's got a case. A few thoughtful moments

on the doctor's part, she'd have gotten some more information, and most probably would have been tested for Tay-Sachs carrier status, as would her husband. Then they'd have had some choices: to try a pregnancy and do prenatal screening and abortion; to try in vitro fertilization and preimplantation screening, only implanting an embryo that did not carry Tay-Sachs; or to use donor sperm—or even egg if they wanted to take those additional risks—to conceive a child without a chance of its having Tay-Sachs; or to skip pregnancy altogether and adopt.

Now how is this different from wrongful adoption? Let's say the woman in the example above learned the baby had Tay-Sachs midway through her pregnancy, but continued the pregnancy and placed the baby for adoption. An unlikely scenario, but let me play bioethicist for a moment—they just love unlikely scenarios. If she were placing because she couldn't bear to take care of a dying baby, and the social workers handling the case either knew that or were too incompetent to find out, and placed the baby with a family that had decided to adopt rather than have a pregnancy because (ta-dum!) they carried Tay-Sachs. . . .

Well, then, suing doesn't seem quite so monstrous.

Wrongful adoption suits have been brought under less convoluted but similar circumstances: the child is ill or dying or will be severely disabled, and the agency should have known that, or even did know it and concealed the information from the adopters. Other wrongful adoption cases have been brought in the context of international adoptions, when agencies knew more about the very awful circumstances the babies had been living in than they shared with the family. As the babies', children's, problems began to surface, the parents sued. Had they known how very badly damaged the children were, they claimed, they would not have adopted.

Maybe that's true and maybe that's not. Maybe these parents aren't such monsters as these cases make them seem. Maybe they do love their children with all of their hearts and souls, but don't know how to take care of them. Wrongful birth and wrongful adoption cases have to be understood in the specifically American context. We don't have national health services or insurance. These cases are a form of malpractice suit; some professional didn't do what they were supposed to do, and some individual client/patient is left holding the bag. The fact is that Americans sue not because we're vindictive or have higher standards for our professional service-providers, but because we *need* to. Sick, hurt, disabled, psychologically scarred children are all expensive. If you had such a kid, by birth or by adoption, and you're not rolling in money, think how fast you'd be looking for a deep pocket.

The incentive to sue is money-driven. If you buy a ninety-nine-cent flashlight and after a day it stops working, you probably just take it as a lesson: doesn't pay to buy ninety-nine-cent flashlights. But if the six-thousand-dollar used car you bought stops working, turns out to be a lemon, you probably can't afford to just shrug that one off.

Landsman titled her article on the strategies mothers of disabled children use to have others value their children "Too Bad You Got a Lemon."[17] That, one mother said, was what it seemed like other people were trying to say to her. Oddly, the new focus on genetics and genetic testing makes adoption almost beside the point; women who birthed or adopted children with disabilities had much the same experience. They loved a child the rest of the world wasn't sure was worth loving. And with all the prenatal testing available, having such a child by birth, no less than by adoption, comes to seem more and more like irresponsible consumption.

6
Talking About Race

I do a *lot* of public speaking—mostly at universities, at professional or academic conferences, that kind of thing. And mostly what I talk about is motherhood-related issues. Midwifery and birth stuff, certainly, work on prenatal testing, and now, having written a book on the human genome project, lots of things beyond motherhood related to genetics: genetic diseases, genetic testing, bioethics and genetics. One-third of that book was about race, the genetics of race. I found it useful, for my own understanding as well as for explaining genetic science and ideology to others, to distinguish "micro" from "macro" genetics and eugenics. At the micro level, people are looking for particular "bad" genes, sometimes whole extra chromosomes, sometimes errant pieces of DNA that more or less wreak havoc on the body. But at the macro level, we have the genetic distributions that define populations, recognizable groups of people, what we call and think of as "race." Which wreaks its own havoc.

The way this lecture circuit business seems to work—for ordinary academics like me, not stars with lecture agents—is that people read your books, or hear you talk somewhere else, and include you when they plan a conference or a speaker series, or whatever. So they generally approach you with a slot in mind, a topic they want covered, and then you can make it more specific or focused as you choose.

One morning I walked into the office and found a faxed invitation from a conference planned in Graz. The embarrassing truth is, I was in an awful mood, having a rotten week for reasons I no longer remember, and I had no clue where Graz was. I started to look it up, and then thought: What difference does it make? They're paying my way to come and see Graz, wherever it might be. They speak German there, that was clear from the heading information on the fax and even from the particular form of the awkwardness of the English. It's somewhere in Europe. So, Graz in September, sure, why not? Just say yes. Felt very daring—saying yes to going who-knows-where. But a large part of the reason I said yes right off was that they invited me to speak about "Race." It was a conference on the body, and the ethics and politics of the human genome project, and they wanted me, *me!* to speak about race. Totally brightened my mood.

The way these genetics-related conferences are organized is pretty standardized, almost formalized. There are variations on the theme of course, but they almost always open with some scientists with a lot of slides, explaining DNA, the double helix, the GAG-A-CAT. (Richard Leibmann-Smith cleverly pointed out that that is all one can spell in English using the DNA letters of G, A, C, T.) Think of that as Act I: it's supposed to be dramatic, lots of colored slides and pictures and stuff, but fundamentally a slow opener—the people who are going to understand and retain this stuff generally have it already; the rest of us have our eyes glaze over in a room darkened for the slide show.

Act II brings on the critics. Not every conference has every category, but I guarantee that there will be someone at the conference complaining that the voice of "____" was missing for whichever category got left out. The range of categories includes: People with Disabilities, People with Genetic Diseases in Their Families (they may or may not have disabilities, but they've got a different row to hoe), Feminists, Genetic Counselors, People of Color, Bioethicists.

Life being what it is, sometimes someone can do two categories at a time: the bioethicist can roll in in a wheelchair. The feminist can be a woman of color. But mostly not. Mostly we are separate categories, and our bodies reflect our topics: the person to speak about disability is *always* visibly disabled. The person to discuss feminist issues is *always* a woman.

So it was cool, way cool, to be invited to speak about race.

Graz, it turns out, is in Austria.

In America the person of color, the person who discusses race, is always of African descent. In America, I am white. In Austria, I am a Jew.

Americans haven't thought of "Jew" as a racial category in a long time. It's actually pretty offensive to American Jews. I remember in my childhood, in the Reform Jewish temple to which we went, they taught us that Jews are *not,* repeat, NOT a race. We are a religion. We are an ethnic group. We are a nation. Hitler thought we were a race, but he was wrong, wrong, wrong.

The wrongness of Hitler hardly requires discussion—that is one dead horse, way beyond beating. But stop and think for a minute: What we were being taught wasn't that Hitler was wrong because he didn't understand what wonderful people we Jews are, what a fine and upstanding race we are, but that he was wrong in thinking of us as a race. Why aren't we a race? Well, because we are *white*.

Ah, the racelessness of white. Whiteness studies, wonderful and insightful books I've read over the past decade or so, have clarified this for me:[1] White folks are white; other people have race. That's what whiteness is: the privilege of not having race, not being bothered with race, being able to afford a gracious color-blindness.

Race resides in the other; race is what other, different, people have. Whiteness thus comes into being as the "regular," the place where race is not. But—obvious, no?—whiteness is a strangely constructed social category, gathering people under one umbrella who have fought to the very death over their differences. Whiteness had to happen in America, had to be constructed to unite all the European settlers, the Dutch and the British and the French and whoever else happened to wander in, in contradistinction to the native peoples and to the Africans being brought in as slaves. All these different European people did not come to America as "white folks." As James Baldwin pointed out, Norwegians did not sit around Norway priding themselves on their whiteness: "No one was white before he/she came to America."[2]

And that is so very true of us Jews. Whatever else we were in Europe, we were *not* "white." Again, from Baldwin:

> It is probable that it is the Jewish community—or more accurately, perhaps, its remnants—that in America has paid the highest and most extraordinary price for becoming white. For the Jews came here from countries where they were not white; and incontestably—in the eyes of the Black American (and not only in those eyes) American Jews have opted to become white.[3]

Baldwin was making this point in the mid-1980s, still a difficult moment in Black-Jewish relations in America.

W. E. B. Du Bois and other black writers had long noted the creation of whiteness, its privileges and benefits, but also its unexpected costs. But it wasn't until the mid-1990s that Whiteness Studies began to make an academic appearance. David

Roediger had written about *The Wages of Whiteness* in 1991,[4] building on Du Bois's insight that there are actually costs to white people in creating whiteness—psychological and even economic, as race divides workers and keeps wages down. And in 1994, Roediger came out with *Towards the Abolition of Whiteness,*[5] taking the point to its logical conclusion: Whiteness isn't doing anyone a whole lot of good, and it most certainly does do a whole lot of harm, so let's get rid of it.

The intriguing journal *Race Traitor* began publishing in 1992, similarly aiming towards a "new abolitionism," the end of the idea of whiteness. In 1995 Noel Ignatiev, a founding editor of *Race Traitor,* published a wonderful book, *How the Irish Became White,*[6] showing just how that group of people "became white" as they came to America. A series of whiteness books followed, including Theodore W. Allen's historical work *The Invention of the White Race: The Origin of Racist Oppression in Anglo America,*[7] but also other books, following Ignatiev, showing how "white ethnics" became white. Mathew Frye Jacobson wrote *Whiteness of a Different Color: European Immigrants and the Alchemy of Race,*[8] showing the pattern of trading up to whiteness that new immigrants used. In 1999, Karen Brodkin specifically addressed the ways that Jews pulled off that transformation, in *How Jews Became White Folks and What That Says About Race in America,*[9] and a 2003 edited collection addresses the question *Are Italians White?: How Race Is Made in America.*[10]

That was the context in which I learned about Jewishness as a religion, a culture, a community, a way of life—as anything, *anything* but a race. Blacks had race. Asians had race. Jews were white.

Whiteness studies are a fresh approach to looking at race, a new handle on an old problem. When I first started studying sociology, in the 1960s, the sociology of race was mostly subsumed under something called "race relations." That is an approach that starts with the idea that society is made up of separate racial groups that somehow "relate" to each other. We studied patterns of relationships between groups, worked up models: assimilation, amalgamation, different ways the groups could relate. The dominant group could enfold the minority till the minority disappeared, melted into the majority. The groups could combine to create something new, the way tap dance grew from the interplay of Irish step dancing and African dance traditions. Or they could exist side by side, like the dishes at the Brotherhood Week celebrations from my own elementary school days: kugel; Irish stew; lasagna, lined up in Tupperware.

Sociology accepted the idea of race fairly uncritically, for the most part. Sociologists were intensely, profoundly critical of the way that race played out, but its existence as a fact of life in the world went largely unquestioned. We developed a sophisticated vocabulary, acknowledging the differences between white ethnics—and between black ethnics—by making use of the idea of the "ethnic group." My yellowed copy of a 1969 dictionary of sociology[11] defines an ethnic group as: "A group with a common cultural tradition and a sense of identity which exists as a subgroup of a larger society." That would be the Jews, the Irish, the Italians, the ethnic groups that lived in my working-class Brooklyn neighborhood.

The dictionary goes on to clarify the distinction between ethnicity and race: "Ethnic groups should not be confused with racial groups. It is possible for an ethnic group to be a racial group as well, but often this is not the case." When it came to defining race, the editors sensibly turned the problem over to another discipline: "An anthropological classification dividing mankind (*Homo sapiens*) into several divisions and subdivisions (or subraces). The criteria for labeling the various races are based essentially on physical characteristics of size, the shape of the head, ears, lips, and nose, and the color of the skin and eyes." It's an anthropological thing, not our problem.

So race, for the sociologists of the 1960s, was defined scientifically, even calling for the language of *Homo sapiens* to define mankind. But even in the sixties, sociologists were not uncritically buying a racial essentialism. The overlapping nature of these characteristics and their essentially statistical variation was pointed out: groups are distinguished by the frequency of occurrence of the racial characteristics. And, rising to a higher sociological standard, the interest in and awareness of racial differences are attributed to "the social and cultural history of the society." But finally, capitulating entirely, "The major racial groups are usually identified as Caucasoid, Mongoloid, Negroid and Australoid." (And it's worth noting that as antiquated and, well, racist, as those four names sound to my ears, my spell-checking program was bothered only by "Australoid." And "subraces" got the red-underline treatment also: haven't we come a long way!)

What sociology was doing forty-some-odd years ago was what most sophisticated, thoughtful, well-read Americans were probably doing. They accepted race as a biological given, a set of scientific categories or divisions of *Homo sapiens* that had seen a lot of bad social use. Nineteen sixty-nine was closer in time to the liberation of the Nazi concentration camps than it is to today. We had only recently taken down the Whites Only signs in America. We had just buried Martin Luther King. The evil that race could bring was beyond question. But the existence of race as a category was perhaps also beyond question, outside of questioning. It existed; what were we to do about it?

The challenges to race as a category have come not only from the social sciences and humanities in the form of whiteness studies, but also, more recently, from the new genetics. While the genetic science of its time was the basis for the eugenics movements of the 1920s through to the climactic 1940s, the new genetics repudiates all of that. There are no races. No such a thing. That's what the new genetics tells us. Human beings cannot be divided up into three, four, ten, one hundred, one thousand different groups.

Give me a moment, missing only the dim lights and the slides, to walk you through the biology of this.[12] The human genome consists of something like 30,000 genes, each made up of many, sometimes many thousands of, base pairs. Each gene has various forms, called "alleles." Almost all of us share almost all of them. We are very closely related to each other. Any person, after all, looks a lot more like any other person than like anything else on earth.

Most of the genetic variation is individual, to be found within local populations: the differences within any groups of Norwegians, for example, the sheer number of different alleles, is far greater than the number of different alleles that distinguish those Norwegians from, say, Koreans. And so it goes throughout the world: The differences that distinguish populations are finite. When counting the whole genome, all 30,000 genes, there are only so many differences. At the level of a population, say Norwegians, you can talk about percentages of shared traits, distribution variations across a continuum. Then you can compare that with another population, like Koreans. A higher percentage of Koreans have this allele; a higher percentage of Norwegians that one.

But you cannot get from there to distinct racial groups, populations that share among themselves and only among themselves a cluster of alleles that would distinguish any individual in that group from individuals outside of that group.

Genetic thinking, this business of allele variation in individuals as opposed to groups, is a lot like sociological thinking.

Take this as an example: Most Americans prefer taking a shower to taking a bath. More women than men prefer baths, but most women do prefer showers. The "bath preference" characteristic is more likely to be found among women, but it cannot be used to distinguish women as a group from men. And it certainly cannot be used to determine whether any particular person is a man or a woman. So it goes with these genetic differences, these allele variations: they can differ between populations, but they can't classify individuals.

So what the new science of genetics has done is refute race as a category. Gone. Doesn't work scientifically. It's particularly hopeless to try thinking of the race categories that Americans care about the most, black and white. Since humankind (*Homo sapiens,* as we scientific types like to call it) arose in Africa, African peoples have the widest range of allelic variations. Little groups, with less variation in them because they were smaller groups, wandered off to here and there around the planet. Given enough time, they turned themselves into Swedes or Germans or Italians or Poles or whatever. Then they rode a boat over to the United States and turned into whites. You're just not going to find a scientific racial system that will get you black and white, Negroid and Caucasoid.

But that won't stop us from trying.

Troy Duster wrote famously of eugenics as coming in the back door.[13] He was looking at the development of social policy and medical practice around sickle cell disease, a blood disorder more common among people of African and Mediterranean descent than among those of Northern European descent. It is this back door that has opened wide and may now be the new main entrance for race in America. Sickle cell disease is understood in the United States as a disease of African Americans. It is, in actuality, equally common among Mediterranean groups, but it is very much thought of and understood as a black disease.

Other genetic diseases are recognized as being more common among other populations: cystic fibrosis among white people, for example, and Tay-Sachs among Eastern European (Ashkenazi) Jews. Remember, what we are talking about is increased or decreased likelihoods of a fairly unlikely thing; most African Americans do not carry sickle cell, but African Americans are more likely to carry it than are non–African Americans. You can see what starts to happen in common-sense thinking: if a disease can be genetic and exists in some groups more than in others, how then can one not think of those groups themselves as genetic groupings? In this way, race is reconstructed biomedically.[14]

This biomedical construction of race has, in an interesting historical twist, been of particular concern for Jews. For a variety of historical reasons, Jews are a highly medicalized group. We were denied access to land ownership in much of Europe and had to find other routes for upward mobility. As educational pathways opened up, medicine beckoned. "My son the doctor" became a Jewish joke, but also a Jewish dream and a Jewish success. For these and for many other reasons no doubt buried in the Jewish psyche, Jews became highly medicalized.[15] You wouldn't know it from me, but studies show that we Jews like medical treatment, seek testing, seek treatment, volunteer for medical management in all sorts of ways, in numbers disproportionate to our presence in American society.

The consequence has been, in the United States at any rate, that an increasing number of genetic diseases are thought of as Jewish diseases. It is not just Tay-Sachs, the most famous and early example of a genetic disease disproportionately found in Jews. In the U.S., breast cancer has been labeled—literally, on the front pages of newspapers and magazines—as a Jewish genetic disease. No matter that breast cancer is itself hardly a good example of a genetic disease at all, with less than 10 percent of all breast cancer patients having the gene for breast cancer. Ashkenazi women were among the first tested in great numbers for the breast cancer genes, and it is Ashkenazi women who are labeled as being at risk for breast cancer.

So it is that race seems to sneak in this back door, and Jews begin to look again like a race group, sharing a host of genetic diseases. I was at a genetics conference in Boston a few years ago, and heard something I'd been both expecting and rather dreading. A young woman described herself as having a rare genetic disorder, something she said was found "in the Jewish race." It was the first time I have heard the conversational use of "Jewish race" in my life as a post–World War II baby boomer. I expect to be hearing it again.

It's not just Jews. We are starting to see the discussion of drug development for different "types" of people, and "type" in the United States most often means race. It gets complicated. The Association of Black Cardiologists was widely reported to be looking to the development of drugs for people who are of African descent—reinventing a biomedical type that recreates race. Remember that blacks in America are an extraordinarily diverse "racial" group, with each individual descended from quite a variety of African, European, and Native American ancestors. But it would appear that blacks disproportionately have some metabolic or other problem that might increase the tendency to heart disease. Blackness is recognizable: blackness becomes the basis for the grouping. Blacks are tested; black heart disease develops as a category, with black pills and perhaps black hearts to follow.

To counter old race-based medical practice that used only white people for biomedical research, and white men at that, newer regulations require diversity. But what does *that* mean? In America, it mostly means race. And race mostly means skin color. There are about a half-dozen genes that affect skin color, and doctors and researchers eyeball people and "race" them, place them in to the "appropriate" racial categories.[16] A dark-skinned pregnant woman gets offered sickle cell testing; a lighter one, cystic fibrosis. There have been a dozen or so articles in newspapers and magazines in the last couple of years in which doctors decry "color-blindness," tell us how they "have to" see race. They need it to do diagnosis. Occasionally someone counters with the story of the white-looking kid who was all but dead of sickle cell complications, or a black kid of cystic fibrosis, because no one had the sense to diagnose him until someone saw the kid's x-rays and lab tests without the kid around. Skin the kid, and any fool could see what his problem was. In his lightness or darkness, he blinded the doctors to the diagnosis.

But most of the stories are warm and pleasant-sounding apologies for having to be race conscious in medicine. That's the back door that Duster was talking about: making race and racial categories legitimate via medicine. It doesn't just affect individual patients in clinical settings, or even drug researchers. These racial categories get created and *sold*. The new genetics, we are told, will bring us individually tailored drug treatments: the variation of diabetes that you might have, for example, combined with knowing your other genetic characteristics, will determine what regimen works best for you. An individualized treatment sounds wonderful—cut back on side effects, increase effectiveness—who would want less? But individualized treatment is expensive.

Think of it like clothing: what you really want is a personal seamstress, don't you? Someone who will get the exact shade of fabric that suits your fancy, put it together with the exact style you've been admiring, size it to your particular body. Ah, joy.

In reality, you know which store or department to go to, to find the most likely choices. You are part of a market segment: read *Seventeen* magazine and you'll find very different clothes advertised than in, say, *Marie Claire,* and different ones in *Jane* magazine than in *Working Mothers.*

So it goes with drugs: the costs of individually tailored drugs are going to be really, really high. The marketing is a nightmare. But population groups, market segments, *race groups*—that could work. One drug could be advertised in *Ebony,* another in *Hadassah Magazine.*

I live in a mixed neighborhood: mostly black, a lot of Haitian people, representatives of the other islands, but a sprinkling of American Southern blacks, and a small number of people from Africa. That's a "black" neighborhood the way the Italian, Irish, and Jewish neighborhood I grew up in was "white." It is a political and a cultural and a social grouping that makes some kind of sense; it's hard to think about it biologically. But a couple of years ago a huge sign went up on my corner bus stop, a sign bigger than I am, asking "Are you African American Diabetic?" and encouraging you, if you were, to participate in a research study at a prominent teaching hospital.

I really don't know what they are *learning* about diabetes in that research, but I do know what they are *teaching* about race as a biological category.

In the very idea of transracial adoption, or mixed-race family, or multiracialism is the hard nut of race. For there to be a transracial adoption, there have to be races for the child to move between. For a child to be of mixed race, there have to be two or more races to combine. To understand and celebrate our multiracial community, we have to see these races that come together so attractively. Not withstanding genetic science or whiteness studies, race is still there in the center—race as a category, race as a fact, a thing.

Race is the most commonsensical thing in the world: it is obvious, present, seemingly transparently clear. When I walk into a classroom, a lecture hall, I almost automatically look out across the sea of faces and check if it's racially mixed. I can be somewhere, as I just was in a housing co-op on New York's Lower East Side, and be taken aback that "This is so white." Or I can go to Hamilton, Ontario, as I did last month, and be pleasantly surprised to find it's not as white as I thought it would be, more mixed, more black folks than I'd expected. (Well, duh, where did I think the underground railroad was going?) I can say these things—this place is so white, that one so mixed—and I can take it for granted that you, my reader, my American reader anyway, will understand, that you can picture the range of faces before me that I saw as "so white" or "more mixed."

Race is a shared vocabulary. But it is not a universal language. I have learned as I travel that not everyone groups races the same way. That's the point I was making about my Jewish racial identity in Austria. But it's also the racial identity of the Maori in New Zealand, or the Aboriginal people of Australia—clearly recognizable, racially identifiable in their countries, vaguely exotic-looking to outsiders. (So my spell checker rejects "Australoid" as a word.)

We in America still experience race as a biological category or set of categories. Yes, that is hotly contested—flatly denied by serious biologists and geneticists, hotly proclaimed by wave after wave of old, new, and newer racists. The race question we still think we can answer affirmatively is: Can you divide the people of the earth into discrete, discernible groupings? But what are the essential differences between the groups? How many of them are there? The classic black, white, yellow and red? The more elaborate ten or thirty or three hundred that physical anthropology came up with at various moments? How many did Hitler recognize?

Race exists for us as a set of physical characteristics, located in the body. Blackness is, as Du Bois called it, in the bone and blood and hair: the color of the skin, the shape of the body, the texture of the hair. But more powerfully, it's in the soul: the souls of black folk, the souls of white folk. Race is a mark upon the body, a set of physical characteristics that are located in the body, but marking something far beyond the body. The characteristics that we call race are passed along, moved from parent to child as physical bits, but they take their meaning as a mark of membership in a community.

Adoption drives this all home so personally for me because Victoria has membership in a community based on physical characteristics we do not share. She does not share the body markers for the community that has marked me. She does not, to put it clearly, look Jewish. And I do not look black.

It's easier to claim her as Jewish, than me as black. In America, Jews became white, but "Jewishness" became a religion, and in America, religion is an option, something one joins or leaves as a matter of choice.

I just saw a show at the Brooklyn Museum, photographs of Jews around the world. The point, as best I could tell, was to show that we are everywhere, and we don't always "look Jewish." Moroccan Jews look, well, Moroccan. Chinese Jews look Chinese. Italian Jews look Italian. Ethiopian Jews look Ethiopian. And American Jews look Eastern European. "Funny, you don't look Jewish" means you don't look Eastern European— you look Chinese or Italian or Ethiopian, perhaps. Not Jewish.

A cousin of mine, someone who has emigrated to Israel and become very, very involved in things Jewish, asked me: "How

Jewish is Victoria?" I was furious. "How Jewish am I?" I snarled at him. Not very. Entirely. Whatever. I "am" Jewish: it's an identity, a culture, an ethnicity I lay claim to, to which I feel entitled to lay claim. I am not religious. I am not very Jewish in my daily life practices, dress, inner or outer life. So how Jewish should my children be? But he didn't ask me "How Jewish is Leah?" It was my black kid he asked about. Her body has marked her as other-than-Jewish.

When Victoria was three or so, among many other songs she was learning was "Hava Nagila." She was singing it in a ladies' room at the beach. A woman stepped out of the stall, smiling, looking over for the little cute kid—and did a classic double take when she saw the particular child who was singing. The lady looked Jewish. Yup. I know what I am saying: I read Jewish in her body; she read not-Jewish in Victoria's. Am I to take offense? Am I to see my child excluded from membership in a community because of what she does or doesn't look like? For all I know, that smiling woman who looked Jewish was raised by a Catholic Puerto Rican family, identifies herself as a Puerto Rican Catholic woman. Can I fault her—or my cousin—for doing what I do when I face an audience and see race?

It is a tangled, complicated relationship that exists between culture and the body. It is not that ethnicity, the way of life, the community, the culture is carried in the blood, in the body, as racist essentialists would claim. But the body is marked with history, and so ripe for claiming by a community. Is that so bad? Of course it has the awful flip side, the dark side of community: some bodies are marked as not belonging, marked as other. Victoria doesn't look Jewish.

This marking of the body is a very powerful argument against transracial adoption. It is a reasonable argument to make: let any white family of any white ethnicity raise the child any way they want to, inculcate him or her with all the cultural lore, values, way of life, songs and recipes, history, all of it that they have and want to share—and if that child's body marks her as black, if her skin and hair and face present her to the world as black, she will have to live in this world as black.

And she damned well better know how. Race isn't just something we talk about; it's something we live.

III

What I Learned at the Schomburg

7
Images

Is there not something unseemly, in our society, about the spectacle of a white woman mothering a black child? A white woman giving totally to a black child; a black child totally and demandingly dependent for everything, sustenance itself, from a white woman. The image of a white woman suckling a black child; the image of a black child suckling for its life from the bosom of a white woman. The utter interdependence of such an image, the merging it implies; the giving up of boundary; the encompassing of other within self; the unbounded generosity and interconnectedness of such an image.

PATRICIA J. WILLIAMS,
The Alchemy of Race and Rights

A 1993 Cultural Studies conference at the University of Michigan used an image, taken from an ad for "United Colors of Benetton," of a black woman suckling a white baby. The University's Women of Color Task Force objected. Patricia Williams[1] was writing in the context of this controversy. What would it mean, she was asking, if we were to reverse the image, placing a black baby at the white breast?

I have spent many hours of my life staring at exactly that, my black baby suckling at my white breasts, and thinking about it. What am I looking at in that reverse image? Unbounded generosity? Interconnectedness? Some weird gendered version of "the white man's burden"? Genocide? A better Benetton ad?

In the work I am doing here, I am going to try to think systematically, theoretically, politically, about that image. It is a powerful, a volatile image. It arouses strong feelings among white people and black. It arouses variously, and sometimes simultaneously, anger, respect, joy, fury, love, and hatred. It is an image whose meaning shifts over time and place, reflecting the color line, the meanings and value of black children and the meanings and value of white women. I am going to use that image, hold it in my mind and ask you to hold it in yours, as I try to understand what it has meant and what it can mean now for white women to be raising black children.

The woman of color raising the white child—as slave mammy or as contemporary nanny—has been theorized, discussed, analyzed, deconstructed, and reconstructed. That image too reflects changing ideas about race and about gender, about childhood, child raising, and motherhood. But unlike its reverse, it is something I think we understand.

For one thing, such a woman is not at all out of the ordinary in the history of mothering. In a sense, she is doing what mothers in patriarchal systems have always done: raising the child who will ultimately have enormous power over her own fate. Mothers of sons in many societies are raising the children who will have the power to throw them on to their husband's funeral pyres or save them, tend to them in their old age or abandon them to fates ranging from ice floes to lions to trying to survive on Social Security payments.

This is the nature of "mothering the oppressor," mothering and raising a child who is of higher status than the mother herself. Since mothers, qua mothers, are held in such low esteem in our own society, their work dismissed as trivial, some variation on mothering the oppressor is a fairly common experience for American mothers.

But what do we know about, how can we think about mothering the oppressed, mothering a child of less-valued status than the mother herself? What images are there for us to call upon? What are the tropes, metaphors, and cultural fantasies available to guide mothering *down* across powerful status lines?

One image is that of the few men who do child rearing and the daughters they raise. How do men raise their daughters? Part of the image that comes to mind is the tomboy, the girl not well versed in "girlness," and the man seeking a woman's touch to help guide the daughter into womanhood. I grew up with a widowed mother, who was involved in a group called Parents Without Partners. PWP included a surprising number of such men in the 1950s, men whose wives had died or, as one inelegantly put it to my mother, "flew the coop." Women like my mother were called on to help out, to teach some of the womanly arts to these girls—taking them shopping for special occasion clothes, teaching them hair and makeup tricks.

There was a sense, though—and who knows how much of this is my childhood memory and how much my reading back now—that these girls were okay, that their fathers were raising them to be strong and competent and good people, if oddly lacking in some of the feminine trim.

Gender is one fundamental cultural hierarchy. In America, race is the other. Are white mothers raising black children, like men raising daughters, similarly equipped to do all of the basic child rearing with only the need of a black hand lent to put in the finishing touches? To what extent is race like/unlike gender; to what extent are white mothers raising black children like fathers raising daughters?

That actually works for me. My situation does feel something like the situations I saw among my mother's men friends who were "mothering" their children. They were doing fine, but they needed help. The kind of help they needed was, in some ways, much like the kind of help I need as a white woman with a black daughter. Fundamentally, we're okay. But there are skills, cultural approaches, experiences, that I have not got, and cannot provide for my daughter. I need a little help from my friends.

But I am a very, very privileged woman. I live in a huge and racially diverse city. I have been able to afford to live pretty much where I want to, in a racially mixed, mostly black neighborhood. I have friends and colleagues and neighbors who are black. I have white friends and family and neighbors who are not the racists I keep reading about, the ones who eventually get around to calling the black child names.[2] I haven't had to grapple with overt white racism in my mothering.

What has it been like in the past, to do what I am doing, to be who I am, a white mother of a black child? Is it imaginable?

For me, this question requires thinking about parenting itself: just what exactly is meant by the word "parenting"? The term has a post–women's movement quality to it in the first place: to "parent" implies some kind of gender-neutral child rearing, when we know that child rearing has been one of the *least* gender-neutral activities we have. So the first thing I have done, as I said earlier, is drop the language of parenting, and speak specifically about "mothering" work. I know that makes a lot of people uncomfortable, some angry. But it is *mothering*, not parenting, that captures the intimate, daily acts of nurturance that constitute raising a child. Like Sara Ruddick, author of *Maternal Thinking: Toward a Politics of Peace,* I am not talking about mothering as a biological relationship or as an identity, but as a set of practices, a form of work.[3] Men can and do mother, but I think we lose more than we gain when we try to use the language of parenting to cover the work traditionally thought of as mothering.

On the other hand, I am deliberately not going to make a distinction between mothering and child rearing. There is a strong tendency in contemporary America to valorize mothering, to distinguish it from less adequate, less loving, less devoted forms of childcare or child rearing. I hear it conversationally, when people critique a woman's child-rearing skills, techniques, maybe especially her commitment to the project: "Well," they say, "that's not what *I* call really being a mother." *Good* mothers, we say, *really* mother. All the rest of the work of child rearing we dismiss.

I am not going to do that. Without an enormous amount of work on the part of one or more adults or even older children, babies and children die. Nobody, the famous Topsy of *Uncle Tom's Cabin* included, "just grows." Any grown person who speaks the language, and manages to function in the world, is living proof of an enormous amount of work. Each was fed, cleaned, trained, and taught. It didn't just happen. It may have been done with loving devotion or with grudging acceptance; it may have been done for pleasure or out of fear; in joy or in sorrow—but work was done. I will call that work mothering. I want to acknowledge its gendered history, and I very much want to acknowledge the simple fact that this work has to be done for infants to live. Calling it parenting does not capture either.

And when you try to look at parenting in a cross-race context, the absurdities abound. White men have fathered the (black) children of (black) women from the time the first European settlers sailed up to the African shores, but this act of impregnation has had precious little to do with any of the mothering or parenting or intimate nurturing of child rearing. So while there absolutely undoubtedly are—and right here in my very own home!—white men actively *mothering* their black children, I'd prefer to call that work mothering and stay clear on what I am talking about.

So what is it that white people, some men and mostly women, are doing when they are raising, *mothering,* their black children? How can we think about that? What images are available to us?

People think in images, in metaphors, in stories. We understand our actions, we understand what we are doing and seeing and experiencing, in the context of the stories we tell, the images we hold. Those images and stories have their own histories. Sometimes we know those histories and sometimes not; the stories and images still have power. They are there to be drawn on, and they have consequences: they shape our understandings and so they shape the stories we are now creating.

In what follows, I am drawing upon the reading I did, most intensively for several months I spent at the Schomburg Center for Research in Black Culture, but sporadically for the last ten or more years, seeking each and every instance I could find of reference to white people mothering—in any and all senses of the word—black children.

To make some sense of all these stories, I organized them, put them together in themes. What I am doing here is simply creating a typology, a description of the various ways this relationship has been imagined, done, thought about. I'm taking this image, the black child at the white breast, the little black hand trustingly placed in the big white one, the white mother with her black child, and tracing it back.

I found I could place most of what I read into three motifs, tropes, or put simply, types: Protégés, Pets, and Trophies. None of them is very satisfying. They're actually rather awful in their own ways. But what is most important to remember is that none of them is unique to adoption, or unique to parenting across race. Look at anybody raising anybody—look at you and your mother or me and mine, you and your child or me and any of mine—and you will find traces of each of these motifs. What is gained from looking back, from looking at this relationship under the harshness of slavery and unabashed racism, is a clarity that highlights some things that are always present but not often seen.

The mentor's relationship to the protégé is more like the traditional role of men as fathers—at least when they were doing a good job. Fathers have traditionally served as a bridge between their grown or almost-grown children, particularly their sons, and the larger world, teaching them, helping them find their place. Fathers share their place in the world with their children, passing on names and identity, privilege, position, and property. That can be a loving gift, something one does out of genuine love and feeling for the child. And it can be a strategic move, a way to solidify one's own place in the world. That has been, after all, one of the recognized motivations for men to have children, to have sons to carry on their work and their name. And, life being what it is, probably this kind of mentoring is most often done out of a mixture of motivations, mentoring the child for its sake and one's own.

If protégés typify the traditional father's relationship with his grown children, then pets typify the mother's relationship with her babies and little children. It's an indulgence, not just indulging the children, but indulging oneself in them. And this too is highlighted, sometimes very uncomfortably so, by mothering across race lines.

All of our children, being who they are, say something about who we are, who we want to be, how we want to be seen. They are all trophies, the third model I found, representing our taste and discernment, the values we have and display. This too is not at all unique to cross-race parenting or to adoptive parenting, but certainly highlighted in this context.

These are, I think, ugly ways to think about ourselves and our children. I certainly don't want to think of *my* children as protégés or pets or trophies! And yet I think there are kernels of truth in those understandings of what it is to raise children, to mother. So here I will explore each of these—safely removed, long ago, and sometimes far away—and then come back to the original question.

What has it been like in the past, to do what I am doing, to be who I am, a white mother of a black child? Is it imaginable?

8
Children of a Diaspora

African American children have been raised in white families since slave days, in a wide range of circumstances. White women have conceived children with their black lovers and raised them. White families have adopted, fostered, and stolen black children with the fullest range of motivations. A white family raising a black child may be engaging in an act of love, or an act of genocide—or it may well be both at once.

One of the definitions of genocide, from the 1948 International Convention on the Prevention and Punishment of the Crime of Genocide, is the "forcible transferring of children of a group to another group." I came upon that definition while reading about the "Stolen Generation," the Australian Aboriginal children who were taken from their homes.[1] It's a story that's been told recently in a movie, *Rabbit-Proof Fence*. What constitutes forcible transfer? The police did it, chasing down hidden Aboriginal children in the bush, images straight out of Australian history, powerfully reproduced in that movie. But it is also a forced transfer when a group is so burdened by its poverty that children are placed out for economic survival.

There are good and moral reasons why any *particular* child may be transferred out. The question of genocide arises with the *systematic* nature of the transfer. Or maybe it's best to look at any problem at its root, where it starts—and genocide starts, arises in its essence, in the construction of racial groups. If a group is targeted as having a biological or genetic identity, more than a social, communal identity, we're well started on the path to genocide. Just by identifying the group, by separating it out, the "othering" has begun. That's the point that proponents of color-blind adoption policies are emphasizing: to "race" the baby, to decide the social placement of a baby based on its body, is to construct race. The baby is raced by its appearance and by its pedigree.

In the United States we have the "one drop" rule, a lasting vestige of the slave system. Slave owners needed to claim all the children of their slaves as their slaves—even those who were also the children of the slave owners. However many the generations of white rape of black women, however white those children looked, they would still be claimed as black, and therefore slave, if they had one drop of black blood.

Given that one drop rule, a baby born to a woman, a baby of her own body, will be "other" if she is white and the father black. The white woman raising her black child—with or without benefit of a black father and family—is raising other people's children. Our race line places her on one side, her children on the other, and that mythical one drop of blood is more powerful than the real blood of her labor and birthing.

American race policy around African Americans has been very different from the Australian situation. The goal of the Australian policy was to remove the children, place them in scattered white homes, and "breed out" the blackness. Something similar happened in the United States with the Native American population. It's a twist on genocidal practice: the Australian government planned on mixed breeds as a way of whitening and finally blending out the Aboriginal population.

African American children placed in white homes, on the other hand, have never been expected to breed out, to become white over generations. It was American policy, even at the height of the liberal movement in transracial adoptions, that the children would remain black. Even when there was unchecked, often entirely inappropriate, placement of black children in all-white communities, it was always with the goal of returning the adopted children in adulthood to the black community. One of the definitions of success in transracial adoption has been the formation of appropriate (read black) racial identity in the children.

In Australia, the question was: "Can white Australians raise children of Aboriginal descent to become (white) Australians?" In the United States, the question was "Can white Americans raise children of African descent to become African Americans?"

While we often talk of racism, there actually is a series of racisms that operate in America. The black-white divide is central in understanding all of it. As I wrote about earlier, most of the time Americans classify people as "white" or "nonwhite," lumping together a host of groups with nothing in particular in common on each side: French, British, Finnish, Norwegians as white, and Mexicans, Haitians, Nigerians, Pakistanis as nonwhite. When we think about the privileges of whiteness, that makes sense. Groups—Jews, Irish, Greeks, Italians—come into American and try to get themselves classified as white. But it might make even more sense to flip it, and think about black and nonblack as the relevant categories.[2]

Adoption follows much the same logic as immigration, and

in the case of the increasingly common international adoptions, the categories collapse in on each other. Are immigrants, or the parents of the adoptees brought in as immigrants, seeking whiteness? Or are they seeking the status of nonblack, differentiating themselves and their children from those in the lowest racial status America has to offer?

That is the way that I see it: other groups, including adoptees, even if not "white," can be assimilated, can move into white America. People of African descent are not permitted that luxury. That is what whole communities of immigrants, like those from the Caribbean, have found: their children quickly Americanized and lost the ethnic identity that distinguished their parents from their African American neighbors. And that is what happens to individual black children born into, or placed by adoption into, white families: they do not become white.

The situation has been different for Asian adoptees, first the Korean, and now the Chinese. The Korean adoptees were, for the most part, raised in white communities. Though not without expressing some resentment, and even some anger at the loss of their heritage, on the whole they appear to be assimilating into white America. It's not yet totally clear what the adult status of the newest group of Asian immigrant adoptees will be, but I do think that these Chinese girls will grow up to be, will grow up to lead the lives of, white American women. Roots trips and cooking classes and "Chinese school" notwithstanding, it's hard to imagine them growing up to join the Chinatowns that our large cities enjoy.

Which is not to say that America has no racism directed at Asians. Sociologist Jeffrey Bussolini studied the case of Wen Ho Lee, the Asian American scientist from Los Alamos who was accused of being a spy. The case brought to the fore what he called "the racialization of Asians," part of the "fervent project to isolate people along ethnic lines." He considered that case in the context of the Chinese adoptions: the romanticizing and sentimentalization of Chinese culture for these children of middle-class white Americans, while Lee, suddenly and harshly "othered" was not even allowed to speak his native language with his family.[3] But with the pressure of their middle-class white parents, I believe that these Chinese girls will, like the Koreans before them, become successfully moved into whiteness. Maybe their presence will change our ideas of whiteness a bit more, letting white people look Asian the way white people can now look Irish, or look Jewish, and still be white.

Children of African descent cannot cross racial lines. As long as the idea of race continues to exist in America, black children will grow up to be black adults, no matter who raises them or where. The black community eventually takes those kids in. They become grown black men and women, raising their own families. American blacks know that lots of their children have a white parent or grandparent, that some of their children were even raised by that parent.

What is it like to be such a child, a black child raised by white people? There have been some memoirs, such as James McBride's widely read *The Color of Water: A Black Man's Tribute to His White Mother*.[4] And there have been some wonderful novels, like Danzy Senna's *Caucasia*.[5] And there's the growing body of books by the now-grown transracial adoptees of the 1960s and 1970s.[6] But I knew there were also passages to be found in books not primarily about white parenting, in novels and short stories, in fiction and nonfiction, about the black people who made it home somehow. I got interested in this autobiography and fiction, this black imagination of white parenting.

The question that sent me to Harlem to the Schomburg Center for Research in Black Culture to participate in their fellowship program was this particular angle on the question of transracial adoption. I wanted to know the history: how the black community, African American novelists, historians, memoirists, and essayists, understood the situation of white parents raising black children. What is our history? Where do we—Victoria and me, families like ours—fit in the long, sad, ugly story of race in America?

As Victoria's white mother, as a white mother of an African American child, I had given a lot of thought to the arguments for and against such adoptions, to the consequences of these adoptions for the children themselves, and for the black community(ies). I'd done what any academic does when confronted by a personal question, a real concern: I read. I'd read the work of Elizabeth Bartholet,[7] herself a white mother of children of color, internationally adopted, and strongly in favor of such placements. I'd read the very early work by sociologists, by Joyce Ladner[8] and by Dawn Day;[9] I'd read the many studies Rita Simon and her colleagues, Howard Altstein and others,[10] had done on the adjustment of such kids, on how they turn out, how they and their adopted families fare. I'd been following that ongoing research since my own undergraduate days, when Howard Altstein's mother, Sadie, was the secretary of the Sociology Department at Brooklyn College. Little did I ever think, as Sadie told me about her son's work, that some day I'd be reading it to help me think about raising my own child. I read the work that Randall Kennedy was doing; his article in the *American Prospect* on "Orphans of Separatism: The Painful Politics of Transracial Adoption"[11] was interesting to me, a work published in 1994, when Victoria was five. That work developed and expanded in his more recent book, *Interracial Intimacies,* published by Random House in 2003.

And beyond "just reading," I'd worked as the dissertation advisor for Heather Dalmage for what became *Tripping on the Color Line,*[12] her book on the experiences of mixed-race families.

I'm a sociologist: the social work approach of Simons et al. and the legal stance of Kennedy interest me, but I'm most satisfied, most comfortable, with a sociological analysis.

And as a sociologist, I had particularly thought about the nature of racial identity and racial community, which underpin all of these discussions of transracial adoption and mixed-race families. There's a developing literature on mixed-race communities, and I was reading it,[13] trying to clarify just what race and mixed race mean in America, what they mean for me, for Victoria, and for the rest of my family, and for families like ours.

The data on children adopted out of the black community tends to support the conclusion that they do well psychologically and socially, and that they do indeed develop a strong identity as African American.[14] How, one has to think, could they *not* in America? They were bound to notice. There aren't as many studies, but the indications are good that children with black fathers, born to and raised by their white mothers, also manage to grow to be self-identified and functioning members of the black community.[15]

These children represent a diaspora within the larger African diaspora, and their search for identity, community, and culture sounds like the concerns of early black scholars in the back-to-Africa movement. They are, as we baby boomers used to say, finding themselves. But as we also learned, you don't really find yourself by going back. You need to know, we all need to know, our story, where we came in, when and where we entered. But for those of this particular diaspora, as well as the larger diaspora, you look back, you gather your pieces, and you move ahead. As Alice Walker said, "the way forward is with a broken heart."[16]

But how? What I wanted to know, needed to understand, was: How do they do it? How do such (grown) children make a life for themselves, come to have an identity as members of the black community, and come to find their place(s) within that community?

There is historical precedent to what we white families are doing when we raise our black children. We too are coming from somewhere, and as with all histories, some of it is pretty vile and awful, some more hopeful, encouraging. I needed to know the history.

In recent years, white families raising black kids, by birth or by adoption, have been fond of reassuring the children that color doesn't matter, and reassuring themselves that all you need is love. I don't actually believe that. And neither do most black folk. Not in America. Color does matter. You need a lot more than love. Where do you find it?

So I went up to Harlem to look.

9
Protégés

As I read through the history of Africans in Europe and America, the story of the protégé came up repeatedly. It was the oldest image I found. Some well-educated, relatively well-off person of European descent takes an African under his wing. The benefactor may appear to be genuinely supportive, trying hard to help the African achieve all that he (and in at least one notable instance, she) can—intellectually, politically, in whatever arena.

There is also this disturbing aspect, maybe a variation on the protégé story, in which the benefactor is essentially conducting an experiment, trying to see what an African could achieve, given the opportunities.[1] This last is like those stories that show up every now and again of people who raise a monkey, chimp, some kind of ape or gorilla side by side with their children, and then reports how the beloved little primate is actually more advanced in this or that motor skill, but behind, more behind, until completely lost, in language and intellectual skills. The experiment is just so hopelessly racist that I don't know what to do with it. I could ignore it, but it taints all the protégé stories.

"Protégé" is itself a problematic concept. "Mentoring" is the more current word, I think, because it focuses on the relationship. I've done a lot of mentoring in my time; I've never had a protégé. I appreciate being mentored, but I wouldn't like to think of myself as someone's protégée. There actually isn't a good word for the object of mentoring; we say "mentee" but, no, the spell checker lights up red again. We haven't got a word for that.

The person who does the mentoring is now called a mentor, but used to be thought of as a "benefactor." Protégés had benefactors. "Benefactor" is a fifteenth-century word, according to the collegiate dictionary my computer handily provides me with, meaning "one that confers a *benefit*; *especially*: one that makes a gift or bequest." A benefactor has power, the power to bestow; a protégé has needs.[2]

Is this role of benefactor, of taking a protégé, a part of parenting? I know mentoring is not unlike parenting.[3] When my children were young, I didn't understand what people meant when they said that being a mentor was like being a parent. But as my children move into adulthood, it begins to make sense. Mentoring is nothing like parenting a two-year-old. But how different is it from parenting grown children?

I apparently lack the gift of compartmentalization. The various parts of my life slop over into each other. Work and family, colleagues and friends, office and home—the boundaries between the spheres of my life are permeable. That's clearest to me when I think about the graduate students I have mentored. I feel as if, in midlife, I have acquired a series of grown children.

A former graduate student of mine came into town once and stopped by my office to say hello. She sat in on a guest lecture, then talked enthusiastically with some of my current graduate students, who had also been in the audience. I was standing on the other side of the room, taking great pride and pleasure in what I was seeing—*kvelling,* we say in Yiddish, and I don't know another word that captures that parental pride and joy. One of my current students walked by, and saw my obvious pleasure. I said: "It's like watching your kids get along, playing well together."

She smiled and went back to the group. I stood there thinking, "I can't believe I said that!"

When I got home that night, I wrote her a note, falling all over myself trying to apologize for saying something that must have sounded so infantilizing, which was not what I meant. . . . But it *is* what I meant. My students got a piece of who they are from how I raised them, and I felt deeply satisfied when I saw them connecting to each other. The current student wrote right back, assuring me she hadn't been offended, that she was pleased to be included as one of my "daughters."

Like family. We use family relationships as metaphors all the time. But sometimes it does rise above the metaphorical and become a way of living, of relating to and caring for people. Is she my daughter? Like a daughter to me? That particular student, no, actually not. But some of the others? I'll be going on Wendy Simonds's family vacation this coming week, meeting her, her husband and kids and extended family in Florida. I'll be there with Victoria, as we have been before. Not only do *I* bring Wendy's cranberry sauce to my family Thanksgiving, but now one of my cousins brings it to hers. Wendy bakes with my challah recipe. I baked one for her wedding. She sat with me in a hospital room, arguing with a nasty nurse for me while I was recovering from surgery. We are like family, like a good family, actually.

And Heather, Heather Dalmage, whose name has come up repeatedly in this book—she taught me a lot about race and mixed-race families. We had endless conversations about the "meaning" of black hair in America, passing references back and forth like the good scholars we are. And when her daughter was eighteen months old, we sat in a hotel room at the American Sociological Association meeting with some brushes, bands, and a jar of grease, and I taught Heather what I know about hair. For months, when her daughter heard my voice on the phone she said "Barbara pull hair!"

This is the kind of mentoring relationship I know, started in power—the modest power of the professor, not the power of the slave owner—but over time grounded in love and need and the body (not to mention the kitchen). Is that anything like the relationship that the European benefactors had with their African protégés? The Africans needed mentoring: it's the nature of the racist system that for any individual African to succeed in any European/American system, they had to have some help. And the stories of so many of the great African Americans include a bit of mentoring here and there by some white folk. Read about Frederick Douglass and you learn that the mistress of the plantation "took an interest" in him. What did that look like? W. E. B. Du Bois had a white teacher who helped. What did they feel for each other? Does any of my experience translate? Did any of these people love their protégés? Did they kvell?

I am not sure this is an answerable question, even if I were a historian with the tools to do it. But let me just briefly look at three of the stories I found in my time at the Schomburg, and see what we can learn from them.

One such story is presented by the life of Ignatius Sancho, who

> . . . attracted the attention of the Duke of Montagu who had among his diversions interests in testing whether, by proper cultivation and a proper tuition at school and the university an African might

not be found as capable of literature as a white person. Sancho, who for twenty years of his life served as the Duke's butler, was Montagu's first protégé.[4]

That's the experiment. Was it more than that? The basic facts of Ignatius Sancho's life are in a brief biography written by Joseph Jekyll in 1782, always given as a preface to the published editions of *The Letters of the Late Ignatius Sancho*.[5] We learn from that about his birth aboard a slave ship in 1729, his baptism as Ignatius, the death of his mother, the suicide of his father, his transfer at age two to the ownership of three "maiden sisters" in Greenwich who named him "Sancho" after Don Quixote's squire, and then the fortunate meeting with the duke. (What those two people really thought about each other, what they might have meant to each other, who knows? But, from what little I have here, it's very hard to make out anything that remotely resembles parenting, mothering, a nurturing relationship.) He learned to read. He wrote. The duke died. The duchess helped. She died. He gambled his money away. He worked as a butler for the duke's son. He set up a grocery shop. He died in 1780.

A somewhat similar story, but intriguing and I guess more troubling to me, in that both the protégé and the benefactor were women, is that of Phillis Wheatley. Her story continues to interest scholars and readers today. There's even a new chamber opera, *The Gilded Cage*.[6] I wrote to the librettist, Richard Olson, but he tells me that the story is only loosely based on their lives, doesn't shed any light on the relationship between Phillis and Susanna, says "more about me than her." Which is probably something I ought to keep remembering. *Me-search*.

Henry Louis Gates Jr. just published *The Trials of Phillis Wheatley: America's First Black Poet and Her Encounters with the Founding Fathers*,[7] but as is clear from the title, his concern is Wheatley as one of the "signifying monkeys," that is to say, the objects of experimentation. Can an African write poetry? Jefferson said no, and the argument got rolling.

I'm not interested in that argument; I'm trying to understand what if anything can be learned from Wheatley's relationship with her benefactors. Here too we have some basic facts. She was born in Gambia, kidnapped, and brought to America on a slave ship, after which she was named, the *Phillis*. When she was purchased on July 11, 1761, she was losing her top baby teeth, so was probably seven or so years old. She remembered her mother, remembered her fetching water. (Did she cry herself to sleep at night, missing her?) Back to the facts: She was purchased by the Wheatleys. She was taught to read and write. She wrote poetry. Susanna Wheatley, the mistress/benefactress took her poetry to England to publish it. (When her work was published, when George Washington wrote Phillis letters, did Susanna kvell?) Some of her poetry is very disturbing: it sometimes seems to imply that her kidnapping and enslavement were good, redeeming, because she became a Christian.

Susanna died.[8] John Wheatley died. Phillis was poor. She had two children. They died. She wrote poetry about that. (I even printed one of those in a book I did once about what it means to lose a baby. I was thinking about Phillis the mother. I didn't think about Susanna.) Back to the facts: Phillis died, about 33 years old, clutching the third little newborn baby in her arms.

What am I supposed to do with that story? I try to imagine Phillis. Imagine Susannah. Imagine them together, over a book, the slave girl and her benefactress. What did they feel for each other? What do I feel for them? That I even care, that I have spent time trying to picture this, imagine this—I'm sure it says more about me than I can ever say about them. *Me-search*.

One more story. Jacobus Elisa Johannes Capitein.[9] The facts: He was born in Guinea. Captured. Sold as a slave. Given by a slave-ship captain as a gift to Jacob van Gogh, a merchant for the Dutch West India Company. Van Gogh was thought to have named him Capitein after the sea captain friend. Traveled around Africa for a while. Then off to Holland in 1728. He was Westernized, educated, converted. Van Gogh, it says in one of my sources, "treated the boy with the love of a father," and had the help of "some famous teachers and of one charming lady." In 1735 he was baptized in the Kloosterkerk in the Hague, given his Christian names, Jacobus Elisa Johannes, and sent to Latin school. He was brilliant.

(I'm trying to stick to the facts, but of course I'm gone. Who was this man, these men? What was the "love of a father"? What did that mean to them? Who was this charming lady? Whom did she charm? Did Jacobus, the African teenage boy, charm her?)

He was a student at the University at Leyden. (I spoke there once. The first time I went to Holland, I biked around the square in Leyden, up on one of those high Dutch bikes, think-ing about travel, worldliness, me in Europe. Not thinking about slaves.)

He studied theology. He wrote a dissertation—a defense of slavery. He quoted the Bible, used rigorous scholarship. The dissertation was called *Political-Theological Dissertation Examin-ing the Question: Is Slavery Compatible with Christian Freedom Or Not?* He decided it was. It was reprinted four times, more than you can say of most dissertations. He was famous. You can imagine why.

But nothing's simple. He argued against harsh treatment of slaves, argued for religious conversion. It's easy for me to be shocked and horrified about how an African child, kidnapped and given away as a gift, could grow into a brilliant scholar who defends slavery. Looks to me like support for every argument I ever heard against transracial adoption citing cultural genocide. But it's *not* simple. Arguing against slavery wouldn't have gotten anywhere. Maybe he knew what he was doing; maybe it was a thoughtful political choice. What do I know? (What I want to know: Did van Gogh kvell? Did the charming lady? Were they proud that day in Leyden when the young scholar defended his dissertation? Were they proud when it was reprinted yet again, when pictures of Capitein and poems about him were all over Holland?)

He went to Africa. He suffered. He saw slavery up close. Smelled the slave dungeons of Elmina Castle. Heard the cries. He wanted to marry an unbaptized African woman. The church said no. A white woman arrived for him on a ship. He married her. He fell into debt. He killed himself. Or maybe that's not a fact. He died at age thirty. Probably he killed himself.

(What did van Gogh think? The charming lady? Did they grieve?)

Three stories, three protégés and their benefactors.

Is this anything like parenting? If my mentoring sometimes feels to me like my parenting, what can that tell me about theirs?

Nothing, I suppose. Times are different. Power's different. Life's different.

It's not what mothering feels like to me, that I know. Mentoring a graduate student does sometimes feel a bit like mothering an older child. It's certainly not like the physically intimate work of mothering a baby. Notice that the children these benefactors took in, took over, were—not so coincidentally, I think—seven years old: the start of the age of reason, the end of babyhood. Phillis's baby teeth were falling out; she was past the point of late weaning.

This kind of parenting is, as I said when I began, much like the parenting that is done traditionally by men, as fathering, and I think it's no accident that it is the earliest form of such relationships, of white folks taking care of black children, that we find documented. Men have traditionally offered their children protection, contacts, education, a place in the wider world, the world outside of the physical nurturance of early mothering. Women can do it too. I have. Susanna Wheatley did.

Does it tell me anything about mothering?

10
The Pet

Joyce Ladner did one of the first sociological studies of the modern practice of formal transracial adoption. The work was done at a time and in a context in which the critical voices of African Americans were much needed and soon forthcoming. Ladner described a family she observed, a white family with older children by birth and a newly adopted black baby. A black woman who knew the family well described the interaction, the relationship, using the imagery of a pet. "They treat him just like a pet dog. You'd think they just got a new pet that they can't wait to show off."[1]

Read without its historical context, Ladner may well seem overly touchy. And I think that's the way her remark struck me, back when I first read it, as the mother of just one child, born to me, crawling around my feet. There is, after all, something of a petlike quality of babies. (And a babylike quality of pets, if you've ever heard people baby-talk their dogs, kootchy-koo their cats.) I am not persuaded that the phenomenon is any more present in cross-race situations than in same-race situations. But so what? As a white mother I can call the white little toddler who is climbing up my leg "you little monkey, you!"—but what am I conjuring up when the toddler is black? My mother regularly, to much family amusement, called my baby brother "Inky," the name of my grandmother's dog—one or the other of them was always underfoot, scooting across the room while she was carrying piles of laundry. Within race, the use of pet or animal terms is affectionate, annoyed, absent-minded, silly. Across race, in a society in which animal imagery has been used as an epithet— and more—for people of color, pet imagery is something else again. Kennedy[2] condemns the "utter subjectivity" of a social worker who reports, after a visit to a white foster family of a black son, "It turns me off a little to see them getting him to perform or do tricks." I think the language of "it turns me off a little" is important here: there is no way to observe these interactions without their history. A white family having their black child do tricks is not going to look or feel the same as the same acts of performing tricks will look and feel in a same-race family.

The history, in transracial, black/white adoptions is slavery. The slavery of the United States, "chattel slavery," was intrinsically—in its very language—related to both the perception and the *use* of people of African descent as animals, as beasts of burden. "Chattel," means "property," and yes, has the same root as the word it most sounds like: cattle. In the slave system, slaves were owned as animals were owned, governed by much the same moral universe.

Slave history, from the perspective of the slaves, is notoriously tricky. It's not as if anthropologists were out there in the fields, collecting data. The narratives have to be understood in their political context—who published them and why. Before the Civil War, narratives were collected mostly for abolitionist propaganda. The closest we come to the more "anthropological" approach are the ex-slave narratives collected in the 1930s, mostly under the auspices of the federal government's Works Progress

Administration, consisting of over two thousand interviews with ex-slaves living in seventeen different states. Like most of the pre–Civil War narratives, these too were collected and published because white people wanted them. The editors of a fairly recent collection of these narratives, Berlin et al.,[3] point out that the interviewers were nearly all white Southerners, many of them descended from the same people who had once owned the former slaves. They tended to select "the most obsequious informants, 'good Negroes' in the euphemism of the day." The informants, for their part, being interviewed during the Depression by government employees, might well have been hoping for benefits and hesitant to offend.[4]

On the other hand, the narratives hardly produce a glowing endorsement of slavery. Scenes of torture, whippings, maiming, abound. There are images I can't get out of my head: a child's head caught under a rocking chair while she was whipped for stealing a piece of candy—a whipping that left her, a lifetime later, as an old woman still stared at for her misshapen face, remembering never having eaten solid food again; children getting more "ordinary" whippings for eating seemingly abandoned food scraps, found biscuits, stolen melons, or for playing with a white child's abandoned doll; a child's hand burnt with an iron, she too bearing her scars into old age.

Interspersed with narratives like that are ex-slaves' memories of always having enough to eat—old people, old *black* people, in the Depression, remembering their childhood. What do you make of it? How do you understand the experience?

I leave that project to the historians. The piece of it that I'm trying to make sense of is the legacy left to Ladner and the unnamed social worker Kennedy quoted: the haunting history of the "pet" image in white parent–black child relations.

Slavery was not a static institution: it changed with a changing economy, with the continuing expansion across the American territory, with a changing world political economy. By the end of slavery, "cotton was king." Cotton replaced the earlier crops of sugar and rice. Those earlier, larger and more profitable plantations had often been run by absentee landowners, and they required a more skilled, varied workforce, such as coopers to make the barrels needed to store sugar. Cotton required lots of brute labor and little else.[5] The earlier years of elaborate systems of house slaves, skilled-worker slaves, and field slaves changed: by the end, most adult slaves were in the fields, and most house slaves were children.

Think of the cotton plantation owners as the *nouveau riche* of Southern society, making their place, inventing their myths, creating their timeless story out of the relatively new cotton plantation world. The story they seemed to tell themselves was that of the patriarchal ideal:

> Emphasizing that their slaves, like their wives and children, were fed and clothed out of the household larder, slaveholders celebrated their special responsibility for the workers they owned, whom they often called "family." Planters draped themselves in the cloak of paterfamilias and consigned their slaves to an eternal childhood, often denominating them "girls" and "boys" until age had transformed them to "uncles" and "aunts."[6]

Understood that way, maybe some of the crazier contradictions begin to add up. Lorenzo Ezell, for example, a former slave, remembers his "old massa" as not approving of the "way some mean massas treat dey niggers" and describes a place in the pasture where his master let runaways hide, gave them something to eat. Lorenzo Ezell only came to understand later that this was part of the underground railroad. And yet this same Lorenzo Ezell says, "In dem days cullud people just like mules and hosses. Dey didn't have no last name."[7]

So what was that "old massa" thinking? Something like a

dog owner who calls the ASPCA on his neighbor? Owning dogs isn't the problem; mistreating them is?

What is it like to be a well-treated young animal? Consider some of these memories:

> Miss Cornelia was the finest woman in the world. Come Sunday morning she done put a bucket of dimes on the front gallery and stand there and throw dimes to the nigger children just like feeding chickens. I sure right here to testify, 'cause I's right there helping grab.[8]

Or this memory of being called in:

> She lift up her voice and holler 'tee, tee, t-e-e,' and Old Master just set upon the hoss and laugh and laugh to see us come running. He like to count up how many little niggers he did have. That was fun for us, too.[9]

Children were called in, and came running, to be fed. Robert Shepherd recalls:

> Dere was a great long trough what went plum across de yard and dat was where us et. For dinner us had peas or some other sort of vegetables, and corn bread. Aunt Viney crumbled up dat bread in de trough and poured de vegetables and pot likker over it. Den she blowed de horn and chillen come a-running from every which way.[10]

That memory, being fed at a trough, shows up repeatedly in the narratives, sometimes in the most matter-of-fact way, and sometimes with a post-slavery sensibility:

> 'Deed chile, you ain't gonna believe dis but it's de gospel truf. Ant Hannah [the slave caregiver] had a trough in her back yard jus' like you put in a pig pen. Well, Ant Hannah would just po' dat trough full of milk and drag dem chillun up to it. Chillun slop dat milk jus' like pigs.[11]

The line between domestic animals and pets is slender, and maybe all the more so when we think about the young animals. Taken out of the field, moved into the home, taken one at a time: yes, attachments form. What happens when they grow up, those adorable little—animals? children? slave children placed by their owners on the ideological border between animal and child?

Sometimes the commitment carried through. One former slave, Mary Armstrong, interviewed as an old woman, remembered:

> Mr. Will and Miss Olivia sure is good to me, and I never calls Mr. Will "Massa" neither, but when they's company I calls him Mr. Will and round the house by ourselves I calls them "Pappy" and "Mammy," 'cause they raises me up from the little girl . . . Old Polly tries to buy me back from Miss Olivia, and if they had they'd kilt me sure. But Miss Olivia say, "I'd wade in blood as deep as hell before I'd let you have Mary." That's just the very words she told them.

And in 1863 she was set free, and set off to find her mother:

> Mr. Wills fixes me up two papers, one 'bout a yard long and the other some smaller, but both has big gold seals what he says is the seal of the state of Missouri. He gives me money and buys my fare ticket to Texas. . . . Miss Olivia cry and carry on and say be careful of myself 'cause it sure is rough in Texas. She give me a big basket what had so much to eat in it I could hardly heft it and another with clothes in it.[12]

Lizzie Williams also had a "loving" owner but with a different ending:

> When I'se right smart size, Missy Mixon, she was Marse Billy's wife's sister, she get Marse Billy to let her have me. She was a good woman. She took me to town to live and make a little white girl out

of me. Y'all knows what I means. I got treated more like de white folks dan de rest of de niggers. . . . But 'twarn't long before Missy send me to New Orleans to nurse de sick child of her sister.

Lizzie was a "little white girl" while that was convenient for Missy, apparently—but when a servant/slave/nurse was needed, that was the end of that. The consequences of losing the "pet" status, the preferential treatment, are devastating when slavery is the fallback. But the status of children as pets, to be petted when convenient, dismissed when not, runs through our culture: "Children should be seen and not heard," we were told when I was a child.

Maryanne Novy puts it starkly in her discussion of *Daniel Deronda,* one of several books by George Eliot that deal with adoption: "The narrator often suggests that Hugo regards Daniel as a possession—at best a pet, at worst an object: 'a convenience in the family . . . this substitute for a son,' that children were treated as a 'product intended to make life more agreeable to the full-grown, whose convenience alone was to be consulted in the disposal of them.'"[13]

In sum, then, the extent to which the pet is a model, an image we have in our culture for thinking about white women mothering black children, depends on the extent to which the black children are more valued than are pets in the larger world. The slave narratives make it quite clear that most owners viewed their slaves as a form of livestock. And as with animals, some become pets. (A similar thing happened historically with dwarves, who were given as pets to royal children.) Slave children were given as gifts in ways that look remarkably like the gift of a pet. And cuteness is a characteristic valued in children across lines of race—maybe especially so. The history of the adorable "pickaninny" and his/her antics sounds a lot like descriptions of pets. The difference is that the children grow up.

* * *

Now go back and reread what Ladner's informant said of the new black baby in the white family: "They treat him like a pet dog. You'd think they just got a new pet that they can't wait to show off." In context—with its history—the innocence of the scene, the little child showing off its cute antics to admiring, even loving adults, is forever tainted.

And yet there is something of value in the pet imagery that I do not want to lose. Taken out of the slave context, is there anything we can learn from pet imagery in mothering?

Mothering any child, but especially a disvalued child, a child the world sees as worth less than the mother, *is* in some ways comparable to pet-work. There is intimate caring, the joys of caring, and yet the object of care is not necessarily valued outside of the relationship.

So far what I am saying is quite ugly, awful. But can it be something else also? People seem to have a capacity to attach, to connect to other people. Every time I say self-evident, dopey things like that, I feel the need to start apologizing, backtracking, base-covering. I hear the critiques, and I am answering a storm of angry people, disdainful scholars, irritated friends. Because there is yet another history here, and that is women's history, the long history of biological essentialism that "naturalizes" women—white and black women—doing nurturing work.

So, yes, I do mean people, and not women. Women may, for a million good and bad reasons that have been discussed at length if not ad nauseam, be more inclined to attach then men. Or maybe not. My point is just that people, men and women, young and old, seem to have that capacity.

No, I do not mean everybody's good at it or very inclined towards doing it. Like all of our human capacities, it shows enormous variation. While I'm not fond of sociobiological explanations, it would seem to make a great deal of evolutionary sense that we "attach" to each other, that we have the capacity to nurture.

Some circumstances work against that: we have the research on prisons and prisonlike situations, on concentration camps, and all the ways and places people have been evil to each other. But we also, even in relatively ugly and awful situations, sometimes reach out to each other. That seems to be encouraged in situations of dependency: when people need us, depend on us, we tend to develop some caring feelings towards them.

It's certainly been the case of people caring for children. Men and women both (and in actuality research has shown this works with nonhuman primate males as well) form attachments to dependent children.

All I am saying is that we, some of us, some people and maybe most people some of the time, have that capacity to attach, to feel a powerful connection to another person. And neediness in that person arouses that feeling of attachment and some kind of urge to help. In some of us. Sometimes.

That feeling is not, it seems to me, entirely "about" the person we attach to. Proof of that: we can do it with cats and dogs, goldfish, birds, sometimes even plants, occasionally even objects. While we know plenty about the heroic dog who runs into the burning building or whatever to save the owner, truth is, plenty of owners have done plenty of crazy things to take care of their dogs. Or cats. It's not, and maybe not even most importantly, the big dramatic things. It's the little stuff: running home early from a party because the dog is lonely. Cooking special treats for the cat. Just knowing, remembering, oddly caring which cat likes broccoli. Or cantaloupe. I had this cat once, just loved cantaloupe. I'd forget from year to year, but each spring when they were back in season, there he'd be, purring, rubbing against me, trying to get at it. What a pleasure it was to leave plenty of fruit in the rind and give him a half to play with, to eat, to drag along the floor. It was a pleasure, that's right, a pleasure for me to give him his treat. I have a friend who used to have a bird. She'd come home in the evening and boil a single strand of spaghetti for him. He just loved his spaghetti, did that bird. And it was nice to do it for him.

Are we crazy? Well, probably. There are starving people in the world, there are people undoubtedly just a short walk from me who could use all kinds of help, and here we are taking care of birds and cats.

That only makes sense to me if we postulate some kind of urge to nurture located in the person, an urge that seeks whatever outlets are available. Or maybe not even seeks — maybe sometimes just *accepts*. This or that little needy thing reaches up to you, and something opens up inside and you do what needs to be done. And come to care.

And now let's ride this along for a bit and see where we go.

This is thought of as a noble, a natural, a healthy behavior when that object is entirely acceptable and socially appropriate. Show those feelings toward your child, and you're a good parent. That virtually defines good parenting, parenting at all. We take that special care for granted, most of us. Eileen Simpson was raised an orphan, and had time and occasion to think about what was missing, what parents were and are for their children, what it is they do:

> They bestowed affection on their children, offered them special tidbits at the table, selected their clothes with an eye to what suited them, took account of their preferences, and were indulgent about defects of character (especially those that reflected their own). Parents felt no need to disguise their preferences: they unashamedly preferred their own children.[14]

The question that begs, for me, is what constitutes one's "own" children. The contemporary American mind is quick to answer in terms of biology: the children of one's own blood, or body, or genes. Adoption is, in our system, some kind of attempt to rise above biology, to conquer the natural with the social.

But no. First off, people have been perfectly capable of defining some of the children who are biologically theirs as not their own children at all: slave owners and overseers regularly fathered children with their slave women, and almost never seemed to feel any need to parent, to nurture, to care for those children. It is harder for women, given the intense physical experiences of the last months of pregnancy and birth itself, to feel disconnected from their children, but it most assuredly does happen. Given the right—or the wrong—circumstances, infanticide by mothers happens. A woman young enough and/or frightened enough not to acknowledge the physical changes and experiences of pregnancy, a woman alone enough, and we have the baby in the trash can, the baby left in the bathroom, the baby left on a mountainside. This too seems to be part of our heritage as human beings, the capacity of mothers to *not* mother, to abandon, to pretend it never happened.[15]

And just as certainly, people have been capable of attaching, deeply, in a way that feels biological, physical, natural, to children who are not their own. Countless numbers of men have been fathers to children who were not biologically theirs without ever knowing it. And countless numbers of women have opened their arms to babies and children and raised them as loving mothers.

The adult is capable of attaching, of coming to feel like a parent. The world judges. In any given social world, a judgment is made about the suitability of that object of attachment. The more worthy the object, the more accepted, valued, lauded, valorized the parenting behavior—the indulgence, preference, *love.* The less worthy the object, the less seriously the world takes the behavior, until finally, me with my cantaloupe-loving cat, my friend with her spaghetti-loving bird, even we have to laugh at it, laugh at ourselves, be clear we are not taking this too seriously.

I had a graduate student once, Patricia Boyce, who did a wonderful dissertation on grieving pet loss.[16] What happens when a beloved pet dies? It was an unrecognized, unappreciated, *illegitimate* grief. People got no support in their loss. She, Boyce, was drawn to the topic when her own cat died and she couldn't seem to concentrate on a paper she owed me. "Why not do the paper on pet loss?" I suggested. And the paper grew into a lovely, fascinating, sociological study of pet loss. And every time I tell people about that dissertation, they wonder about its writer: Was she a lonely, sad old lady? A social misfit of some sort? No, a happily married young woman with a baby, actually. She just loved her cat, you know. And it was interesting to her, how people do, actually, love their pets.

When that kind of love is shown to a child "of one's own," all is well with the world. When a person of lower status, charged with caretaking a child of higher status—mammy or nanny—shows some of that behavior, then too all is well. The behavior is seen as endearing, valuable, charming, and not unnatural. So much is that behavior valued, and even more so the sentiment that underlies that behavior, that women who do not feel it have learned to fake it pretty acceptably. Some come to feel the attachment; some not. All who want to keep their jobs come to show it.

When a person of higher status cares for a child of a lower status—along race lines in a race-stratified society, or, to take a different example, a healthy parent caring for a profoundly disabled child, the mothering work is seen as "selfless." Think about the language we use for the mother who is lovingly caring for her far-from-perfect child, the mentally retarded or physically disabled child. People say of that love, of that nurturance: it's noble, generous.

In truth, it's as self-indulgent as any other form of love and care. And so what? This self-indulgence is not something we should feel bad about, but something we should revel in. The deepest of human connections are formed in the most mundane acts. It is in the work of nurturance, Heather Dalmage reminds me, in the *doing* of feeding, changing diapers, cleaning up vomit, that the possibility for the deeper connection is born. Heather heard a colleague, a man who is a father of grown children, say that in the moment a child is born a parent has the most love for the child, that it won't be that strong again. She heard that and felt sad for him, sad that he missed the piece of parenting that counts, that the deepest connections are created, not born.

When a child, a healthy child, is born to you, you don't distinguish, you're not *asked* to distinguish, the narcissistic part of your love from the altruistic. When you take care of that child, no one asks you *why*. But direct that nurturance towards a child the world has made clear it will not value, and not only motivation but the very legitimacy of your actions are up for question. It's true of love for the disabled child, and it's true of love for the "rescued" child, the child taken out of a third-world orphanage, out of slavery, or just out of a contemporary American ghetto and into a middle-class white family.

The joys of nurturance, the self-indulgence of parenting, the pleasures of mothering are made apparent when their legitimacy is questioned. But it is in those acts of nurturance, and the joys and pleasures they give, that the basis is set for lifelong relationships, for watching the child grow, become his or her own adult self, separate, move on and out and off, as children do.

The pet/owner relationship is defined by limited time and by an unequal power relationship that never changes. So, sure, I had this cantaloupe-loving cat, and my friend had this spaghetti-loving bird, and it was kind of nice, satisfying for us. But neither cat nor bird ever grew up to get its own treats, let alone to offer us some.[17] A pet's needs, interests, demands, and aspirations are relatively static: not so with children. The commitment to a child that we understand as mothering is unlike any other commitment in its expectations (yes, I know, not always met) of untempered, unmitigated, unqualified acceptance. The benevolent control over a pet—if it becomes tedious you can give it away, let it escape, put it "to sleep" if you want to—is there for as long as it pleases. The commitment to a child may flourish in the intimacy, the play, the pleasures of petlike nurturance, but goes way beyond that.

Something grows out of intimate care, the nurturance a mother gives a child, that is far beyond its own self-indulgent, petlike beginning.

> (Oh, my little monkey, my little angel, my baby, delighting me with your tricks and antics, satisfying my soul with your contented sleep-smile: you are my baby. And in countless hours of care and intimacy, in endless hours of nurturance and, yes, indulgence, we form a bond, we create a connection. Yes, my pet, you are and will always be my child.)

11
The Trophy Child

The "trophy child" is a peculiarly modern idea. Conceiving of any child as a trophy probably requires a more straightforward self-indulgence in parenthood than was imaginable in earlier times. Parenthood has to be seen very much as a choice, something one wants to do, for a child to be a trophy. And then for a black child to be a white person's trophy requires in addition an awareness of whiteness, an awareness of race and racism, and a struggle to rise above that.

The trophy child is a kind of variation on the pet. The trope of the child as a pet focuses on the inherent joys and satisfactions of nurturing. But sometimes—maybe always—people are nurturing a particular kind of child, not just for the sheer joy of loving, but because it says something, about themselves or about the kind of world they want.

Heather Dalmage points out that some white people use a black child as a statement. Having a black partner, being in an interracial family, adopting a black child—these can be statements of one's own "cool," one's own nonracism. She compares it, in a sense, to the men who sometimes walk around with huge snakes draped over their shoulders. It is a pet, but having such a pet is a statement of masculinity.

Many pets are statements, consumer items, status symbols of one sort or another. Having such a pet tells you something about the owner. Looking specifically at the modern phenomenon of transracial adoption, does having a black child serve some of the same function?

Certainly it can, and arguably this was some of the motivation behind the major shift in transracial adoption practice in the 1960s. White people in largely white cities and suburbs, in largely white states for that matter, found a way to participate in the civil rights movement by adopting a black child. This is absolutely not to say that these people did not love the children they adopted, did not raise them with great care and the fullness of parental love. But the child they chose to offer that love to was chosen for its blackness, and how can that not be a statement about the chooser?

One of the more astonishing examples of the trophy child comes not from a white family adopting black children but from a famous black woman. Josephine Baker set out to adopt twelve children from around the world. She wanted to create what she called a "Rainbow tribe."[1] She was in her late forties, married for seven years, when she began this family. Her first plan had been four kids, one of each color: black, white, red, and yellow.[2] She adopted the first in Japan while touring in the spring of 1954, but ended up with two "yellow." "She brought back children from her travels as one might bring back souvenirs."[3] She first wanted all boys, thinking, for reasons that are none too clear to me, that she would avoid problems in adolescence.[4] For the white child, she adopted a two-year-old from an orphanage in Helsinki, Finland. Her husband wanted an American Indian but she told him, "They're very hard to find. . . . We'll simply have to be patient."[5] Israel was unwilling to part with Jewish boys, and she finally gave that up. She got her Jew from France instead. A North African boy and girl, sole survivors of a massacre, joined her family. Her Indian child came from Venezuela, sick and malnourished, in 1959. The twelfth came from France, the child of a Moroccan mother. But she was apparently still gathering them; "with her characteristic generosity"[6] she brought a Hindu girl from a Belgian orphanage and gave her to her sister.

There are so few examples of Black people adopting white children. It is interesting that she had to go to Finland to do it. But is someone as famous and rich as Baker still "not white"? It is reported that she found some resistance in Colombia, where her lawyer told her that according to local belief, white people stole black babies to drink their blood. Baker replied in astonishment that she was black herself. The lawyer explained that to the Colombians, she was not: her wealth made her white. It's not only in Colombia that enough money buys one honorary whiteness.

Baker apparently really loved her children, raised them as a family. That's important to remember when we think of pets or trophies. We're looking only at a motivation for entering into a particular kind of parenthood. But people can and do love their children, no matter what enticed them to enter parenthood. Women who have been raped have been known to love their children; surely those who chose them as fashion statements can.

Pearl Buck was doing something similar, if apparently less intentionally planned to prove a point or make a statement.[7] She too adopted children from around the world in the immediate post–World War II period. Her children included the babies that African American soldiers fathered with German and with Japanese women during the occupation. Her "rainbow" family also served as a statement about family, the "family of man," and the joys of brotherhood in the aftermath of the war. She didn't seem, from her writings, to have set out to make that kind of statement, but the behavior of a well-known woman was used in the mass media of the time to reinforce those values of family and universal brotherhood.

In her study of Chinese adoptions, Ann Anagnost found a case curiously similar to Baker's. In her work, Anagnost was focusing on privilege, the ways the differently privileged people of the world connect in the global economy of adoption:

> Perhaps I should not have been so surprised when, in my field research in China in 2000, a 25 year old lawyer expressed her fantasy of adopting one child from each of China's 56 officially recognized national minorities and then of going to Africa to bring back a child or two to China to rear. She reasoned that her professional status gave her the economic means to give these children a better start. . . . But in so doing, I suggest, she is also expressing a newly imagined means of assuming a certain class privilege in which she can move effortlessly across racial and national divides—to be a new kind of citizen in the world. What this example suggests to me is the possibility of "doing good" without ever questioning one's own privilege.[8]

It requires a position of privilege to begin to think about "collecting" children. The trophy child says something about who the parent is; this kind of collection is one type of trophy. The "rainbow tribe," as Baker called it, is an attempt to remake the world, with the family as a little UN, the parent(s) as visionaries.

Rebecca Walker presents herself as a different kind of trophy child: a mixed-race, *Black White and Jewish* child, in her autobiography of that name. She's not, she reassures us and herself, a "tragic mulatto":

> I am not a bastard, the product of a rape, the child of some white devil. I am a Movement Child. My parents tell me I can do anything I put my mind to, that I can be anything I want. . . . I am not tragic.[9]

A "movement child," a child born of a particular, hopeful moment in the civil rights movement when black and white activists, like her white Jewish civil rights lawyer father and her black mother, thought they could make new people for a new world. On her side of the story, Alice Walker, Rebecca's mother, writes:

> If North America survives, it will not look like or be like it is today. One day there will be, created out of all of us lovers, an American race—remember how Jean Toomer, whom we sometimes read to each other in Mississippi, was already talking about this American race, even in the Thirties? We will simply not let the writers of history claim we did not exist. Why should the killers of the world be "the future" and not us?[10]

That was the energy, the power, that pushed forward a whole generation of "movement children," some of them born to black/white couples who broke the law of their states by loving and marrying, some of them adopted by white couples who went through the state's legal processes.

The idea of a new race, a raceless race, keeps resurfacing. An exhibit in the winter of 2004 at the International Center for Photography showed the photo montage of the "new American," a woman created by mixing the racial characteristics of all the groups blending in the new mixing pot.[11] This bloodless morphing, this computerized mingling is, I suppose, the post-modern version of miscegenation, the mixing of the races as embedded in older, blood-based race models. And while we think of the word "miscegenation" as an ugly racist term, it actually has a rather interesting history. The word was coined in 1863, in a pamphlet:

> The word is spoken at last. It is Miscegenation—the blending of the various races of men—the practical recognition of the brotherhood of all the children of the common father. . . . All that is needed to make us the finest race on earth is to engraft upon our stock the negro element which providence has placed by our side on this continent. We must become a yellow-skinned, black-haired people, if we would attain the fullest results of civilization.[12]

The pamphlet was a hoax, created by Democrats seeking to discredit the (abolitionist) Republicans.[13] A variety of abolitionists, including the Grimke sisters, Lucretia Mott, and others, endorsed its views, although recognizing it wasn't good timing politically. So while it was trying to show people the awful lengths to which abolition sentiments would go ("But would you want your daughter to marry one?"), it actually did reflect one stream of thinking at the time, as now: hybridity is a good thing.

One of the sweeter if stranger books I found at the Schomburg was called, I kid you not, *Run, Zebra, Run.*[14] The book jacket describes Leon Harris, the author, as active in the NAACP, and the hero as a "white skinned Negro, born of a white mother and a colored father." By page 37 those parents had died, and he was raised by a French sea captain and his wife. When he tried to "be a Negro, it seemed he could not be the right kind of Negro. . . . Most of them ('colored girls') considered him 'stuck up,' a smart-aleck and an egotist."[15] This is a 1959 version of the problem of the black person raised by white people and unable to "talk black, act black, be black." By the end of the book, he'd resolved his problem, identified as a black man. And married a white wife. The book ends with his little daughter saying:

> "Daddy, we're just people aren't we?"
>
> Husband and wife glanced at each other. Had a little child just solved the nation's most difficult problem? "Yes, daughter, just people. We're all growing up—just people—Americans—together."[16]

In the pathos-ridden language of Rebecca Walker, in the hopeful imagination of Alice Walker, or in the maudlin fiction of Leon Harris, the thought remains that somehow a little child shall lead us. We will make this new child, this child beyond race, and she will take us to the new world.

It's this funny Benetton ad thing: race exists to surpass itself. We recognize race, but only to go past it. We celebrate race, we take pleasure in it, as we overcome race. It is a way of thinking about race that involves *not* thinking about race, denying its significance, its politics, and its history. We are all just people— black, white, yellow, or, as some people like to suggest, green or purple. Our variations, they say, are just meaningless colors. This is both a celebration of color and a denial. "Color" becomes "colorful," meaningless, apolitical.

This approach, or model, or image for the white parent raising the black child is to ignore blackness. A baby is a baby is a baby. That could not, of course, be more true. In each and all of the daily acts of nurturance, the race of the baby is completely beside the point. Diapers and diaper rash, breasts and bottles and baby food, early language acquisition, peek-a-boo, skinned knees—these have nothing to do with race.

But blackness is a quality assigned to the child, even if not to the relationship. The child has to have the oft-discussed "survival skills" of a black person. At its extreme, the slave child has to learn how to be a slave. The subservience, self-protection, street-smarts—whatever it is that the white society demands of that child, the child has to learn it somewhere. And as the child grows, larger and larger loom the societal expectations about race.

The real movement folks, those who continued to work long past the early days of marches and bus boycotts, got past that Benetton, color-blind, all-in-it-together thing pretty quickly. In a racist system, you're not going to all join your multicolored hands together and sing race away. The work got harder.

And the work gets harder for the trophy children. Just as we all have to grow up and realize we're not the best-beloved pets of the whole world—only, if we were very lucky, our parents' best-beloved pets—so too do children who start out as trophies have to grow up to take their place in the world.

12
Imagine

As so often happens in life, I didn't find what I was looking for. I was looking for how the children found their way home, how these black children raised by white people reentered the black community. I found these protégés and pets and trophies. It's depressing. I was looking for something positive, some "role models," some images I could relate to. Susanna Wheatley and Josephine Baker just aren't doing it for me.

Sometimes I can't even stand myself. I'm like some pathetic Anne Frank, declaring her belief in the basic goodness of people as she's being herded off to the ovens. She said:

> It's a wonder I haven't abandoned all my ideals, they seem so absurd and impractical. Yet I cling to them because I still believe, in spite of everything, that people are truly good at heart. It's impossible for me to build my life on a foundation of chaos, suffering and death. I see the world being slowly transformed into a wilderness, I hear the approaching thunder that, one day, will destroy us too, I feel the suffering of millions. And yet, when I look up at the sky, I somehow feel that everything will change for the better, that this

cruelty too shall end, that peace and tranquility will return once more. In the meantime, I must hold onto my ideals. Perhaps the day will come when I'll be able to realize them![1]

Like poor Anne, I want to believe in something. For me, it's the connections between people, our ability to weave together. I believe, yes I *want* to believe, that ability stems from motherhood, from the connection out of which we grow. Some feminist colleagues accuse me of being too essentialist. Maybe I am. I believe that people essentially—in our very essence—can and do want to take care of each other.

I argue all the time these days about war and its causes. It's not about natural aggression I argue. Desperately. We're not aggressive creatures who break out into wars if the UN or some treaty doesn't stop us. What actually goes on in wars, I love to jump up and point out whenever this "war is inevitable" thing starts, is intense bonding. Soldiers fight not out of outwardly directed aggression, but as acts of inward protection. They fight in order to take care of each other. It's actually the case I think, I want to think, that those little stories of Christmas Eve truces do happen, will happen, given a chance. Every now and then the fighting does stop for a bit, and they share a cup of tea. That's the natural part, I feel, not the fighting. The bonding within the troops I am sure of: that's what drives war activity. How much you have to do to turn people into killing machines against each other, how much work that takes, I'm still not sure.

How much work does it take, I am asking, to get people to be cruel to each other, and especially to children? How much work does it take to view a child, a human child, as property, as service, as worse than just "not human," because so much of animal treatment is itself inhumane?

I know all about how unutterably awful the plantation women were. I got that. It's class and race and gender, and it's all too much.[2] Their husbands went off to the slave quarters and made babies, and no, the mistress of the plantation was *not* nice about that.

But was it always like that? Weren't there also women like Mieps, the woman who smuggled stuff in for the Frank family? There actually were good Germans too.

There must have been good white women, and men, and they must have sometimes nurtured where they weren't supposed to.

They didn't leave records. Maybe they never existed. But we know there were white mothers of black children[3] who wandered off and left whiteness and "let thy people become my people," women who became "the color of water."[4] Some of those women didn't have all that much whiteness to lose, anyway: Irish, Jewish, lots of bottom-of-the-heap white ethnics thrown in with the African Americans in inner cities.[5] Not *all* the mixed-race babies were from black women with white fathers.

I didn't find the white slave-owning woman who raised a black child. Tom Hayden said, when history fails, use imagination.[6]

I picture her. She's not on a big plantation. Maybe her husband owned one or two or three slaves. That's what most slave owners had, just a slave or two, not huge slave quarters out back. And she's not rich. She's got her whiteness and her slaves, but not all that much more. She's had this woman slave, who died giving birth or shortly thereafter. There's this new black baby. And she, this white woman of my imagination, had a baby herself not too long ago. The slave baby is hungry. Its mother is dead and it's hungry, and this baby is worth money. She can't afford to let it die. She puts it to her breast. The baby doesn't understand slavery, race, power, evil. Just milk. The baby sucks and grows. The woman nurses.

What does she feel?

Imagine.

IV

Weaving the Pieces

13
Home from the Schomburg

So what exactly was it that I was doing in the basement of the Schomburg library? What was I looking for, really?

The proposal I sent to the Fellows Program at the Schomburg Center for Research in Black Culture, a part of the New York Public Library system, was to "immerse myself" in Black fiction and autobiography, finding and cataloging the discussions of black children raised in white families.

Well, I've got the stories. I know there are more, but how much time could I spend in that basement? I'm not a library type. My family laughs at that, my mother especially: How could I be a scholar, and so dislike libraries? I like them in the abstract, the idea of them, of course. But I buy books all the time that I could have, should have, taken out of the library. And there I was, buried, trapped, stuck in that library.

Outside was Harlem, a near edge of Harlem, a cleaned-up, early-gentrified slice of Harlem. It's funny, really: When I got on the #2 train up there in Harlem, there were almost no white people on the train, just a smattering. Then we went through the length of Manhattan and the train got whiter, then on through to Brooklyn and it got blacker again, and finally, at my stop, the last stop on the train at Flatbush Avenue, I'm almost always the only white person on the train. I got off, walked past the Jamaican patty shop, the black hair-care products shops, down Glenwood Road to my house. And got back on that train again a few days later, back to Harlem, back to the Schomburg, to try to understand "black" culture, life, community, children.

What I said I would not do, what I so, so do not want to do, is write a memoir of my experience as a white woman raising a black kid. Or actually, now that I look at the proposal, it was not to write one more memoir of a white woman discovering race and racism.[1] I read a bunch of those, and with all due respect and appreciation, I do not appreciate the genre. At the best, they do "raise consciousness." But more often they just offer some proof that America is still racist, trotting out some moments when the author's consciousness was raised, and all in all, telling us that racism exists: you can believe me, I'm white and I'm saying so.

But I *am* a white woman, I *am* raising a black kid, and I *am* encountering race and racism, and whatever it is I write, it's bound to be my own story. I could put a lot of sociological theory behind that sentence, not to mention some lit crit talk if I really wanted to, but I'd prefer not, if you don't mind. It's just in there with all the discussions of identity politics, grounded knowledge, shifting perspectives, a touch of Foucault, and a soupçon of Bourdieu.

So what I had was a pile of stories of black people raised by white people, and good sociologist that I am, I put them in a typology, a grouping of stances or approaches to understanding the relationship of white people mothering—in any and all senses of the word—black children.

Towards the end of my stay at the Schomburg, I wrote the first draft of this historical work, the section you just finished reading in this book, and presented it to the Schomburg Fellows, a group of young black scholars, the crème de la crème of American black scholars. I was there, an old white sheep among the young black lambs, as an "independent scholar," an unfunded fellow, made welcome, given my desk in the basement with the others, access to the stacks and the library services, but most importantly given a space in the group, a place in the fold.

I was terrified.

When it was my turn to present, I was simply, flatly, terrified.

I presented my ideas: the meaning of mothering, and why I am using that word for the activity of intimately rearing a child, whether it is done by a mother by birth, another woman, or a man. We talked a long time about the gender stuff, the stuff I always get called on, about how to conceptualize this oh-so-gendered work in a nongendered way. So that took half an hour, but I was on familiar territory.

Then I presented my typology, my discussion of cultural images of black folk raising white children. There have been a number of examples of white folks taking black protégés, and is that parenting? I talked it through, with some of these stunning examples.

We talked, as much as time permitted, about what it means to raise a child, what parenthood, motherhood, fatherhood mean or could mean when race lines are crossed. We talked about pets, about children as adorable and cute and a fun project, evoking great emotional attachment—but so do cats and cockatoos. We talked about how English uses the same word, "adoption" to describe taking in a child as your child, or a cat as your cat. How a white person showing off the talents of a little white kid looks one way, but make it a black kid and it may appear to be something very different. Is it?

We talked about the trophy, how totally terrific it is in some circles to have yourself a black kid of your own—how cool is that? I don't just have myself some black friends, hmm-hnn, not me, I got myself a black kid, and aren't we just something?

And then, finally, we talked about what it is to be the mother of a black child. When you are the mother. When that is your child. When you mother that child and that defines who you are, the mother of that child. When you've put your eggs in that basket, when your future lies there with black kids, with the world black kids live in and will grow in. When who you are is kind of besides the point, when you've reached the limits of how much white privilege you can extend to your kid, and you're standing there watching the kid go forth into the world, as a black woman or a black man. We talked about that, me and these fine young black scholars, and one of them, one who has some kids of his own, had the last word:

"Barbara, we're proud of you."

Oh, god, is that what I was there for? I had a moment of recoil from my own pathetic self. Is that what I was buried in the stacks of the Schomburg seeking? Approval? It's OK what I'm doing, how I'm doing it? Is that what I have been seeking here?

Or was it—his statement of pride, my shock of acknowledgment of my own neediness—what Heather Dalmage says it is: acceptance? To be accepted is to be made part of something, to be allowed to enter the community. Was "Barbara, we're proud of you" an acceptance? Who, after all, do we have a right to be proud of, other than "our own"?

To weave together a family as we are doing, taking a child marked as one thing and raising it in a family marked as another, is to weave together the two communities themselves. A person marries across the racial border, or adopts across that border, and it is just possible that a bridge is created. That was a moment when a hand had been offered across the bridge.

Too often, it seems to me, people try to put the weight of that on the child, expecting the child to bridge between worlds. The back of a child should not be a bridge, should not support the weight we're asking. It's the adults, those of us who are supposed to be the grownups, who need to make the bridges, need to move ourselves between worlds.

And that, of course, is what I've been trying to figure out all along: how we form communities, families, connections between individuals and groups of people.

I went up to Harlem to find myself, in a way—to find my history, and it was pretty awful, all in all. It's a risk we all take when we look for our history, and in this particular case—the history of white people raising black children in America—it's no surprise that it's awful. I think we all need to know our histories, however ugly they may be. It's part of understanding who and what we are, what we are doing, how we are understood by others, how we fit into the world. But we are more than our histories.

All of my grown life (like many women of whatever age, I grew up in the course of having and raising my first kid) I have been exploring, intellectualizing, examining, unpacking, thinking about motherhood. And race and adoption, adoption and race, sent me back to the drawing board in a new way, made me ask a lot of the same questions all over again. Mothering across race, mothering through adoption, and doing both at once, opens up all the basic questions of motherhood, of family, of relationships, love, intimacy, and connection. And that's what I'm trying to figure out: how we're connected, how we weave family. I live it; I know we *do* it. But—to complicate the obvious—how?

I've looked at the institutions that frame our mothering: motherhood itself, adoption, race. I've looked at the history.

And now it's time to look more at the journey. How are those of us who are doing it now, who are white people raising our children of color—especially, race being what it is in America, raising our black children—making those bridges?

Back downtown, back across the more literal bridge, back home to Brooklyn to look.

14
Going Places

We think of opening up our lives to our children, making space for them in our lives. But it's the other way around too, as they make room for us, stretch the world to let us fit in somewhere else, open up new places for us. Have a kid, and you end up going places you'd never have gone—from Chuck E. Cheese's to an operating room, from the *Nutcracker* to an unfamiliar church, from the planetarium to your own sister's—places and moments you might not have had without them. We make our children, but they make us; we make room for them, but they make room for us.

Children make friends and we become embroiled in the lives of other families: baby-sitting while someone else's grandmother is in the hospital, going to religious services in honor of someone else's new babies. They have science projects and art assignments that drag us off to zoos and museums. They reentwine us with our own siblings and parents in new relationships that never would have come about without them. They take courses in things we never heard of, and new languages are spoken in our homes; they get jobs we've never thought about, and new pages of the newspaper start making sense. They bring home music and movies—and we may beg and scream for them to turn the volume down, but we hear things we wouldn't otherwise have heard. And they enter into new relationships, and we have new families again.

It's impossible to discuss parenting, having children, without falling into one cliché after another—this is a much-thought-about thing, after all, this having of children. Many compare it to a journey; that's not new either.

It's the nature of travel that we want to share when we come back, and many parenting books are basically travel guides. Some are memoirs of trips taken; some are guidebooks. We've been there, and the things we've seen! The things we've learned! Parenthood takes you to places you've always dreamed of, but also to places you'd never imagined.

There was a lovely piece written some years back that was passed around among many of us who were interested in prenatal testing and selective abortion.[1] It was about Down Syndrome babies. Having a baby, the author, a mother of such a baby, pointed out, is like planning a trip to Italy. You read the guidebooks, you study, you fantasize—the Leaning Tower! Michelangelo's *David*! The Sistine Chapel! You make all of your plans, pick out all the fabulous, magnificent places you will go. And somehow, the time comes, you board the plane, the journey is about to start. And as you swoop down for a landing, the captain says, "Welcome to Holland!" You're on the wrong plane, you've gone to the wrong country. The glories of Italy are not to be yours. You're stuck in flat Holland, mourning and hurt. But after a while, you look around. Holland has tulips. Holland has windmills. Holland even has Rembrandt. It's not Italy. But it is lovely, with charms of its own.

That's what it's like, she thought, to have a baby with Down

Syndrome: It is not the journey you thought you were taking. But yes, it can have joys of its own.

Is having a black baby when you're a white woman like having a baby with Down Syndrome? No, of course not. And yes, actually. People with Down Syndrome are disabled, have real problems, can be sick, can die young. Some of their problems are socially caused, the results of bad societal attitudes and poor social facilities. But some are just there, inherent in the condition.

Being of African descent in America is like that in that it shares the stigma, the social condemnation, disvaluing. It's not like that in that there's nothing wrong with the baby, the problem is entirely with the world into which the baby is born, not the condition of the baby's own life. But stigma is stigma, as Erving Goffman[2] famously pointed out: the stigma of a disability shares much with what he called a "tribal" stigma, the stigma of race. For a parent who does not share the stigma of the child, raising that child is a journey to a new place. You become what Goffman called one of the "wise," the outsiders who come to truly understand that other world.

And so we have a genre of travel books, the journey white parents take when raising a black child in America. They discover things they'd only heard about: racism, even actual racists (they turn out not to be extinct after all). The parents who write these books share the journey, share what they have learned. And like so many white colonizers of black lands, they think they've discovered something. They go along well-marked trails, are taken by experienced guides, and call it all a discovery. It is a journey of discovery.

Each new child takes you on a new journey: no two of them are the same. Only parents of an only child think they understand parenthood. Have a second, and you realize you don't know as much as you thought you did. My first two kids could not have been more different from each other; the knowledge carefully gleaned from raising the first was only occasionally useful on the second. The adoption social worker spoke seriously to us: What if the child we place with you is not like your other children? I laughed. What's left? I thought I'd seen it all. But not.

I'm not talking about issues of race or of adoption now. I'm just talking about yet another kid with yet another set of issues. Taste. Style. Personality. Skills. Interests. All that stuff that distinguishes us from one another. Leah loved beet baby food. Can you imagine? Beets! Victoria made a face. Pears—Victoria loved pears. Daniel likes to cook, has since I can remember. Leah will lick the beaters, thank you. Victoria enjoys the kitchen. Daniel sprawled out when he slept, kicked us half off the bed even as a newborn. Leah needed to be swaddled, wrapped like a blintz, as my mother taught me, arms bound against her, or she'd wake herself up and cry. Victoria needed to be held bent over my arm while I rubbed her back. God knows what a fourth child might have taught me.

And on top of that, there's race. A white woman, a white family, raising a black child is on a journey. Race only means something, only exists, because of racism; if it weren't stigmatized, there would be no race. At the adoption agency they made us take parenting classes. We were the only ones who had kids, the only ones not drawn there by infertility. There were five infertile white couples, one mixed-race couple, and us. We raised some questions about race, about difference. A young (well, young compared to us!) woman jumped in, "Yes, Yes, what about that? What if we get a baby who looks Italian or something, and we look so Irish? Don't we owe that child something about her Italian heritage?" The social worker leading the class was flustered, uncomfortable. The black man in the mixed-race couple came up to us after class, talked about being the lightest in his family, being different, and said that it's not that big a deal.

But difference *is* a big deal, when it is marked as race. It is even a big deal when it doesn't get marked as race but just makes the adoption obvious. I know "matching" has gone out of style in adoption, and for good reason, but there is a difference between an adoption that slips by and an adoption that every kid in a playground can recognize: "*That's* your mother?" or "That *can't* be your mother!"

When the line you're crossing, the barrier you're hurdling, is not just difference, meaningless individual brown eyed/blue eyed variation in a sea of whiteness, but the race line, you are off on a particular journey of discovery. Of course you will learn more about race—and racism—than you knew.

The thing most of us white parents learn right away when we bring home our black children—from adoption agencies or our own births—is that we are white. No doubt I've always been white. But I never thought to describe myself that way, never thought about myself as white. That is what it means to be white, not to have to think about how white you are. But now? Someone I haven't met says they'll pick me up at the airport and I casually say, "I'm a tall, gray-haired white woman." I think of myself as a white woman now. Sorta. I also forget how white I am. Sometimes it almost surprises me, my whiteness, when I see it in a mirror, when I have my hand on Victoria's dark skin. Raise a black child, and you gain whiteness: you see yourself as white.

But raise a black child and you lose whiteness: you are not and never will again be white, not white in that raceless, taken-for-granted way you used to be. Maureen Reddy, a white woman married to a black man, mother of black children, put it perfectly: "I *look* white, but that white skin conceals my inner life. This feeling of being costumed in one's own skin, of 'mas-

querading' as white in public, may be the only thing white partners of black people, and especially white parents of black children, share regardless of the other differences among us."[3]

I am most struck by my own whiteness not when I'm in a
mostly or all-but-me black setting, but when I'm in a mostly
white place. When I'm at an academic conference, it happens:
things are being said, assumptions of whiteness are being made,
and I look around, trying to make eye contact with someone so
we can figure out how to deal with this, how best to respond—
and there's no one there trying to make eye contact back with
white-old-me. Contrast that with Victoria's experiences being
in mostly-white settings: total strangers, black strangers,
stopped her on the street in Germany just to say hi. When she
was a baby and we were together in very white places (the north
of Holland, say), I'd get that sometimes—a black person just
stopping to say hi to me. But no longer. I walk in my own white
body now, alongside her, as she walks along in her black body.

I brought Victoria along to a home-birth, midwifery meeting one time a few years back, and there were a couple of black
midwives there. There are some black women involved in that
movement, but, for lots of good reasons and some not so good,
there are not many. Victoria came up to me, kind of startled, and
shyly pleased: the two black midwives, walking together past
Victoria in a hallway, had smiled and said "Hi, Sister." They were
just pleased to see her there, the same way she was probably
pleased to see them there. But me: I was pleased to see them, but
I was no comfort to them at all.

There have been more dramatic moments of confronting my
own whiteness. I live in the police precinct made famous by the
rape of Abner Louima, a Haitian man taken into custody and
sodomized with a broomstick. We in New York have had quite
a few bad police brutality cases these last years. I came out of the
subway station one warm afternoon, and two white cops were

arresting a young black kid, apparently for jumping the turn-
stile. The kid was struggling, the cops were grabbing at him—
and from nowhere, from everywhere, a circle of black women
gathered around. They just stood there; they didn't interfere
with the cops arresting the kid, they didn't argue with anyone
about anything, they just stood there, encircling, watching.
They were clearly there to see to it that no one hurt that kid.
They were there as watchful mothers. I started to sidle up, held
off, moved forward, moved back—I look like the mother of one
of the *cops,* not the kid. I dithered. If I join the circle, will the
cops take it as reassurance? What will the other women think?
Where do I belong?

I stood back, behind the women, stood there as long as they
did, till the kid was settled down and things seemed back under
control all around. Maybe I should have just joined in that circle. Doesn't much matter: they were doing fine without me, and
if they'd needed help I'd have been there. But for me, it was a
painful confrontation with whiteness and the limitations of my
body, the skin in which I am masquerading.

All of us white mothers of black children share that, the confrontation with our own whiteness, the "masquerading" as
Reddy called it. But we certainly don't all experience it in the
same way. France Winddance Twine did in-depth focused interviews with ten white women in Britain who had birthed and
were raising African-descent children.[4] Racism in Britain is
sometimes different, sometimes shockingly recognizable to
Americans. All of these women had confronted the problem of
racism in their extended families: verbal abuse, rejection, refusal
of assistance, racist language. Not what one wants for one's children from Grandma and Grandpa. Some cut ties with their own
parents; some engaged in continual negotiations; some put up
with it and tried to find a way of convincing their children that
not all whites are racist.

In that way, adoptive parents are at something of an advantage; those who know that their families would be racist and rejecting have lots of time to make cool, level-headed decisions. Most people who know that's what they would confront probably just opt out of those adoptions. It's hard to imagine someone deliberately placing herself in the situation Twine describes for two of her interviewees, so distressed about the relationships with their parents that they were clinically depressed. Hesch and I were asked by the adoption social worker to think about how our extended families would react and if we were "prepared to deal with it." (God bless 'em, we've got a great family. One less problem in the world to deal with.)

We made a choice to have a mixed-race family; it's as if we got on the plane wanting to go to Holland in the first place. Not every white parent of a black child wanted to go on that journey. That's obviously true of women who have short-term relationships with black men and end up alone and pregnant; it's also true of people who, as the language has it, "fell" in love, sort of wandered into a mixed-race relationship and all that follows. But it's also the case that not everybody who adopts a black child does so because she/he particularly wants a black child. You might think that every white person who adopts a black child is a political, race-aware, activist of some sort. But not.

Nora Rose Moosnick interviewed American women who adopted white, Asian, and black children, and found, much as one might expect in America, that race is tied to cost: "A White baby will cost you this much, international this much, and a Black baby I can get real cheap."[5] Or as one mother put it:

> I do get a little bit tired of being held up as a poster child for race relations. I just adopted these kids because I really wanted to be a mother. It's not a political statement. These are the kids. This was

one of the easiest ways to adopt at the time. It was financial[ly] not a huge stretch. It was one of the least expensive, most streamlined ways of adopting.[6]

The good side, I suppose, is that she is clearly not collecting trophy children. On the other hand, I'm thinking she is going to wake up clueless in Holland—or Harlem—one of these mornings, taken on a journey for which she is shockingly ill prepared.

15
Culture: Celebrating Diversity

We just finished Passover. Twenty-four people for a formal, many-course dinner. It takes a week just to put away the dishes.

Talk about trophy people! We take enormous pride in the variety of people and, particularly, the number of languages we gather around the table. It's not that I go looking for people to invite based on the language that they speak; we're not collecting people like trophies. And yet. . . .

It started innocently enough. We were in the Netherlands on my Fulbright, back when Victoria was five and Leah was thirteen. We did a Passover seder there for my Dutch friends. It turned out, as does happen now and again, that the seder night was on Good Friday—the Last Supper was a Passover seder, so there's always that overlap. So it was an interesting, ecumenical experience—there are relatively few Jews left in the Netherlands, and my Dutch friends knew almost nothing about Passover.

Passover celebrates the Exodus of the Israelites from slavery in Egypt. It's a home-based holiday, with the celebration taking the form of a service (called a Haggadah) read at the dinner table—the dinner is called "the seder." It's a shoo-in, you can see, for a do-it-yourself kind of holiday, reinterpreting, subverting, borrowing, elaborating the text to incorporate whatever you want. So we've modified, used the holiday to celebrate all such flights to freedom from all kinds of slavery. Back maybe twenty years ago now, I held a seder at which I asked people to bring readings about anything they felt represented the spirit of the Passover celebration, and that's become one of our traditions. Over the years we've had readings on American slavery, gay rights, Cuba, the Watergate papers and freedom of the press, disability rights, the fall of the Berlin Wall, Anne Frank, the lives of mentally retarded people, feminism, Haitian liberation movements, poetry on prayer and on the Gaza Strip. It's been interesting.

So there we were in Groningen, a city up at the top of the Netherlands, doing a seder for Dutch folk. There's this one central piece of the seder, called "the four questions," asking, "Why is this night different from all other nights?" and elaborating on the four differences in what and how we eat. We always sing it in Hebrew—nonsense syllables to me because I never studied Hebrew—and read it in English. We had a Dutch Haggadah—it was 1995, the fiftieth anniversary of the liberation of the Netherlands after World War II, and someone reprinted copies of the Haggadah that had been prepared for the newly released Jews. I asked a friend to read the questions for us in Dutch, just to hear it.

The next year, Leah—rightly proud of her Dutch—read it for us back at home in Brooklyn. Idly curious, I asked Carolle Charles, my Haitian colleague who always attends our Seders, what it sounded like in Creole. She translated. My mother said: "I bet you don't know what it sounds like in Yiddish!" and she translated. We were off and running. At a peak year we've had maybe ten or more languages, and, all told, about eighteen I think—including Farsi, Korean, Thai, Hindi, American Sign Language, and the more routine range of European languages.

Each year I "rewrite" the Haggadah, make whatever edits and changes we've decided on, catch some more of my typos. At this year's "post mortem" the next day, sitting around the table, Daniel and Leah and I talked about what changes needed to be made after this seder. One was to acknowledge the meaning behind all these languages, or as Leah put it, make it into something more than "Ooooh, Turkish!" So I wrote a couple of lines about diaspora, that Jews are a people of a diaspora. And since, when I'm not making Passover and cooking, I'm writing this book, it made me think.

Diasporas usually happen for pretty awful reasons. People don't just pack up and leave home without a good—read: a pretty awful—reason. But diasporas are also mixed blessings; whatever evil might have impelled them, some beautiful things come out of them. That's really what we're celebrating at our seder: all of my friends and family, products of so many diasporas, come together to create a Passover seder—to weave a family, really.

It's a celebration, with a dark side. I think of the stories of the diasporas we represent—slavery, pogroms, failed revolutions, wars, famines, every horror people can possibly inflict upon one another. Only my friend Maren, who came from England to study and stayed on, has no such horror tale lurking in the background (but then, having spent six months in England, I have a sense of the cultural oppression that she was fleeing). But what fun we have hearing the same phrases read in Creole (slave uprisings, unthinkable poverty), Farsi (revolutions and religious fundamentalism), Irish (potato famine and British imperialism), Yiddish (don't ask!).

There is, there has to be, this tension between the celebration of diversity and the causes that bring people together from disparate places. It's the truth at the macro level when we look at the United States, land of immigration; and it's the truth at the micro level, whether I'm looking around at my seder table or, yet more micro, when those of us in families formed by adoption across borders look around the dinner table. Almost always, nothing good started this, however wonderful, glorious, joyous, enormous fun the end product turns out—our nation at its increasingly rare best, our families at their most ordinary.

This is indeed a country of people in diaspora. We're almost all, relatively speaking, just off the boat from somewhere. At my Passover seder, the Haggadah says:

> We often have at our table a big chunk of the history of our planet and the people who ride it. We sit here, living testimony to the history of oppression. Trace back families and biological histories of the people at this table: many of us descended from people who came to this country in ships fleeing oppressors. Others came in chains in the holds of ships, dragged here by oppressors. And we sit here together, constructing family, celebrating the freedoms we have and the freedoms we strive to achieve, for ourselves and for the rest of the world's people.

That phrase, "families and biological histories" is supposed to cover some complicated territory. Our families are, and are not, our biological histories. In her children's book about "where babies come from," Pearl Buck has little Johnny ask, "Where was I before?" And when his mother answers, "You were in me," he pushes harder. Before, he wants to know: where was I *before*? "I was as tiny as a seed once too inside my mother, but still you were in me and I was in her and she in her mother and so it goes back to the very beginning of everybody."[1]

That's the lovely story we who adopt do not get to tell: we haven't got that unbroken line stretching back. We don't quite know how to go back, to trace our paths backwards with adoption. There's a school exercise they often do, teaching children geography and probably a bit of something about American diversity at the same time. They ask the children to stick pins in a map showing where their families came from.

Jaiya John was a black child adopted by a white family and raised in, of all places, Los Alamos. There were of course some Mexican families, but on the whole, places don't get much whiter than Los Alamos, a town so white that even the Jews aren't exactly white:

> Until high school, I was one of only five or so other Black children in Los Alamos, whom I saw around town only now and then. Two were adopted into White or Jewish families. Two others were sisters whose parents were a Jewish man and Kenyan woman. . . . Los Alamos High School had about 1,600 students when I attended, and the number of Black students. . . . hovered around eight.[2]

Late in elementary school he faced the map project:

> The teacher laid out a large map on the floor in the center of the classroom. The map was of the entire world, showing all the continents and oceans. . . . I was horrified. When I realized what we would be doing, a wave of panicked heat rose in my chest.

His shame of Africa, a place off the end of the known universe, a "jungle," battled with his sense of betrayal. He stood there with his pin: *"Where do I come from? Which group is more of me: my adoptive family's ancestors or my Black ancestors? Who in the hell am I?"*[3]

The teacher rescued him, told him to use his adoptive family as his family, their geographic origins as where he "came from."

I contrast that poor child off in Los Alamos with Leah, cosseted in a Quaker school in Brooklyn some twenty years later. She came home with that school assignment just weeks after Victoria arrived. She needed to know where we "came from."

She called her grandparents and looked on the globe for Russia. And then she looked on the globe for Africa. I do grant you that she was clueless as to just where in Africa she should stick her pin, but it was clear to her, looking at her sister, that our family also comes from Africa.

This story is offered not as a testimony to our fine parenting or the joys of a Quaker education, but to a real shift in the zeitgeist of ethnicity, a shift partly because of place (Brooklyn is *so* different from Los Alamos) but also because of time. We now —my cohort of adoptive parents, parents in general these days—teach our children to celebrate and enjoy their "diversity," their "heritage," their "culture" and "ethnicity" and biological "roots" and whatever else we can think of to call it.

And just what is this heritage we celebrate in our adopted children? What is it that the parents of the Chinese girls are celebrating with their pandas, that all of these adoptive parents, with the foods and music and folk tales and clothing, are bringing home with their children from all over the world? Is it culture? Does a baby have a culture? We're doing this celebration of heritage for children who left their native lands long before they learned to speak, let alone developed food preferences for things Peruvian or Chinese. Where does this culture reside in the baby?

Obviously part of the reason we're celebrating diversity is in response to just the kind of situation poor Jaiya John found himself in: color-blind liberalism just didn't work. By now, enough years have passed since transracial and international adoptions started happening on a fairly large scale that the adoptees themselves have been heard. Their books and stories are practically a genre unto themselves, including both personal memoir and more academic studies.[4] While their experiences are wildly varied, as families inevitably are, some things come through clearly. Children see and experience race in America, and that needs to be dealt with in the family. Black, Asian, and other identifiably nonwhite children in white communities experience racism. They deal with name-calling, rejection, teasing, and sometimes worse. Coming home from that to someone smiling sweetly and saying "color doesn't matter" just doesn't cut it.

The color-blind approach to the racism has been to focus on the (very true) fact that lots of children, most children, will be teased for *something*. One kid is teased for being fat, one for wearing glasses, one for being in a wheelchair, one for having a lisp, and one for being a Chink. Is one of these things not like the other? Or is stigma just stigma?

Disability rights activists have drawn heavily on the African American civil rights movement for both ideology and practice. Being called "crip" is not a whole hell of a lot different from being called "Chink." In both cases the teasing is about the child's membership in a disvalued group, and the solution is to be found at the level of the group. Irving Kenneth Zola, disability activist, sociologist, and white father of a black daughter, tried his hand at fiction. In one of his short stories, the narrator, a white father in a wheelchair, is in the park with his black daughter, who is being teased for being "brown."

> "Why did they do that Daddy?" ... "Because they're assholes," I thought to myself. But that was my anger getting in the way, so I waited until I was in better control. "Well, Mandy, look around here at this field. Do you see any black people or people with disabilities?" [The child shakes her head no.] "Since there aren't many of us around, we look and seem different. When people who aren't black or brown or who don't have physical disabilities meet us, often they don't know what to do. In a sense they're frightened and so sometimes they run or turn away, or sometimes they get angry, or sometimes they just tease us or call us names."[5]

What Zola did, in his fiction, in his advocacy work, in his scholarship, and in living his life, was to address these issues politically, to bring black, brown, and disabled people onto a more level playing field. "Mainstreaming" kids with disabilities, making public space accessible, is much like racial integration. It solves the individual problem of teasing at the structural level, by removing the basis for the teasing. Being brown or disabled is just one of the ways people can be in the world—and if there are enough such people around, any child can see that.

If you don't focus on the structural, political aspect of this, as Zola always did, and just reduce it to individual variation, meaningless teasing that everyone experiences, the child is left vulnerable and ill prepared for life in a racist (and ablist) world.

But what if you focus on making difference acceptable, without looking at the political? That, I think, is the path that our "adoption nation"⁶ is taking, celebrating "heritage," without a political/social-change context for it. It's not just adoptive parents who are discovering the joys of ethnicity. We are in what some have called an "ethnic revival," a renewal of interest in heritage. While once there was an expectation that America would be a melting pot in which new immigrants would immerse themselves, losing their individual ethnicity in the great American mix, the new approach is more one of multiculturalism.

Multiculturalism or diversity is rooted in the idea of different "kinds" of people. To think of gathering a diverse group of people—for a seder, for a hiring committee, a family, a nation—you have to think of people as being of disparate types. You have to have the "boxes" from which you draw the people, the categories. So you can't get to diversity without making those categories—the very categories we then try to rise above in our diversity. That of course has been the critique of affirmative action programs: they require us to acknowledge the significance of race if we want to decrease its significance. But affirmative action is again the political arm of this issue. The ethnic revival is far from entirely a political phenomenon.

In part, the new appreciation of ethnicity can be understood not as a political but as a marketing phenomenon. We have reached the end of the "mass market" approach; marketing now is all about segmentation, dividing the market up and targeting segments. "One of the most successful of the segmenting strategies," according to Marilyn Halter in her study *Shopping for Identity: The Marketing of Ethnicity,* "has been to target specific ethnic constituencies."[7] As consumer goods become more and more standardized, brand loyalty is harder to maintain; instead, advertising has developed the emotional sell, or as one "multicultural brand manager" put it: "In order to reach the marketplace's pockets, you have to reach their minds and hearts first. How do you do it with one advertising fits all? You need to get on the home turf of that person. What's home turf? It's culture."[8] So everything and anything—not just ethnic foods but banks, telephone companies, chewing gums, airlines—sells itself with ethnic pulls, ethnically marked consumers sitting around enjoying the products in their own ethnically delightful ways.

Once Americans were supposed to be vaguely ashamed of any foreignness, any "old country" customs, foods, accents that lingered. Now we celebrate these differences, revel in them. "In an age that celebrates diversity and multiculturalism, it has become almost a civic duty to have an ethnicity as well as to appreciate that of others."[9]

Ethnicity isn't just a duty in this context: it's a right. Halter says:

> Perhaps nothing better illustrates the extent to which the ethnic revival has permeated our culture than hearing the renowned baby

and child care expert Dr. T. Berry Brazelton proclaim: "every baby should get to know their heritage." In the fundamentals of end-of-the-century American child-rearing, roots training comes even before potty training.[10]

That is the context in which heritage has entered the world of adoption: something our babies and children have a right to have. The problematics of this have probably been most obvious with the Chinese adoptions. On the one hand, those parents have done a wonderful job of celebrating Chinese culture with and for their children. Chinese schools are flourishing. Pertman, in *Adoption Nation,* says in high praise: ". . . the parents also seem to be ensuring the continuous, long-term infusion of Chinese culture into our country by teaching their children about their homeland, its customs, and its traditions from the time they are infants."[11]

Adam Pertman feels that adoption is a revolution, "transforming America." Americans adopt more children internationally, he tells us, than do the inhabitants of the rest of the planet combined.[12]

> One of the genuinely noble, enriching aspects of the American sensibility—notwithstanding the intolerance of some narrow-minded people and political movements—is its celebration of people's connections to their past. We marvel at the beauty of an African-print dress, revel in the music at a Latino festival or an Irish step dance, savor the delights of Asian restaurants, incorporate the expressive words of other languages into our own.[13]

I find myself searching for six recognizable expressive foreign words for bullshit.

You tell the thousands of legal and thousands more illegal immigrants coming from China, living in slums, crowded, without access to the most basic of services, trying to make it on tips as delivery boys and waiters, that the parents of the four or five thousand Chinese baby girls adopted into America each year are keeping their cultural flames burning in "our" country.

The parents themselves realize the enormous contradictions they face; they want their daughters to be proud of their heritage, proud of their culture—and yet it is that culture, that heritage, that rejected them, made them available for adoption in the first place. Son-preference is not the part of the culture they want to teach. They are doing what we all do, certainly what I do when I celebrate Passover—search through my heritage for the pieces I can live with, the parts I want to save, discarding the rest. But what have we got when we're down to kneidlach and won tons?

Ethnic celebration is certainly an improvement over color-blind liberalism, but ethnic celebration collapses quickly into triviality. An adoptive mother Moosnick interviewed in her study of women who adopted white, Asian, or black children said: "And when we do think about a third child, it's like let's make it a totally different race and country so we'll have another excuse to travel and learn another culture and way of cooking."[14]

Ethnicity becomes yet another consumer choice, as people sift through their heritages to pick the one or two they would like to celebrate—Irish-German-British families focusing on their Irish heritage, people with that almost mythical Cherokee great-grandmother celebrating their Native American roots, an Italian grandparent becoming an excuse to enjoy a trip to Italy in a special way.[15] And adoption becomes part of that.

But in America, all of these different ethnicities are not placed on equal, level playing fields. We want to show our children that they are—and they *are*—all beautiful, each in different ways, with their different colors and hair textures, their different abilities, and disabilities, all of them. In a book Pete Seeger did for children, there's a picture that shows all kinds of people gathered together.[16] There's an old guy in a yarmulke and a beard, an Asian woman, a dark guy in a turban, an African woman in flowing robes, even a white guy in a suit. It's his image of community, all the people of the world coming together. But in reality, if they start talking, it's going to be in English, isn't it? This is a kind of diversity that we can share with children, to show them how the world ought to be, but we know it's not really like that, not a real community of everybody together. In the real world, we welcome that diversity when it spices up our lives without really changing anything, not shifting any real power around.

If one ethnicity is good, maybe two are better. Adoption is only one way we get multicultural families, and Danzy Senna, author of *Caucasia,*[17] writing in *Half and Half: Writers on Growing Up Biracial and Bicultural,* satirizes "The Mulatto Millennium": "Strange to wake up and realize you're in style." She fantasizes waking up in the new millennium and finding "mulattos had taken over: they were everywhere. Playing golf, running the airwaves, opening their own restaurants. . . ."[18] Danzy's fantasy goes to the dark side, being picked up by the mulatto police, criticized for having, in her youth, claimed her blackness in reverse racism over her whiteness. She argues back:

> Multiculturalism should be about confronting racism and power, not about plates of ethnic food . . . all this celebration of mixture felt to me like a smoke screen, really, obscuring the fundamental issue of racism, and for that matter class divisions. It seemed to me we spent so much time talking about kimchee and grits, we forgot to talk about power.[19]

Kimchee and grits, the Four Questions in Hindi, these are the fun, the joyous sides of our diasporas and our ethnicity. We're right to celebrate them. But we mustn't forget to talk about power.

16
Identity: Pride and Joy

I only ever agreed to speak publicly about transracial adoption one time in my life.

It was one of those situations where I just couldn't refuse.

Heather Dalmage had been my dissertation student. Which is to say, I had the great joy and pleasure of midwifing while she birthed her first major piece of work, *Tripping on the Color Line*.[1] She was writing about families that cross the color line. Her original thought was to do her work on multiracial people and black-white couples. But she was part of that adoption reading group I mentioned, and she began to see that my situation, as the white mother of a black child, was not altogether different from hers, as the white wife of a black man. Oh, sure, in some ways there's nothing comparable about the two. But in others. . . . So she added transracial adoption into the mix, looked at mixed-race families formed by adoption as well as by marriage.

For the most part, my job as dissertation advisor was to do what any good midwife does: nod and smile, pat and reassure. Yes, yes, you're almost there. Every so often there would be something I could do that might be of actual use—a reference to suggest, some editorial comments, the right question at the right moment. It moved along smoothly, at least for me. But there was one point over which we struggled. Heather did not want to identify herself in the project, did not want to let her personal life intrude. Oh, no, I kept pushing—that will never do. Can you imagine anyone ever reading this when it's a book and not going to look at the author's photo to try to figure you out?

It seemed to me then, and still seems now, that the reader *has* to place the author, has to know who the author is. A person cannot, I am sorry to say, move outside of her body. If one could, I could go visit Israel *not* as an American Jew, or could have visited South Africa during apartheid *not* as a white, to see what's going on. But no, wherever you go, you schlep your body with you. If Heather were a black woman, transracially adopted, she would be standing in one place; as a white woman, now the mother of two black children, one by birth and one by adoption, she stands somewhere else indeed. We struggled over that for months. Maybe years, I don't know. I won.

So then, when she was off ensconced as a professor at Roosevelt University in Chicago, organizing a conference on mixed-race families, and invited me to speak about transracial adoption as an adoptive mother, what exactly was I supposed to do? Oh, no, I claimed. I can't talk about that really. It's not my research, you know. It's private. It's Victoria's life too. Oh, sorry, Heather, really, I can't.

You can imagine how big that went over.

That conference was, as conferences so often are, bunched in the middle of too much travel. For me, a couple of trips a month is a lot, as much as I can handle. And we were right up at my limit. What set my limit was less my level of exhaustion than my family. Victoria was the little one: she was nine. The trip right before the one to Heather's conference was to Europe, to the Netherlands. Victoria was usually a good sport about my travel, content to have the different kind of family time she had when I was gone, eat beef without my almost-vegetarian objections, and watch too much TV. But this time, not. She raged. She dumped out the contents of my suitcase, yelled, roared. Cried.

I got on the phone, made last-minute changes, got her a ticket to go to Chicago with me for Heather's conference. Left for the Netherlands promising, *swearing,* she'd be on the next trip with me.

So a few weeks later, there we were, off to Chicago, land of the Chicago Bulls, tee-shirt shops, deep-dish pizza, and, oh yes, a conference.

I've always enjoyed traveling with my kids, and tried to take each kid alone on a trip of some sort pretty regularly. And in some ways, this was a good choice; Victoria liked Heather, and the conference crowd was appealing, all those members of mixed-race families. Since attendance basically consisted of adults, I am not sure what a child saw. There were lots of people of all colors, but so what? We can see that on our street. I saw a lot of people I recognized as interesting combinations: black and Asian, black and white, whatever. I couldn't tell what if anything was registering for Victoria. I know she enjoyed the sneaker shopping, lunch at a pizza place, souvenir shopping, hanging out with me. But when I had to be at a session, Heather's husband or one of her students took charge of Victoria, entertaining her for much of the working time.

What I did *not* want was for Victoria to be attending the sessions. It was, I thought, inappropriate. She was a kid, not ready to intellectualize race, mixed-race families, the politics of the census categories, and, most definitely, not ready to hear a heated debate on transracial adoption policies.

But that's what I was in for. CSPAN was interested, and our

panel was facing into cameras. We had one of the foremost researchers in the field, one of the people who have collected all the hard data over all the hard years. We had someone from the National Association of Black Social Workers who had been involved in writing the original, famed statement opposing transracial adoption. We had a gentle, soft-spoken but determined advocate of transracial adoption in the form of a young black woman who had been so adopted. And then we had me.

What I really worried about was Victoria walking in in the middle of this. I did not want to have her listening to me debate the legitimacy of my motherhood, on a stage in front of a huge crowd and a television camera besides. I had more backup plans in place than you can imagine, people who would be with her every minute, doing something, anything, making sure she didn't wander the building and find her way to me.

It was, as I said, the first time I'd ever presented on the issue. I'd only actually been to a conference or session like that once or twice before. It was not, as I kept saying, my "area." And yet I could quickly see how this goes. The rest of the people had been doing this for so long, they all knew their parts. The researcher cited data. Numbers, numbers, numbers. More numbers. Transracial adoption works. The adoptees are psychologically normal, fine, happy, well adjusted, thank you. It works. Want some more numbers?

The social worker raged. He made all the good, legitimate points, and some of the less valid ones. Children need role models, need to learn how to deal with race in America; white parents can't teach them that. And so on. That works for me, yes. Those are real problems. I'm with you. But he also, literally and truly, called transracial adoption a form of genocide. I know that is *not* in the official statements; I know that the black Social Workers have been accused of saying that and did not officially do so. But he did. Genocide. I had just spent unconscionable amounts of money on a last-minute flight, walked all over downtown Chicago buying the most perfect pair of sneakers to be found, was running back and forth between this set of meetings upstairs and a kid downstairs, was overstressed, overspent, overtired. If this be genocide, surely there is a less labor-intensive way to do it.

My head was spinning. I gave my talk, actually pretty much read it—something I don't often do—so nervous was I about the whole situation. It was basically the piece that's in this book on "our story," on how I profit from American racism, about how we need to refocus upstream. I had thought hard over every word, wanted to be careful, balancing everything I needed to balance: my privacy and my child's, my politics and my behavior, my obligations to Heather and my own deep misgivings about participating at all. I sat down, much relieved to have that over.

The young black woman spoke. And everything clicked into place for me. My eyes filled. Not with joy. She was articulate, thoughtful, well adjusted, psychologically healthier than I am, no doubt. She praised her parents, and all parents like hers, who rescued children from poverty and gave them fine educations. She dismissed the need for such parents to be tested on, to be held accountable for knowing, black culture. Plenty of black people don't celebrate Kwanzaa, don't know the names of ten famous black women, whatever. She thought it would be better if *more* black kids were upwardly mobile via adoption. And race didn't matter.

Ah. Genocide. Got it. She's psychologically well adjusted, happy, content, and gone. Gone from the black community as surely as if she'd been exiled. She *had* been exiled.

Of course, part of me is going to be happy if *any* of my kids are that poised, professional, accomplished, happy with me, with their lives. What mother's heart wouldn't rejoice in all that?

But that's not what made me sit there trying not to cry before the CSPAN camera. It was the fear and the grief that I was feeling, that maybe *that*—her cheerful, empty-headed exile from her own blackness—is the cost of this project.

If she were my black daughter, I'd be devastated.

So that's the awful situation I was in: success, as the researcher was defining success, and as the young black woman so clearly displayed success, was failure. And the social worker, whom I honestly felt like smacking upside the head, accusing me of genocide and all, was right. In his own crazy way, he was making more sense than anyone. And yet, clearly not: there's no way my relationship with Victoria has anything to do with genocide.

The problem, any sociologist can tell you, lies in the level of analysis. The adoption researcher and the adoptee were speaking at the psychological level, at the level of identity. The social worker was speaking at the level of structure, of social system, of *power*. As a mother—as an individual woman living her life—I have to function at that psychological level most of the time. I had to buy my kid a ticket to Chicago because of "separation issues"; I had to buy particular types of sneakers because of "bourgeoning adolescent identity issues." Those are all very real, very important parts of life. I've spent enough time dealing with those things, believe me, I know what I'm talking about. Anybody mothering a child would know that. That stuff matters.

But ask any politically aware person, any activist, any sociologist—just *think* about it for a minute—and the other stuff matters too. Race isn't only about identity. It's about systems of power. Raising psychologically healthy, intelligent, lovely children, black and white, isn't of itself going to change those systems.

There's been enormous concern in the United States about

the "labeling" of people, a concern focused in part on the census categories, but more generally on the various forms we fill out in applying to schools, jobs, and the like. We're asked to label ourselves, to put ourselves in a category, to check off a box and identify ourselves. And lots of people resent it; they don't want to be "boxed in." Some people resent the whole thing on principal: we're all human and that's all that counts. Some resent particular category systems because they feel they personally deny those categories by their existence—for example, people who are not simply male or female, but both/neither/ something else again. And what about the age categories: maybe I've lived fifty-six years, but what if I feel thirty-six? Or seventy-six?

But most of the discussion, of course, hasn't been about the age or sex categories, but about the race/ethnicity labels. It was a lifetime ago, but back working on my master's degree in the early 1970s I was studying attitudes towards the then-new women's movement. I was doing quantitative work—surveys with college students. And I wanted to see if there were ethnic differences among students in their feelings about feminism. College students just then didn't want to check off those narrow "identity" columns. So instead, I devised a question that said: "Families are part of different ethnic groups. Below are some ethnic groups commonly found in New York. Check whichever ones your family is part of." And then I listed the ordinary range and an "other" for good measure.

That worked. The students checked off a box or two or three, I learned what I wanted to know, and it was kind of interesting. I was interested in race/ethnicity as *cultural,* the way people get their ideas about things, like feminism, via their ethnicity. Culture is a third level of analysis, neither reducible to the psychological nor interchangeable with structural. Culture is what we call all of the beliefs, values, knowledge, skills, language, cus-

toms, the way of life of a social group. It's really culture, or selected, *edited,* parts of a culture, that people are drawing upon
when they celebrate ethnicity.

Think about someone doing a study like the one I did in
about ten years, when the Chinese adoptees are in college. Many
of these girls are being raised by feminist parents; they will
probably show feminist attitudes, think girls can grow up to be
anything they want to be, and so on. That will be a reflection of
the culture of their adoptive parents. But the girls will probably
identify not only with their parents' category, but also as "Chinese" or "Asian American." The Asian features that mark their
bodies give them an *identity* that does not necessarily reflect
their *culture.*

Black or Asian or other children of color whose mothering
is coming from white people are in much the same position
whether they are born to or adopted by those white folks. If race
isn't biological, so you can't sensibly call one person "more"
Asian or "pure" black or "full-blooded" Indian,[2] then we're left
with the psychological, the cultural, and the structural. Identity
has to take all of those into account. Sandra Patton, concluding
her book on (black) transracially adopted people, comes to a
definition of identity that makes enormous sense to me:

> In my view, identity formation is shaped by the biological, embod-
> ied aspects of being, the cultural meaning systems available to in-
> dividuals, and the public policies, social institutions, and political
> economy of the society in which a person lives.[3]

If you look black (the biological, embodied aspect of being)
in America, you're going to have to deal with blackness. When
you have white family—by birth or by adoption—you're being
raised, at least in part, to think the way white people think
(within a cultural meaning system of whiteness). And ultimately you're going to grow up beyond your family, to stand on

your own, to take your place in the world (in the social institutions and political economy of the society).

The problem addressed in the American discussion about labeling has largely been about personal identity, specifically the rights (and of course it was bound to come back to rights again) of people to claim the identities they choose. Maria P. P. Root is a psychologist, and "the leading published authority in America on the developmental and social issues raised by the 'biracial baby boom,'" according to Intermix, a UK-based group for mixed-race people.[4] She's written a "bill of rights" for racially mixed people, and Intermix claims it as their motto. It's been reprinted widely, used in classes and discussion groups, all over the United States and elsewhere. Root does claim a politics for what she is doing. She groups her rights into "Resistance, Revolution and Change." Here are the three groups of rights:

RESISTANCE: I have the right:
>   not to justify my existence in this world
>   not to keep the races separate within me
>   not to be responsible for people's discomfort with my physical ambiguity
>   not to justify my ethnic legitimacy

REVOLUTION: I have the right:
>   to identify myself differently than strangers expect me to identify
>   to identify myself differently than how my parents identify me
>   to identify myself differently than my brothers and sisters
>   to identify myself differently in different situations

CHANGE: I have the right:
>   to create a vocabulary to communicate about being multiracial
>   to change my identity over my lifetime—and more than once

> to have loyalties and identify with more than one group of
> people
> to freely choose whom I befriend and how[5]

I guess that's a psychological kind of revolution: incredibly, powerfully important for the individual, and maybe opening up the possibility for social, structural change. Or maybe not. It opens up the space in which one could subvert whiteness, undermine racism. But it also opens up the space *not* to do those things.

The thing about being black in America—or Jewish in Nazi Germany, black in apartheid South Africa, Aboriginal in Australia—is that you don't choose your identity. It's assigned. So having the freedom to claim your own identity could be very *personally* liberating for "mixed-race" people, without being at all revolutionary at a larger level. It could give them a privilege of whiteness: the privilege of not being identified by others. Of course I'm all in favor of anyone's rights to identify themselves any way they choose, change those identities over time. But if that actually worked as a political strategy, any lynching could have been stopped by the black guy just speaking up and claiming a white identity—lots of them had white fathers or grandfathers or great-grandfathers. Or, in a more contemporary mode, in these days after the civil rights movement, is claiming a white identity going to help a black man catch a cab in midtown?

So it's a great idea at the individual level, but is it just going to leave some other, "really" black person behind?[6]

Katya Gibel Azoulay studied Black Jewish people—adults who had one Jewish and one black parent—to learn how they think of their identity. One of her interviewees, identified as "Belinda," was among those who insist that "they think of themselves as human beings and refuse to privilege race in their lives."[7]

Belinda talks like someone who fully accepts the bill of rights Root has proposed.

Asked about racism, Belinda says:

> I refuse to let it dictate my life. . . . It's never been an issue as far as *my* self goes. If it's an issue for somebody else that is their problem. It only becomes your problem if you. . . . let it become your problem.[8]

Azoulay notes that Belinda is "light enough to pass or be misrecognized as white" and sensibly wonders if Belinda makes a connection between her racial ambiguity and "having the freedom to defer race as incidental."[9] Of course that's a good sentiment, a good psychological strategy, not to let it get to you. But are black people in America free to just *refuse to let* racism dictate their lives?

The joy of ethnicity, the ability to play with identity(ies), assumes an equality of categories. If all the ethnicities/racial categories are sitting there in the marketplace, and "choice" is a matter of kente cloth versus Nottingham lace, small brass Buddhas versus little Madonna statuettes, grits versus kimchee, then we could indeed shop for ethnicity to our heart's content. My father's mother's sister married an Italian man: that's where my spaghetti sauce recipe comes from. Whoo-ee, I'm authentically Italian! Why not?

But if you think, as I most certainly do, that there is still racism in America, that all of these ethnicities are not equally displayed before us, then not all play is equal. When we choose between equally valued ethnicities, then we are perhaps in the realm of play, of consumption, of individual choice. When we choose upwards, discarding a lower-valued race/ethnic categorization for one of higher value, then we are in the realm of "passing," or "being an Oreo," or "selling out." And when we choose downwards, then perhaps—at its best—we're subverting whiteness, being a "race traitor" in the best possible way.

The relations between African Americans and Jews in America are a particularly good lens for thinking about this. The relations between these two groups in the United States have been thought about, written about, talked about endlessly. A selected bibliography on the topic covering the period from 1752 to 1984 runs well over one hundred pages.[10] Jews really have had some very awful times, even in the United States. The Klan spoke of blacks and Jews in the same breath. The first Jew to be lynched in America, forty-seven years before Leo Frank, was S. A. Bierfeld, who ran a dry goods store in Franklin, Tennessee. He and his black employee were lynched in 1868.[11] Jews, as I discussed elsewhere, just didn't become white until recently; CORE, for example, founded in 1942, was set up as an interracial movement composed of blacks, Jews, and whites.[12]

But Jews did get to become white, pretty much, in the United States. The process of moving up meant moving out, away from blackness. For a long time, Jews held a position in poor black neighborhoods very much like that of the Korean grocery owners we heard so much about in the Los Angeles uprisings: they were the ones, just one notch above, who were on-site. Jews moved up into the middle classes in New York and became teachers; the New York City school teachers' strike of 1968 focused attention on Black-Jewish relations in the city. We started hearing about Black anti-Semitism, Jewish racism. It got ugly.[13] And of course, all the while, you had African Americans and Jews marrying, raising kids together. You had the "movement babies," as Rebecca Walker[14] describes herself. Others have written about their black-Jewish families, including James McBride,[15] Hettie Jones,[16] Naomi Zack,[17] and Jane Lazarre.[18] Read any account of mixed-race people, and black-Jewish combinations keep coming up.[19]

Katya Gibel Azoulay is the American-born daughter of a Holocaust-surviving Austrian mother and a Jamaican father. She spent twenty-one years living in Israel. She says, "To be Jewish and Black and interracial . . . is a standpoint position from which to challenge racialist nationalism and misguided prejudice."[20] People in America who are the children of Jews and blacks are seen as looking black and not seen as looking Jewish. The biological, embodied aspect of being reinforces the black, not the Jewish identity. And most people in those relationships are not raised to be religiously Jewish; they're not, as people sometimes say of people like me, "very Jewish." So how do they understand their Jewishness? Mostly it seems to be about their whiteness, but it's more than that. "If it came down to it and there was another Holocaust, I'd be taken in two seconds,"[21] said one; and another: "well, I'd better accept the fact that I'm Jewish whether I want to or not because if Hitler was here today, he would take me as soon as he would take someone else."[22]

From the standpoint of people who are made constantly aware of their blackness, Jewishness is an identity one claims *because* it is disvalued. It's not as if they're actually worried that Hitler's coming back, that anti-Semitism is a big fear of theirs. Being Jewish is an obligation; from yet another of Azoulay's informants, "link(ing) anti-Semitism in Europe and the Holocaust with slavery in the United States":

> For me personally—what makes it so important for me to carry out traditions is what my actual great-grandparents went though on both sides; what they went through and what they stood for—it just seems like I can't just turn, turn back and go on, "Oh, I'm just a light-skinned person, a light-skinned black person."[23]

If they're coming around with yellow stars, then yes, these Jews too know they will step forward. That stepping forward—

claiming the identity precisely because it is disvalued—is a political act, not just playing. There's a story I gather is apocryphal, but I've heard it all my life, learned something from it: The Nazis entered Denmark and the Jews were supposed to put on the yellow star. The morning of the decree, the king of Denmark came out of his palace with a yellow star around his arm; all the Danes put them on.

And the other morning, Victoria told me she read an article in *Seventeen* magazine about a Jewish girl in Brooklyn whose car was defaced with swastikas. We talked for a few minutes, standing at the bus stop, saying how weird that was, how awful. And then Victoria said to me, "You know, I ought to wear a Jewish star. People don't know I'm Jewish." I'm proud to be that kid's mother.

This then is the thing some of us worry about in the mixed-race, multiracial movement. Most often the disvalued race is the one that the society is recognizing. It's a problem if a claim to mixed race becomes a way of moving more people into the nonblack category, which is fine for them, but doesn't do anything for the people left as black. That's what made so many black people annoyed with golf star Tiger Woods and his "Cablinasian" comment on TV's *Oprah Winfrey Show*. Asked about whether he identified as African American, he said that Cablinasian was what he came up with for himself when he was a kid, recognizing his various family ties (Caucasian, Black, Indian, Asian). It's not fair to blame him, beat a dead tiger and all—he did say it was what he said as a *kid*—but in celebrating his various heritages he was, in a way, taking away from the black community's ability to claim him as their own, his success as theirs. Contrast that with Halle Berry's Academy Award speech when she was the first African American woman ever to win the Best Actress award. Berry listed some well-known African American actresses who should have received that award and never did, and claimed the moment for them, and for "every nameless, faceless woman of color that now has a chance because the door tonight has been opened." Halle Berry has a white mother. Let me tell you, watching that—I would have been real proud to be her mother!

17
Entitlement: That Can't Be Your Baby

Parenthood is based on an endless series of contradictions: we have children because, at least in America today, we *want* to. We want the something-or-other we think it is that children will add to our lives. We want an experience or bunch of experiences that come with children. We want to experience ourselves as parents. The children are, then, inevitably, a means to something: a means to the experience of being a parent that we want in our lives. The ethicists tut-tut over anyone being a means for anyone else: people are to be valued for their own selves. And most assuredly parents *do* value their children for themselves, for who they are, and not as a means to an end. And yet they have children in the first place because they want the experience, and so the children *are* a means, a pathway to the experience of parenting.

The contradiction, I think, is between the fantasized, planned-for child, the child we want to have so we can be the kind of parents we want to be, doing what we want to do, and the actual child who shows up in our lives. For most parents, and certainly for most mothers, that child who actually shows up, the child we have, becomes a—maybe the—central force in our lives. We give up so many of our dreams—the little daily ones of a clean house, quiet evenings, an uninterrupted phone call—and sometimes the larger ones. Parents, mothers especially, have a long history of sacrificing whatever needs to be sacrificed for the child. Sometimes it seems as if it's one's own life that has become the means, as the needs of a child turn a life upside down.

And that's an interesting thing right there: The children are bit players in the movie of our life. We star, and some kids are slotted in from central casting somewhere. "She lives in Hawaii with her husband, two children, and a dog," it says on the back of the novel; President Johnson or Ford or Lincoln had—how many kids, was it? But in the lives of our children, we are bit players, or at best maybe character actors: his father was a lawyer; her mother encouraged her talents; his mother's dreams spurred him on. We're some groundwork, some explanation of motive, a fill-in, the back story.

So much of the tension occurs as the story shifts, from one generation's to the next's, as the kids cease to be bit players in our movies and begin to direct their own. Welcome to adolescence. It starts at around age two and maybe ends when the kids settle into their own middle age, receding to background in their own kids' movies. My mother says kids should be buried at fourteen and dug up again at twenty-one—and those certainly are the worst years, the hardest part of the struggle over who gets to direct this movie. By fourteen or so they've got enough strength and competence that they can have some control; by twenty-one a lot of what we had in mind for our children is accomplished or a lost cause anyway. They're off living their lives and we're grateful to be kept informed. We'd like to see the rushes while some editing can still be done, but we're clearly not running this show.

What does adoption, and especially adoption across race, change? Nothing. Everything.

For many adopters, probably most, the planned-for child grew and grew and grew. The planning stage stretches out endlessly. For many of the people who adopt, there's the dawning realization of infertility, the prolonged struggle against it, and finally the reconciliation to what is so clearly in most people's minds, the second-best choice, the remaining option of adoption, "when all else fails." And then there's the endless adoption procedure itself, with its paperwork and interviews and classes and meetings and more paperwork. For middle-class white people, there are not many "accidental adoptions," babies left on the doorstep. That's a whole lot less true for poorer women and women of color, who sometimes do actually have babies pretty much dropped on them, babies and children they may formally adopt or just take in, and take on, for however long the need lasts.

But stick for a moment with the highly popularized image of adopters, the middle-class white couple of "desperate infertility" who turn to adoption. They give up imagined baby after baby as they move through this process, and by the time they come back from China with an eight-month-old, or get matched with an American black baby, there's not much resemblance between the baby they thought they were going for and the one they've got. And yet: they are all the same.

In the short story "Dream Children" by Gail Godwin, a nurse, exhausted from working double shifts, accidentally brings in a baby from the nursery to a woman who had had a stillbirth the night before. The grieving woman brings the baby to her breast, holds it, and I suppose thinks all that happened yesterday was the nightmare from which she's finally awakened. The nurse, realizing what she's done—and faced with having to go and take that woman's baby away from her—is suddenly swept with the realization of how interchangeable all these mothers and babies are, that it really doesn't matter which baby goes to which mother. The babies are all bit players, all sent from central casting, or the central nursery, entirely interchangeable. Bundles.

Look through family photo albums of new babies: there are some portraits there, some photos of the baby, its face caught in the camera, close up. But there are usually many more photos of mothers mothering, fathers fathering, grandmothers grandmothering, grandfathers grandfathering, aunts aunting, uncles uncling: people greeting, and holding, and displaying—displaying the baby, displaying themselves in this new relationship, displaying themselves in this new role. The bundle that they cuddle, the mouth into which they push a baby spoon, the face belonging to the little fingers they hold as little feet first try standing—there is something generic about that. In families where the babies look alike, people often identify the photo by the others in it: that's Uncle Sam, so that must be Hilary as a baby; that's the old kitchen, so that must be Ellie as a newborn.

I have a friend who loves my son, adored him as a baby and little child, she really did. She came in from out of town once while he was in nursery school, a little toddler. I sent her off to go pick him up, surprise him, see his class. She hesitated, and finally, because she's my friend and she loves me and trusts me (not to do this, probably, tell this story to the whole world) she confided her fear: What if I don't recognize him? What if I don't know which one he is? I had to laugh: I'm famous in my family for not recognizing faces (someone has to keep whispering to me all through movies, yes, that's the same guy from the last scene; no, that's a different woman), so I knew just what she meant. And I knew the solution: he'll know you, silly! Because all these little children—yes, they do all look alike, more or less.

But we organize these children into the same categories we use for all people: by gender and by race. Gender in children is largely the province of the costume department and props: no one can tell the clothed two-year-old boys from the girls without those clues. Race is, as ever, in the eye of the beholder, but there it is: the black kids, the white ones, the Asians—by broad categories or by local arrangements, we group the kids into the categories by which we have organized our society.

Think about the nurse who mistakenly brought in that baby to the grieving mother: the mistake is made possible by an assumption of whiteness. White people who hear that story see the universality of the babies because they assume whiteness everywhere. If the nurse had picked up a black baby and walked into a white woman's room, picked up a black baby and walked into an Asian woman's room—if the baby and the mother didn't "match" racially—she'd have caught her mistake in the doorway. "This can't be your baby," she'd have thought.

"Oh, this can't be your baby." Can't. Cannot. Logically impossible? Inherently wrong? Out of bounds?

But for some of us, that *is* our baby, yes indeed. It can't be, but it is. We've crossed a racial boundary in our motherhood; by partnering with a man across the race line, or by adoption, we have a baby that "can't be" ours. Our baby is not the generic baby in our family photos: ours sticks out. Ours can be spotted with the most casual eye, jumping out of photo after photo. White folks playing: dark baby. White folks at a picnic: dark baby. White folks in front of a church, a store, a car, a beach, a mountain, a house: dark baby.

I think anyone who's ever done mothering, any man or woman who's taken on the responsibility for a baby, must have questioned their own entitlement, their own *nerve:* Who am I, just who do I think I am, doing this? I remember in my labor with Daniel—before there actually was a "Daniel" for me—the doctor offered to do something to "speed things along," and I

thought: hell, no, I'm not ready to be someone's mother. I remember my first quiet moment alone with Leah, who was so, so
beautiful, and thinking, oh my god, please don't let me screw
this up.

I birthed those babies at home; I have no memory of the doc
from the first birth or the midwife from the second leaving, no
memory of a door closing and being on my own. I was at home,
with a houseful of family and friends, and the reality, the responsibility, crept up on me slowly. People who give birth in
hospitals and birth centers do have a stronger memory of those
first moments when it's all on you: being wheeled to a hospital
door, and left there to go out into the world with your baby, or
walking into your home and closing the door behind you: it's
us, now.

Adoption is like that: someone hands you a baby and you
bring it home. Just like that. After god knows how many hoops
you've jumped through, hot coals you've metaphorically walked
across, after you've created far more pounds of paper than there
are pounds of baby—somehow, at the end, it's all of a sudden.
The hospital-birth people have been angry about the "drive-
through deliveries," the speed of it all. Their complaints really
haven't been all that much about the "recovery" from the act of
giving birth per se (except of course the Cesareans, who do get
more time) but the abrupt transfer of responsibility for the baby.
Nurses feel they haven't got enough time to teach new mothers;
new mothers may feel overwhelmed, learning it all so fast.[1]

In adoption we get our babies and, instantly, they're ours.
We take them home—or to our hotel room in some foreign
country, the little oasis of home we create for a while—and suddenly: that's your baby. While we feel oh-so-overwhelmed, we
adoptive parents actually haven't fared badly. We do as well as
other new parents. It's not, when you come down to it, all that
complicated: people hire fifteen-year-old kids to baby-sit, and if

they can do the tasks, so can we. You put the right stuff in one end and clean up what comes out the other, and basically, that's it for a while. Hugging, cuddling, singing, rocking—you'd be surprised how quickly we pick that stuff up, how easily it comes to most of us, men and women, boys and girls. Higher-pitched cooing, eye contact, if that stuff isn't instinctual to human beings (*human beings* I said, not "mothers"—I'm not talking about "maternal instincts"), it sure gets learned easily enough.

And with the doing of those mothering tasks, with the feeding and holding and cleaning and caring, comes the other kind of caring, the deep, solid attachment we feel for our children—and they for us. I do think there is something biological in that attachment. I think in adoption, especially in the adoption of very young children and babies, some kind of instinctual thing clicks in for people, and it's easy to attach. I don't think we're rising above our biology, above nature to privilege nurture, but working with our nature. We're social, communal animals.

From my background in the home birth movement, it's long fascinated me how little American society does value and work with the natural, the biological in baby care. Contrast these two scenes, thinking about how much biology matters:

It's 4:00 a.m. September. Late September. Victoria's a month old. You look in my bedroom. We're tangled in the sheets. Victoria's in between Hesch and me, her empty cradle by my side of the bed. I'm wearing a nightgown that's open to the waist, twisted around me, my breast exposed. Victoria's suckling. The "nurser," a contraption that consists of a plastic bottle of formula worn around my neck with two tubes that extend to my nipples, usually taped into place with surgical tape, is mostly empty, lying on the headboard bookcase. I've been using that to bring my milk back in for this baby, giving her enough formula to keep her sucking. She's suckling on mostly nothing now, just at the breast, not getting much more than tastes of milk. I'm more asleep than awake. Hesch is snoring, one arm stretched out over her legs.

And this one:

A few blocks away, a baby sleeps in a crib, in a room to itself. Down the hall in their bedroom, the mother and father are in their bed, asleep. She's still recovering from a Cesarean section. There's a baby monitor by the side of the crib, and a speaker on their headboard. If the baby cries again, they'll hear it, and—if they think it's time— one of them will warm up some formula, fill a bottle, and go into the baby's room, feed it, and put it back down in the crib.

Does biology matter? I think it does—I think the immunities the baby is getting from whatever breast milk an adoptive mother does produce, the immunities and comfort the baby is getting from skin-to-skin contact with adults, the feedback the baby is getting as it stirs in close contact with adults—I think these things matter. I think baby monitors, like sonography, tell the parents the baby is OK, but they don't give the baby anything back. Fetuses are getting their comfort, their contact, their connections. Babies need that to continue for a while, need to feel connected.

Adoptive parents can do just as good—or just as bad—a job of attaching, connecting, bonding, and nurturing their babies as mothers by birth can do. It may well be that an adopted baby grieves the loss of its birth mother: most often we're not offering continuity from the moment of birth, a familiar voice, body. I remember sobbing with Victoria one night in her first weeks, when nothing I did, *nothing,* seemed to comfort her. It was the middle of the night, and I thought, "This poor baby needs her mother!" And in the calm of day, I spoke to friends whose babies had cried just as inconsolably in the arms of the women who'd birthed them. It may actually have been much the same thing: a hospital birth, a few days of nursery care, many arms and smells and sights and sounds, another adjustment to home, a confused baby. American birth practices, American hospitals, put all new babies in much the situation adopted babies are. And we work it out, take a few days or weeks even, but we work it out. Babies adjust. They're flexible, adaptable. Give us a bit of time, a couple of weeks of mothering work, and yes, those really are our babies.

And then we open the door and go back outside.

Parents of racially matched adopted babies and children often share the funny stories of how people say, "Oh she looks just like you." Babies do, it seems, come in just so many types: the Winston Churchill, the Alfred Hitchcock, the Plucked Chicken. Those of course are the white babies. "Resemblance" between a newborn and a thirty-year-old is always kind of a stretch, an imaginative leap. We're back to the reality that they all look alike, so they might as well "look just like you!" It's something parents seem to like hearing, so it's something casual acquaintances, strangers at the supermarket, and day-care teachers can offer.

Not so for parents of unmatched babies. When a baby crosses a racial border, it seems very hard for people to see resemblances, even when they actually are there. A white colleague with a black husband gave birth to a daughter who does, really, look just like her, but she said people always assume the baby was adopted, and ask, "Where does she come from?"

It's rather like a little problem in cognitive dissonance, the theory from psychology that says people have a hard time with contradictory evidence, and work hard to make sense of it. White people are supposed to, expected to, have white children. A child of color is supposed to, expected to, have a color-matched mother. When the match isn't there, when it's not obvious—what do you see?

Mostly people don't see the relationship. But sometimes they make a few adjustments in what they see. As Judith Lorber likes to put it, "Believing is seeing!"[2] White mothers of multiracial babies say that white folks often see the baby as tan, dark from the sun. My white cousin, married to a Mexican man, says that's how people saw her children when she was alone with them: "My, they're tan!" A friend who lived in a very white suburb with her multiracial black/white daughter said people were always telling her how tan her baby was getting, sometimes admiringly, more often critically, having read the sunscreen information. These are children who, in another context, in a Mexican or black neighborhood, would have been instantly ethnically recognizable.

And sometimes it's the mother whose race category is reassigned. I was at a professional meeting with a very young Victoria on my lap. I'm not unknown at these meetings. I was sitting in the second row. I spoke up and asked a question. And at the end of the panel, I walked up to one of the women who'd just presented a paper, to continue our conversation. Now it's true that it was summer and I actually *was* tan. But still. She stared at me for a minute, then laughed, and said: "Oh, it *is* you! I saw you and thought, 'That black woman looks a lot like Barbara Katz Rothman.'"

At one level, these are just a bunch of silly, funny stories, speaking to the skills we have to develop to "present as family," the ways we work to make family obvious. But at another level, they can be understood as a form of what Heather Dalmage describes as "border patrolling," a form of *borderism*: "Borderism is a unique form of discrimination faced by those who cross the color line, do not stick with their own, or attempt to claim membership (or are placed by others) in more than one racial group."[3]

White border patrolling is the more ordinary racist phenomenon. White women's bodies are the grounds upon which racists have staked their battle: protecting the "purity of the white race." Women who give birth to their black children face far more racism than those of us who adopt ours, but most white mothers of children of color can recount for you some racist experience. And of course virtually all of our children can.

The borders, as Heather Dalmage shows, are patrolled on both sides. Multiracial people and transracially adopted people (and yes, oftentimes they are the same people) face pressure from the black community as well as from the white. There's a pressure to prove oneself, to show just how black you really are. It involves the much-discussed pressure on high-school kids to not "act white." Kids with white families are bound to do some acting white, using white language or aesthetics. These are issues that Victoria is facing now, as a teenager, moving into high school:

> I'm teased by other black kids because I talk "white." And I know exactly what they mean. Their definition of talking white was speaking with good grammar, the result of living with wealthy white people, being able to afford fancy schools with fancy teachers. But what hurt me the most is that when I actually gave a damn and tried to fit in or make friends, I was not being myself, and all because of who I was raised by.

And we all know that no one, no one on earth, knows how to apply pressure like high-school kids do.

Heather Dalmage's conclusions after interviews with adult multiracial and transracially adopted people are optimistic: "Once acceptance is granted, demands for proof of blackness ease—at least within a given neighborhood or community."[4] Yes, when you first move into the black neighborhood, the black school, you're going to have to prove yourself. But, as parents have been telling teenagers for a very long time now, it does get better.

The border patrolling of the kids takes the form of having to prove their blackness. For the mothers, the border patrol is about the legitimacy of our motherhood: that can't be your baby. Cheri Register named the problem in the title of her book about border-crossing adoptions: *Are Those Kids Yours?*[5]

White folks with children of color get that question not just from white folks, but on all sides. "Are you a social worker?" I got asked once on the subway, by a black woman. "No, she's mine," I said. And held my breath. Is she going to be OK with this, or am I going to have to defend my motherhood? And she smiled, relieved: "I thought maybe you were bringing the baby to foster care. Good, she's got a home. Nice to meet you." And she walked off, smiling.

When white people asked those kinds of questions of me, I was unsure just how to respond. If I claimed Victoria mine by adoption, I felt as if I was disavowing the legitimacy of having had a black husband/lover/partner. The adoption question is routinely asked by whites of white mothers who birthed their black children, and often does seem to be about maintaining "racial purity": "If women who appear to be good turn out to be polluted, white border patrollers get nervous."[6] But if I refused to acknowledge adoption, then I was disavowing the legitimacy of motherhood via adoption. And every adoptive mother can tell you about being asked about the "real" mother. I asked a colleague who was the white mother of black children by birth how she handles the question, and her answer—which I had great fun using—was "tell them you're the nanny."

That is my variation of "wearing the yellow star," accepting whatever is the lowest status on offer so as to be as subversive as possible. Whatever you want to think I am, I'm not going to participate in your dumping on others: people who adopt, white women with black partners, nannies.

But I, along with most white mothers of children of color,

am much more comfortable being subversive, being nasty if I have to, with white people. The racism of white people is something I just do not have to tolerate, not for a minute. Border patrolling from the black side is far more complicated. "Reverse racism" is a made-up idea; you don't "reverse" racism the way you reverse traffic, north to south, south to north. Again, all these groups—white, black, African American, Irish, Jewish, Chinese, Mexican—they're not all laid out on a level playing field. Border patrolling is about loyalty and betrayal: betraying the powerful is subversion; betraying the oppressed is something else again.

Those of us who are raising our children of color by adoption may feel vulnerable to accusations of having used our white privilege to get these children in the first place, and then taking them from their heritage. Like white women who date or marry black men, we stand accused of taking away people who "by rights" should belong to black women. If it takes a village, we've taken a child from the village.

Moosnick, comparing mothers who adopted white, Asian, and black children, found: "Mothers, in particular, of Black and Biracial children voiced the sentiment more than the others, that they were not the exclusive owners of their children."[7] This isn't an altogether bad thing; she also found "those women most willing to acknowledge that their children belonged elsewhere were most likely to work for racial change."[8] White women raising black children in a white neighborhood put their kids in a more difficult situation, and that of course challenged their sense of motherhood, but the white woman raising black children in black communities confronted "minority women's evaluations and appraisal of her mothering skills."[9]

It's not easy, being judged. Anybody doing mothering work has experienced some of that: Don't you think the baby's too warm/cool? Isn't she too young/old for that? Isn't that dangerous? (To the last, Hesch always used to answer: "Nah, we only lost one out of the last four that way.") Being judged when you're confident, as Hesch was of being safe and careful, is one thing. But being judged when you're feeling a bit wanting, when you are less sure of yourself, that's very hard.

I used to let the kids go shirtless on hot summer days; three-year-old girls in little short pants seemed OK to me. Leah and a friend were walking with Victoria around the block and a man she didn't know, one of our Afro-Caribbean neighbors, stopped her: "That child should have a shirt on!" "No," Leah reassured him, "my mother said it's OK." And his response: "I don't care what *your* mother says, it's not OK with *her* mother." He was holding Victoria to the norms of his community, his cultural standards. Leah came home laughing, she and her friend just cracking up eleven-year-old style about how funny it was—*my* mother, not *her* mother!

Me? I put a shirt on the kid after that.

Being judged and evaluated on one's mothering competence isn't always pleasant, but it's not always unhelpful either. Sometimes, you know, the baby *is* too warm or too cold, too young or too old for whatever it was, sometimes something is more dangerous than you thought or noticed. It can, actually, be helpful. And, even if you're doing everything perfectly, just perfectly, you still can't do it all on your own. Much has been written of the communal mothering that black women do: the "othermother" as Patricia Hill Collins calls it,[10] the community of co-mothers described by Carol Stack as "all our kin," in her book of the same name.[11] It seems to me I've needed a community of mothers—including foremost Hesch, who actively mothered our children along with me, but extending to our mothers, my stepfather, my friend Maren, various friends and neighbors, all along.

When the child presents a new set of issues, something beyond your experience or competence, then of course you need some extra help. This is true when we're talking about individual variation: a child who wants to learn a skill the parents haven't got, a child whose personality challenges this particular set of parents, a child with a particular ability or disability. And it's very, very true when the child crosses a race/ethnic border.

These othermothers are a mixed blessing. France Winddance Twine studied white mothers of mixed-race children in the United Kingdom, and found that:

> The African Caribbean community was both a site of affirmation and a challenge to mothers of African-descent children. Not all members of the African Caribbean community supported interracial relationships or sympathized with the plight of poor white mothers struggling to raise their children. White mothers who identified the African Caribbean community as their reference group and source of support described how they felt the need to constantly prove their maternal fitness to Black Caribbean women.[12]

But they also got the help: "they learned the range of skills associated with Black family life including cooking, discipline, haircare, music, décor, and dress."[13] And they got something more important than just skills, what one mother spoke of as "the sense of being comfortable, not estranged around Black people—feeling okay with Black people, and not alien to them. Do you know what I mean?"[14]

I do, yes, I do know what she means.

The black community is one place where white mothers can get their affirmation, their sense of entitlement to their children, but they have to work for it. There's another community that offers some of the same things, with lower costs to the mothers: the multiracial community.

Ananya Mukherjea was working with me as a research assistant at an early stage of this project. I'd emerged from the basement of the Schomburg, knowing all I wanted to for now about the history of white women raising black children, and wanted to know a bit more about what's going on out there right now. Ananya Mukherjea spent time online, gathering what she could find. Some of what she found was, of course, the growing body of scholarly literature. But she also found many online communities, many chat rooms and support groups, and the electronic evidence of the more "live" and less "virtual" counterparts.

She found it unsettling. The mothers, she pointed out, seemed so desperate for this kind of support, expressed such joy in finding it. The children, she found, were often lumped together as "of color," indicating to Ananya that it's really about the mother's race, and not the child's. The mothers wanted to find "families like theirs," "children like theirs" for role models for their children. But how do you define a "child like yours"? Is the key thing the blackness of the child or the whiteness of its mother?

I should imagine children and families need both: the children do probably benefit from exposure not just to lots and lots of black families, or Chinese families, or whatever race/ethnic label will be applied to that child, but also to mixed families, and specifically to families with children like yours, with white mothers.

In her recent work, Heather Dalmage has been studying the multiracial family organizations, and she's not altogether pleased with what she's finding. Whites may be turning to these groups precisely to avoid the feelings of judgment, and maybe worse, that they fear from the black community.

> Much of the demand whites express for comfort is couched in a language of avoiding the perceived threats against them, that is, whites

as victims of racial hostility. . . . reaching out to blacks is beyond the realm of comfortable and safe possibilities. In circular fashion, then, separation and isolation allows whites to build their world-views around their own projections (fed by a steady diet from the media and other mainstream institutions), and their own projections, in turn, cause them to want to avoid interaction.[15]

What she finds is that the white mothers—and it is most often mothers—"fail to grasp the connection between their deep desire for racial comfort and the reproduction of whiteness."[16]

It's understandable why any of us would turn to "people like us" for comfort, support, and advice. A roomful of white parents of black children is one place where I will never hear anyone say, "That can't be your baby." And for early childhood at least, that's probably all the child needs. Children want to see themselves as like the others, "kinda the same," as Sesame Street had it. But children grow up, and must come to terms with their own, personal, extrafamilial place as adults of whatever identity is written on their bodies. Heather Dalmage concludes that "instead of exploring their own white racial identities, these parents seek comfort with other white parents, and the onus of race and white supremacy remains on the shoulders of their children and all people of color."[17]

They are asking the children to be the bridge.

18
Hair: Braiding Together Culture, Identity, and Entitlement

> Everything I know about American
> history, I learned from looking at Black
> people's hair. . . . It's all in the hair.
> LISA JONES, *Bulletproof Diva*

I started this project wanting to do a book about hair, about how white mothers learn — or do not learn — to do hair for their black children, particularly for their black daughters. I wanted to write *The White Mama's Book of Black Hair*. Maybe I will someday.

I started collecting passages out of novels, memoirs, short stories, essays, mysteries, works of history and fantasy, of polemic and of self-help. I have files and files now, passages from a few sentences to a few pages, and not a few books besides, on the doing of black hair. Hair, I have found, is more interesting — and more provocative in multiracial settings — than is skin color. Color just *is;* hair must be done.

In the doing of hair, one does race. Race is constructed, celebrated, despaired of, enjoyed, feared. Hair is a test to be passed or failed, a trial to be endured, an intimate moment to be shared. In memoirs of those raised within the African American community[1] and those raised by white people,[2] hair and the doing of hair emerges as a focal point for the discussion and for the experience of race.

It was Victoria's hair—her beautiful, thick, tightly curled African hair, and the responses it evoked more from black friends, neighbors, acquaintances, and perfect strangers than from white—that drew my attention to hair as a point of connection between black women. When Victoria was little, I'd be with her at a playground, a park, a fast food place, waiting for a bus, outside a nursery school at dismissal time, and from somewhere, from *nowhere,* some black woman would come up to me. Nice beads—did you do that? Or: Who does her hair? Or: I had hair like that—I cried on hair days.

I had Victoria with me at a sociology conference, and a nationally renowned black feminist sociologist, seeing Victoria for the first time, all done up with "Mickey Mouse-ear" pom-poms blurted, "Oh, Barbara! She has bad hair!" We stared at each other, equally shocked that she'd said it, and then burst out laughing.

I had Victoria with me on a Fulbright fellowship to the Netherlands, in a northern city, waiting on line at a bank, and a black woman—the first I'd seen in that city—materialized beside me to talk about Victoria's hair. I thought: Someday I'm going to go to the moon and the only other person there will be a black woman with a comb, a jar of grease, and a story.

White people—especially but not exclusively those of us raising black children—need to know these stories, need to know the politics and history of hair. Not knowing has consequences. A well-meaning white teacher read her class a book about nappy hair[3] and practically started a riot. In New York

City the schools that black kids attend are rotting before our eyes, the books and the roofs alike falling apart. The reading scores are a shame and a scandal, the whole system is in perpetual turmoil, and as Abiola Sinclair noted,[4] more parents showed up to shout their anger over a book called *Nappy Hair* than had shown up at PTA meetings all year, maybe all decade.

There was a time when I would have thought that was overreacting.

The history and politics of hair is the history and politics of race. The devil is in the details. Picture the slave woman helping the mistress of the plantation: try to remember those famous images from the movies you've seen of the slave woman, her hair wrapped up, covering her shame with rags, while she is brushing the white woman's "crown of glory." The Black Barbie arrived a century later (finally! Hallelujah and the hell with gender politics!), but she had long, straight, flowing hair, the very same hair that white Barbie has. One of the wealthiest and most successful of African American women *ever* made her fortune starting with the straightening comb; what can we make of Madame C. J. Walker when we try to teach our daughters pride in their foremothers?

White people raising black children confront race history and its contemporary consequences as they groom their children. Hair demands attention: the hair of a black girl requires an average of two to four or more hours of work each week. A relatively simple style can be braided in an hour, but will need to be redone frequently. A more complex style may last for several weeks, but will require more hours to put in—and almost as many to take down. Undoing a black kid's braid is not a matter of just running your fingers through and shaking it out. These hours force upon parent and child a confrontation with difference: a white parent, grooming black hair, is physically engaged with race difference in a way one rarely encounters in any other interaction.

Adoption agencies now routinely ask white people doing adoption or foster care to learn something about black hair. As well they should. But white folks, raising black kids or not, need to know this history. We white women are doing something when we casually flip our hair back, run fingers through it, toss our heads in that way that white girls have that black girls mock. With pain, sometimes. I've seen black women—grown, educated, professional, competent black women—brought to tears by the sight of a black girlchild putting a scarf on her head and "pretending" hair. "Shaky hair, I want *shaky* hair," a black friend's black daughter said. And her mother's eyes filled. There's a history here that we need to pay attention to.

There has been, over the last decade or so, a growing scholarly attention to hair,[5] and specifically to black hair.[6] There have been wonderfully curated exhibits and art books on African and African American hair.[7] There have been books that combine practical information with politics and history.[8] There have been biographies and novelizations of the life of Madame C. J. Walker, America's first black millionaire, founder of a company that brought employment to thousands of African American women, and whose work has been a bone of contention among scholars and activists ever since.[9]

So what is this all about? And now, if the rest of you will be so kind as to excuse my elaboration of things you know very well, I'm going to address myself to my white readers, to those who have never taken a comb to a head of African-descent hair, who have no clue that "bad hair" has traditionally meant tight or nappy or African hair, and "good hair" meant looser, more European-style hair. The ordinary, pervasive race segregation of America means that most white people, including those who will grow up to be mothering black children, do not grow up in intimate contact with black friends. White girls don't usually have the experience of helping their black friends do their hair, the way they've done their white friends' hair.

The management of hair—the literal combing, plaiting, and grooming—presents a series of challenges for white parents of black children. There are of course the simple mechanics of hair technology, ways to take care of hair that curls so tightly it can "lock," knot up beyond the possibility of combing out. This is not something that people of European or Asian descent have usually had to deal with. Really curly European-type hair can get knots, get matted—but truly, this can be different. Velcro sticks to tight black hair; as a little kid Victoria got the Velcro closures on her down jacket stuck on her head, and they had to be slowly, painfully peeled off. It's glorious, magnificent, as it says in *Nappy Hair*: "God wanted hisself some nappy hair upon the face of the earth,"[10] and truly it is a wonder to behold and a thing to celebrate. But you have to know how to take care of it.

It's hard to discuss this bodily difference without sounding essentializing. Of course lots of African American, African European, and other peoples of Africa and the African diaspora have hair that is much like European or Asian hair, and people who are members of the white world may well have pretty kinky hair. Such is the nature of all bodily difference—it's across a continuum, and there's all this wonderful mixing going on besides. That said, the ignorance of white people about black hair (and black people about white hair) is still pretty striking.

Black people in America have less opportunity to remain ignorant about white folks. White people's products are mainstreamed. That is, pick up any popular-culture magazine, watch any ordinary television show, and you will probably see adds for white people's hair products. Black hair care, on the other hand, is specialized, found in *Essence* more than in *People*.

Even so, it's interesting what gets taken for granted and what pockets of ignorance remain. A young black woman, one of the students in the almost entirely black high school where Hesch teaches math, came up to him as he was seated at a desk, and ran her hand along his long fly-away gray hair: "I wanted to do that for so long—I wondered what it felt like."

We had Victoria's friend Ashley with us on vacation up in the Adirondack Mountains of New York one year when the girls were about seven or eight. Where we were staying, a rustic cabin on a lake, was a pretty white place indeed. Ashley knew lots of white people of course. But she'd apparently never seen so many *wet* white people before. She wasn't the kind of kid who asked a lot of questions, mostly just quietly observed things. But this seemed to be really bothering her. She came up from the lake one evening and worked up her nerve to ask: "Why, uhm, what's the, I mean, why does some people's hair, when it's wet, get so, uh, like *little*?" "Little"? I was confused, but Leah caught it: white people's hair, she explained, doesn't have much curl to it, so when it gets wet, it gets flat like that, hangs down along their heads.

Black people's hair, when it is wet, "turns back," fluffs right up—if it hasn't been chemically treated, it just pops back up into a soft cushiony mass. I look at hair that has been hot-combed straight, and when it gets wet, it reminds me of one of those resurrection plants—it returns to its glory, becomes *alive,* when you wet it. There is something willful, exuberant, energetic there in that hair. There's a little spot, right at the back of the neck, where the hair rarely grows long enough to really straighten. It's called "the kitchen." Henry Louis Gates describes it:

> If there ever was one part of our African past that resisted assimi-
> lation, it was the kitchen. No matter how hot the iron, no matter

how powerful the chemical, no matter how stringent the mashed-potatoes-and-lye formula of a man's "process," neither God nor woman nor Sammy Davis Junior could straighten the kitchen. The kitchen was permanent, irredeemable, invincible kink. Unassimilably African. No matter what you did, no matter how hard you tried, nothing could dekink a person's kitchen.[11]

These days white people seem fascinated with the intricacies of black hair. What does that Afro feel like? How do those long braids get added in? How do you get the beads to stay in? How long does that take? What makes those whadaycallem, *dreads,* stay in? Sociologist Ingrid Banks found that many of the black women and girls she interviewed resented the intrusion on their private space that white people's curiosity represented. And the white people sometimes feel that the black women are just being mysterious, not wanting to explain, closing themselves off. And sometimes maybe they are. That too comes with a history:

> I'm insulted, especially when white people come up to me and say they like my hair because I've had to listen to (their) value judgments to create who I am for so long. I don't want (them) to validate or not validate me. (Their) opinion has no bearing on what I choose to do anymore.[12]

The history, as all black/white history in America does, goes back to slavery. White masters, one historian suggests, could tolerate the skin color but not the hair of their slaves,[13] and Orlando Patterson agrees that hair was a more potent signifier than even skin color: "Hair type rapidly became the real symbolic badge of slavery."[14] The slave owners didn't even call it hair, but referred to it as "wool,"[15] in keeping with the animal imagery used for slaves.

That sets some context for the long history of straightening—hot combs, lye, relaxers, all kinds of attempts to get the kinks out, get African hair to lie flat like European hair. Madame C. J. Walker was one of several entrepreneurs who developed creams and lotions to protect the hair from the ravages of the hot comb—originally (pre-electricity) a metal comb you could heat over a fire and comb through the hair to straighten it. The heat, as you can well imagine, was uneven and hair got burnt all the time. One of the most recognizable hair styles of all time was the product of such an accident: Billie Holiday was getting ready to go onstage when she burnt off a big patch of hair on the side. She sent someone out quickly to a florist and pinned an orchid in place.[16] A star was born.

Straightening was politicized from the first. Madame Walker never used the word "straightening" at all—she was selling products to make hair healthier, stronger. But the battle was on. In 1937 a white writer called straightening an "insult" to the blacks. Garvey denounced it as an affront to race pride. Du Bois came to Walker's defense and said that was oversimplified, that straightening was no more an insult to race than was curling—something white women did all the time.[17]

But insult or not, race self-hatred or not, some kind of straightening—the hot comb, chemicals—became standard hair care for most African American people all the way through to the 1960s, when "Black Pride" and "Black is Beautiful" broke through that barrier.

I saw *Hair* on Broadway in 1969, and probably have most of the music of that show stored somewhere in the back of my brain. People of my generation do not have to be told that hair is political. We had *that* fight with our parents. I'm still having it; summer is starting as I write this, I turn fifty-six next week, and I just had Victoria help me put a nice purple streak in my gray hair (she's got blue and Leah's got green). My poor mother. It never stops. "I know, I know," she sighed when she saw me, "It's only hair."

It's only hair when white kids from Liverpool let it get shaggy, when white kids in Boston wear it long and straight, when white kids in New York spike it with gel, when old white women tint it blue or dye it purple. When Black people (and now I do want that capitalized, now I *am* talking about a cultural, political movement) refused to straighten their hair, it wasn't "only hair." It was about refusing to bring your body into line with a white standard.

Sometimes it seems as if the hair is the only thing people remember about the sixties. Angela Davis has found herself "reduced to a hairdo." She's written about it:

> I am remembered as a hairdo. It is humiliating because it reduces a politics of liberation to a politics of fashion; it is humbling because such encounters with the younger generation demonstrate the fragility and mutability of historical images, particularly those associated with African American history.[18]

By the 1980s, the Afro itself had gone out of style, which of course meant that it first came to be seen *as* a style more than as a political statement. But it actually seems to have worked as a statement: black women may be straightening their hair again,[19] but it doesn't mean what it did. Banks found, in her interviews with black women and girls, that especially for the younger women, straightening isn't about self-hatred or identifiably Eurocentric standards. Maxine Leeds Craig, in her work on black women, hair, and beauty ideals, similarly finds that the self-hatred idea is too simplistic these days.[20] Now, not surprisingly, hairstyles are more about individual, consumerist choice. Discussing hairstyle and empowerment, one young woman talked about what it means to just do the opposite of what your family tells you to do: "So it's about the choices and your ability to make those choices that brings empowerment."[21]

The ability to make those choices actually required a lawsuit.

In the 1980s, black female employees successfully sued American Airlines and the Hyatt Hotels over a policy that did not permit braids. The suit was a public relations success too, covered by Oprah, the *LA Times*, *20/20*, and more,[22] bringing the issues of black hair to "popular" (read "white") attention.

So now there are all these choices: braids, cornrows, box braids, extensions, straightening, short Afros, beads, dreadlocks—a veritable cornucopia of hairstyles to choose from. Americans, including African Americans, tend to think of all those styles as "African." It may not be quite that simple:

> My "Afrocentric" twists, which had evolved from my 1994 natural, were decidedly "Western" in South Africa. As disconcerting as it may be, the truth of the matter is what we think is a "black thing" in the States is often an "American" thing when viewed from the continent.[23]

It's not just black hairstyles that are being imported to Africa, it's the slang, the clothing styles, the music, the backwards baseball caps and the baggy jeans, and all:

> There was a time when I would have found all this diasporic, transatlantic cultural mixing a testament to black creativity. Now I fear it is nothing more than the end product of market hungry capitalists, eagerly proffering superficial representation of what it means to be black in America for the sake of profit in America *and* Africa.[24]

What is being sold is "African American culture." It is blackness as an ethnicity to be celebrated.

And here we have one of the more interesting conundrums I've ever dealt with, a bind between identity and culture as played out in the body.

In much of the more recent feminist writing about black hair, the ignorance of white women is exemplified by a stupid thing Susan Brownmiller once wrote.[25] She had no clue what "bad hair" meant to black women, and wrongly assumed it was pretty much what bad hair means to white women: limp and stringy. That is one thing you don't have to worry about with black hair. "Bad hair" of course meant—and yes, this is ugly and problematic—African hair, and "good hair" meant more European-like hair. By now there have also been volumes on African American and other African-diasporic colorism,[26] which is not one of the more desirable aspects of African American culture. It is understandable, rooted in slavery and racism, but still, not a good thing. For someone like me, without that history, tight, kinky black hair is *simply* beautiful. It's *magnificent*.

And that's where I was until Victoria was almost a year old, and the doorbell rang one August evening. "It's time." It was the sixteen-year-old kid from next door. "My mother sent me. She said to tell you it's time."

Her mother and I had talked—Victoria's hair needed some doing. It was bad enough that I was taking her to the beach with me and not shading her. The kid was getting darker and darker. As was I, but Victoria's always so far ahead of me there's no catching up. She was a glorious plum color. God, I loved that. I'd grease her skin, I'd slather her in oils, but no, I would not stop her from getting darker.

Her hair, though. The soft fluff that was her hair. I carried her in a Snugli, a front pack that had made it through Leah's infancy and hers—they hadn't invented such a smart thing when Daniel was a baby. I took her to work, taught my class with her asleep in it. I'd have my morning coffee and corn muffin while she slept in the Snugli and I got ready for class: yellow crumbs fell into her hair. Fell down, down, down into the soft tangle of her hair. I thought I'd have to vacuum the child. But it was time. My neighbor was right. No little black girl has a soft fluffy head like that. It needed to be "done." It was "undone." Untamed. Wild. I *liked* wild. That's a white aesthetic: soft fluff of hair, unbound.

I permed my own hair around then—I had no time to deal with my hair in the morning, and I envied Victoria hers. I went to the hairdresser and told him to make it as tight as you can. I was like "Eliza Jane," from a song by Vance Gilbert about a love between a black man and a white women: "What hair you didn't cut or perm you had braided back, hoping that your predetermined genetic situation might be mistaken for being black."[27]

I was also like a lot of other white women who have black kids: I liked it unrestrained and wild. And I wanted *her* to like it. I wanted my child to love her body, her self, her blackness, just the way she was. You see a lot of black children of white mothers with wild hair. I've come to spot them now on the streets. But now, to my eye *now,* they look "motherless."

And that's the conundrum: the little soft baby Afro, the wild young-girl hair, is intended by the white mother as a celebration of difference. It ends up being a disregarding of culture. A culture has developed—out of the experience of the hair itself, out of a response to racial denigration, and also out of self-love and pride and joy—that tells people how to deal with that hair. And loose, unbound, wild—that's not it.

When you listen to white folks who are raising black kids talk about it, they sometimes pride themselves on *not* doing their kids' hair. They're not the ones who are going to braid that little head of hair into submission. And for sure, they're not taking out the hot comb. White folks are too cool to straighten. They're teaching the kids to love themselves, they say. And maybe they are. But they're not teaching their kids how to be black in America.

It's trivial, I'm sure. It is, after all—and as my mother has come to accept—only hair. And yet not. It has something to do with identity, culture, and entitlement: it brings all those things together for me.

Way back towards the beginning of this book, I compared white people raising their black children with the men my mother knew through Parents Without Partners who were on their own, raising their daughters. My mother sometimes stepped in and helped—took a kid shopping for a party dress, and yes, maybe even to get her hair done.

I grew up in the fifties. Girls wore skirts with pleats, blouses with ruffles, and they hadn't yet (one of the great ironies of all time) put a "permanent press" setting on the iron. We wore a lot of labor-intensive clothing. We didn't yet have the rebels who wore jeans (we called them dungarees) and tee shirts (they were underwear) to school. I think that the rebellion against all that restrictive, time-consuming clothing was a good thing. But I don't think it was motherless girls who should have been the ones to do it. Their fathers had to find a way to get the ironing done, to tie the most perfect big bows on the party dresses, to keep their daughters from looking motherless.

And so it goes for me: my black friend could cut her daughter's hair into the only Afro in the classroom; I had to see to it that Victoria looked just like all the other black girls in the kindergarten class.

Black boys and men certainly have their hair issues as well. And in border-crossing families, that can indeed be a big hurdle. Any discussion of any black person raised by white people seems to have a few pages on hair, and the boys clearly don't have it easy. Jaiya John devotes five pages to discussing how he and his white mother tried to manage his hair in Los Alamos, with the nearest competent barber—a barber who'd done black hair—two hours away. He used humor a lot. That helps. ("What's that stuff you put in it? Anti ignorance cream. It's not working.")[28]

Many of the mixed-race, black/white families in America are white women and black men, and in those families one assumes the men just take their sons off to the barbershop. For the trans-racial adoptees and the single white women raising their black children, even if the black barbershop isn't two hours away, it's probably experienced as a fairly impenetrable place. For white women, try this little experiment, as I have—just walk into a black men's hair shop to ask a question, anything, even "Where's the nearest pay phone?" That is just not a place it's going to be easy to walk into for people in our bodies.

Hair is a place where a white mama is going to need a bit of help.

I am so, so unendingly grateful to the kid next door, and to Barbara Ellis, the mother of LaShaun, Leah's best friend from elementary-school days, and to the several kind and lovely women at our local beauty shops. The first two taught me the basics of black hair care. They sat down with brushes and grease and bands and taught me. I am a slow learner, and this took more than one lesson. And the others, the professionals—they didn't shame me in front of my child. They accepted my ama-teurish work as amateurish, not white. I'd read and heard so much—for instance, about the hair stylist who told the black daughter of a white woman, "You never, never let a white woman touch your hair! They don't know what they're doing." I was in dread. But no, I didn't face that.

I went in alone the first time, and said (gulp), "My daughter is black, she has kind of long, tight hair, and we want it braided for a special occasion. About how much would that cost?" I was asking about dollars because it seemed so much more acceptable than asking what I wanted to know: "Is this going to cost me emotionally? Are you going to give me a hard time? For having a black kid? For being moderately incompetent in the hair department?" (Though actually, by the first time I had it professionally done, I must say I wasn't all *that* bad.) By the time I walked in with Victoria, I wanted them to be expecting us, so any explanations, issues, concerns were taken care of, over and done.

The first woman I remember doing Victoria's hair, for a wedding I think it was, did a great job, and then took me aside and said, "My mother never did learn how to handle my kind of hair. I had real tight hair, and my mother never could do it. My brothers still remember how I used to cry and cry, try to hide on hair day. That's why I became a hair dresser—I love to do right by little girls."

I suppose, because she didn't say otherwise, that her mother was black.

I remember holding Victoria, alone at night, after that very first time she'd had her hair done. All the fluff was gone. My first two babies had been pretty bald. I can still almost feel in my hand the shape and texture of a bald white baby's head. And I can feel too the soft fluff that was Victoria's infant head. That first night, all tightly braided and bound, little ridges of hard hair and bumps of soft scalp felt so foreign. It was, I suppose, what people felt with a boy's "first haircut." (Daniel was a child of the seventies— did we cut hair then? It kinda got trimmed a bit, as I recall. No dramatic shaving off of little blonde baby locks, like in the books.) Years ago, when boys were kept "babied" for longer, somewhere around two or three, very abruptly, their parents cut their hair and dressed them "like boys." They were transformed. And that's what that first braiding felt like, a transformation. Was that my baby?

But the eye and the hand adjust, and yes, that is indeed your baby. The one with the cornrows, the beads, the head of "little balls," the star-shaped parts, or the zigzag rows. Or even—and this was yet another big adjustment—the one who's been hot-combed! Victoria went over to Ashley's grandmother's house one day, and came back hot-combed straight. That was the moment when I got hit head-on with the identity/culture conundrum. Was I going to call up Ashley's North-Carolina-born-and-raised, umpty-umpth-generation African American grandmother, and tell her I don't approve of hot combs? That I am trying to preserve a healthy black identity and self-love in my child, so spare us the straightening? I don't think so.

Hair was not a natural talent for me—I once snipped off a tiny (really, it was *very* tiny) piece of Leah's cheek while trimming her hair. But in the last fifteen years, I have not only learned how to manage a hot comb (I hardly burnt the kid at all, really), but I've braided and beaded hair like you couldn't imagine. I've braided Victoria's hair, the hair of white kids on the lakeside beach in upstate New York, of little German girls, Dutch girls, a Norwegian kid on a ferry between Sweden and Denmark—I've become quite the hair maven.

And something funny happened in all that time. I developed more than just a skill, as valuable as that is. I developed a bit of an eye, an aesthetic sense for black hair. I see it in a way I didn't use to, appreciate it in a way I couldn't have before. I understand about hair now. I went off to England and Germany with Victoria and I brought a hot comb, and enough beads, bands, and grease to last the months we'd be away, but I was looking for those black women to talk to about hair. Hair would be our way into whatever African-descent, African, or Caribbean community we could find. If I get to the moon and that black woman shows up with her brush and grease, I am ready—I know what we're talking about. I'm still masquerading in this skin, but I'm starting to realize that I'm not the same person. I've been transformed too.

It's easier to see change in someone else. I watched it in a friend, a white mother by birth of a black child. She too used to love the wild curls. And then she too learned to braid, to take proper care, community-standards-appropriate care, of her daughter's hair. The child is "mixed"; her hair is curly, but not beyond what you sometimes see in a white kid. My friend said one day, a couple of years after she'd been braiding her kid's hair: "What do white women with white kids do with hair like this?" She could no longer imagine how you manage it if you don't braid it. In two years, what she saw, *how* she saw, changed.

That kind of change is going on all around us in America. It's the process of assimilation, as cultures blend together. In a family that crosses borders, that assimilation can happen right in our homes, but it's not unique to us. Richard Rodriguez has written a lot about assimilation, how cultures blend together in the United States.[29] An interviewer asked if he was "in favor" of assimilation, and he said, "I am not in favor of assimilation any more than I am in favor of the Pacific Ocean or clement weather. If I had a bumper sticker on the subject, it might read something like ASSIMILATION HAPPENS." Culture, he points out, is fluid: "Culture is smoke. You breathe it. You eat it. You can't help hearing it—Elvis Presley goes in your ear and you cannot get Elvis Presley out of your mind."

Rodriguez recounts the interactions between Laotian Hmong refugee kids and Mexicans in Merced, California. The kids don't like each other. The Laotian kids were complaining: "They were telling me that the Mexicans do this and the Mexicans don't do that, when I suddenly realized that they were speaking English with a Spanish accent." Rodriguez talks about how he has gotten used to the colors Chinese Americans paint their houses in his home city of San Francisco—colors he once thought of as garish. Now, he says, he's become Chinese: he sees photographs of rural China "and I see what I recognize as home. Isn't that odd?"

Lennard J. Davis is a hearing child of deaf parents. I've read his work,[30] listened to him talk, and he sounds to me like a child of immigrants. He had a home language and home customs, and some issues moving between the world of home and the world outside. He didn't know, for example, what that odd noise was that buildings sometimes seem to make—the cooing of pigeons. He didn't know that because deaf people don't know that, and Davis was raised Deaf. Not "deaf" as in unable-to-hear, but Deaf, as a member of Deaf culture. Within Deaf culture these hearing children are acknowledged as members of the community, called "CODAs," children of Deaf adults. They are native speakers of ASL, American Sign Language. Leah learned ASL, and works as an interpreter. She's gotten very good at this. But it's not just about skill with a foreign language. I've watched it change her. She's become more expressive, learned to use her face, her whole body when she speaks—even when she's just speaking English. She's becoming Deaf. Isn't that odd?

And me? I'm assimilating into a new culture too. In some part of my soul, I'm starting to turn into a Black mama. I've got white skin and white privilege, but it becomes more and more of a masquerade. I got on this journey, the "plane to Holland," the trip to the new places Victoria's taken me to. I'm still me, of course—I know I'm a middle-aged white Jewish woman. But I went to a book party for Barbara Seaman, and while someone was praising her I called back a soft "hmm,mmm, she *is*" response—and remembered white folks don't do that. I look at Victoria growing up, talking about maybe doing her hair in dreadlocks, or (I know I completely deserve this, and anything my mother has to say about it is fair game, but *oh no!*) possibly shaving a Mohawk for the summer, and I'll *miss* doing and talking about hair.

Masquerading in this white skin, I've *become* the woman with the comb and the jar of grease looking to start a conversation.

19
Weaving a Way Home

Victoria once, as a little child, angry, overburdened perhaps, said—screeched, I guess would be the word—"I wish you'd never told me I was adopted!" We've come a long way in our "adoption nation" since the days when that was even possible, since the days when we thought children *shouldn't* be told. Adoption isn't a looming family secret, and adoptive families aren't trying to "pass." Border-crossing families, nonobvious families, are actually rather fashionable in some places now. We celebrate the diversity of our families, and there is much there to celebrate, in the new and different ways we're creating families. The mythical suburban 1950s family has perhaps lost its grip on our imagination—and not a moment too soon.

We've gotten better about thinking of the family as something other than a natural, biological unit. Family didn't use to need a lot of justification—it wasn't a choice. But now it is. A woman doesn't have to become a mother, a man doesn't have to produce sons, let alone daughters. If we have children now in America, it's because we want to. Or think we should want to.

When family was more clearly mandatory, in very traditional, patriarchal societies, adoption as we know it wasn't necessarily acceptable; it didn't meet the needs family was supposed to meet. As family became more a chosen way of life, adoption became a more acceptable route.

It helps to think of the needs of men and women separately here. Family became optional for men before it became optional for women. A man didn't have to produce sons to be a "real man" in industrialized America, as the economic role of children shifted from assets to liabilities. But women did feel enormous pressure to produce children, to become mothers. "Producing children" and "becoming mothers" separated. And so adoption was a kind of power for the powerless, a way for women to become mothers when the production of children didn't make all that much difference to men. But family has become more important for a lot of men too—family as a psychological space, family as a place of meaning in the world. And so men too—men married to women, men married to men, men alone—are more willing to mother, more willing to adopt, more willing to devote themselves to loving and raising children. Parenthood in America, for middle-class people at least, women and men, has become, as Ann Anagnost phrased it, "increasingly marked as a measure of value, self-worth and citizenship . . . which, incidentally, fuels the desire for adoption as a necessary 'completion' for becoming a fully realized subject in American life."[1]

And so we think less of family as a biological, hereditary unit, and more of family as a psychological unit, a haven, yes, but more than that, as a space where we can find meaning in the world, where we can do things that *matter*. It's a very private place, that family.

But that private space is in a larger world. I have a friend who taught ESL, English as a Second Language. She said if she never read the newspaper at all, she'd know what was going on in the world; she just had to read the roster of her new class, and she'd know where the trouble spots were on the planet. Is that what we are doing with adoption as well? We have to think about where the next group of large-eyed, beautiful, needful, war-ravaged, poverty-afflicted orphans is going to come from. Where are the "hot spots" that will produce the babies that Americans will lead the world in taking home? Where, within our own borders, are we producing the kind of need that creates the babies that we so warmly welcome?

Adoption has as its public face, meeting the needs of children, what used to be called "childsaving." But there are cracks in this public face, a shift in focus from the needs of children to the needs and interests of adopters.[2] After World War I, adoption was increasingly marketed to infertile couples, as a way to meet their needs for parenthood.[3] And that is very much today's understanding of adoption: a beautiful way to form a family. It is only inside of that perspective that the notion of a baby shortage makes any sense at all. If adoption were about helping parentless children, then the absence of children in need would be entirely a good thing, wouldn't it? But adoption became increasingly a way to meet the needs of middle-class white people for the children they needed to complete themselves as families.

When the kinds of children they wanted weren't available, they began—with good old American initiative—to look further afield. They began crossing borders of one kind or another.

When having a child—and even the particular kind of child you have—becomes a matter of choice, when you get to choose the object of your mothering work, it raises some questions about not only the objective of mothering (Why are we doing this? In whose interests?) but about the process itself: Just what is it that we are doing?

* * *

Private lives, families, intimacy, the stories of our lives, are always happening in a time and a place. There's always a context. History frames biography.[4] That's a whole lot easier to see when it's someone else's biography. The relationship between Phillis and Susannah Wheatley only makes sense if you know the history of slavery, know what was going on around them. That's obvious. The relationship between me and my children, you and yours, that too is happening at a particular historical moment—and that's a lot harder for those of us in the thick of it to see.

There's something about mothering that seems so timeless and universal. And maybe it partly is. It's that timeless part of it that makes me able to imagine that slave-owning woman suckling the orphaned slave baby. But I know that it's not all in the body, that there is this larger political, social context in which even our most intimate moments occur. Wendy Simonds and I have worked together over the years, and she points out to me where I get too "essentializing" about motherhood, skate too close to biological determinism. I can see Wendy's handwriting scrawled across this page and that whole section on "imagination": COWS!!!—our shorthand for the longer, social, feminist critique of essentializing motherhood.[5]

What I've been doing in this book is tracing the tensions between the intimate, personal lives we lead and the social contexts in which we lead them. I can feel the "cow" in me—the universal nurturing mammalian experience. And I can feel in me the contemporary American woman, so far removed from that. I am raising my children, as we all are, in a world in which "commodification—the process of transforming things into objects for sale—has become a totalizing cultural force," in which we live not just in a market economy, but in a "market society." We have to think about what that means, "for the things that we hold most dear, for our most intimate relationships, for our understanding of what it means to be human."⁶

Many people have been thinking about how the market society affects family. Arlie Russell Hochschild has been struggling with this, as a feminist and as a sociologist, for a long time.⁷ As women escaped the traditional family, the confines of that awful 1950s suburban mothering, who was there to step in? Caitlin Flanagan, from an almost flagrantly antifeminist perspective, has been writing about the problem in *The Atlantic Monthly,* praising Erma Bombeck and the competence of suburban housewives, and claiming that "Serfdom saved the women's movement."⁸ She's got a point: the people who stepped in were hired to do so. They were nannies. And given the way the world works, those nannies were mostly women of color, some of them from the same places from which we adopt our children. Americans pluck one child out of poverty to raise, and hire a woman mired in poverty to do a lot of the work of raising it. As my great-grandfather used to say, wonderingly, sometimes despairingly, in a long drawn-out musical way, "America!" Go figure.

We live in a world in which race still exists, in which racism explains a lot—different infant mortality rates across nations and across zip codes, playground taunts, wars, hairstyles, immigration patterns, where "babies come from," and where nannies come from.

We're watching the process of whiteness expand to include more groups, but we're not yet seeing the end of whiteness. It may well be that the Asian children and the South American children we're adopting will grow up to be white. But as long as whiteness exists, the children that some of us are raising will not be permitted whiteness.

That is the world in which we are living, the world in which

—and *for which*—we are raising our children. We cannot truly understand our families, what it is we are doing in that private space of home, if we do not raise our heads up and look around at that outside world.

Mothering is always about raising children in one world for another. One of my friends is the last-born child of Holocaust survivors. After they were liberated and gathered the remnants of family, her parents came to the United States, settled in Brooklyn, and—a testimony to life and renewal—had another child. Their little Yankee, they called her: the American child, the child of the new world. She grew up, as children of immigrants do, with a foot in each world. Yiddish at home, English outside, endless discussions about safety and freedom and what "everybody does" and what "we don't do."

But is that so different from the way we all grow up, the way we raise our children? Aren't they all the little Yankees, raised for the world in which we'll never be at home, the land of the future? Salman Rushdie writes about "imaginary homelands": "It may be argued that the past is a country from which we have all emigrated, that its loss is part of our common humanity."[9] It takes someone who has experienced loss and emigration to see that, to see how universal it is.

All knowledge is knowledge from somewhere. Every way of knowing the world is grounded, placed, located. When we're smack dab in the middle of things, sometimes it's hard to see what's there. But when we're off to one side, we might get a better view, a clearer angle of vision. That's what adoption does, that's what mothering across the racial borders does, and that's what the two of them combined do: they give us a vantage point.

Anybody mothering a white child in America is doing just that: mothering a *white* child, just as anybody mothering a black child is engaged in that project: mothering a *black* child. We're always mothering the race,[10] creating and recreating race in America in our mothering. But white people rarely see it. Black people tend to be more aware of it, from their own marginalized position, but even they don't necessarily see how much of what they are doing is located in the politics of race.

When I was at the Schomburg, speaking to the Fellows, I spoke to some of the little, daily differences of raising white and black children in America. I'd heard, from so many black friends and white friends raising black children, that storekeepers are quick to accuse black children of shoplifting. It was thus very important that Victoria learn never to give the appearance of shoplifting. She came up to me in a store once, a child of maybe three or four, with a little stuffed animal in her hand. "Look!" she was showing me. We were in upstate New York, she may well have been the only black person in that store. I took it from her and walked her back and said "We can look, but we can't touch things we haven't bought."

One of the Schomburg fellows stopped me: "That's just polite! That's got nothing to do with race!" I remembered Leah and Daniel in stores, picking up things to show me, carrying toys around and begging, whining. I had to teach them to be careful, and not drop things, and not damage fragile items, and all that. But I do remember sorting it out at the cash register sometimes: "Yes, you can take this, but no, not that." It was a privilege of whiteness I'd never, ever thought about while raising white children. A privilege of whiteness this young woman at the Schomburg never even *knew* about. I raised these children years apart. I never had to stand there and look at two kids and say, "You, the black one, put that down! You, the white one, you can hold it." But there it was, eight years apart, but no less real. I raised white children with the taken-for-granted privileges of whiteness, and a black child without. It gives one perspective.

Adoption, mothering across racial borders, they do that, they give you perspective. You could learn a lot.

But mothering isn't about learning; it's about teaching. We have to learn about the world to teach it to our children. Raising kids keeps us young, we say (while it ages us, grays our hair, and wrinkles our foreheads). It keeps us young because it forces us to encounter the *now* and the future, doesn't permit us to be mired in the land of the past.

That sounds reasonable, doesn't it? You have to be part of the world you're trying to raise your children to live in. So what if I say this: You can't raise your children in a Deaf world if they're going to grow up to be hearing. Lennard J. Davis's Deaf parents had to prepare him for the hearing world, didn't they? They had to see to it that he had hearing teachers and friends, people to correct his spoken language as they, automatically, as parents do, corrected his Sign. He had to have people who could explain that pigeon-cooing noise to him, soothe his childhood fears about strange sounds. It's only fair, reasonable.

Now try this: You can't raise your children in a hearing world if they're going to grow up to be Deaf. These have been fighting words for a long time. How much of Deaf culture do hearing parents owe deaf children? Is the simple fact of physical deafness something that gives the child a right to the heritage of Deaf culture? Or can deafness be "overcome" and the child totally assimilated into hearing culture?

And now, of course, move it to race: You can't raise your children in a white world if they're going to grow up to be black. Maybe our Asian children can grow up to be, for all intents and purposes, white, totally assimilated. But that is not what is happening in the immediate future for our black children.

What is there, beyond protégés and pets and trophies, to give us a model for raising black children in white America? There are Black mothers, the mostly women and some men who have done it, who have learned, and who can teach us. We white mothers can go to them. Because eventually we're going to have to *become* them. If you're the mother of a black child, you have a black mother's concerns and needs—and, for a while at least, a white mother's privilege. For a while, your black child will have a white family, the protective cloak of your whiteness cast over the child. But eventually, that child goes off, as children eventually do, and your whiteness won't do a thing for that kid.

A child, I've said, should not be a bridge. If we want to conquer the racial divisions of America, we should not be asking little children to lead us. You don't send children places; you have to take them by the hand. If your child is going to grow up without the privileges of whiteness, you'd best learn what those are.

But blackness in America is not defined entirely by the lack of whiteness, the lack of white privilege. It's also a culture, a number of different cultures, African American, the many and varied Afro-Caribbean, and other African-descent communities that live in America. The way to learn a culture is to be part of it, to become "acculturated." That's more than learning to cook ethnic foods, or dance ethnic dances, or even do ethnic hairdos. It is to undergo a transformation, to become someone you were not.

And the first thing you're likely to become is angry—very, very angry. Racism does still exist in America. Yes, I am saying that, and yes, I am white, and yes, you can trust me, and yes, I know that was the one thing I didn't want to say. With all of the black people in America telling us about racism, we don't need white people to confirm it.

But those of us who profit from American racism—those of us who have the children and all of the joy and wonder they have brought into our lives—have had a chance to see the face of racism from a different angle than most white people do. And we have more than just an obligation to fight racism. We have a stake in that fight.

Fighting racism, Ananya Mukherjea[11] reminds me, is a life-long work that will inevitably be frustrating and painful, and so cannot ride on abstract notions of justice alone. You have to be a saint to have that kind of strength, to maintain a lifelong commitment to the cause of righteousness, knowing full well that it won't be accomplished in your lifetime. To keep fighting the good fight, you need to feel personally compelled. And love can give you that strength and conviction.

Love—it does not conquer all, no. Our children need it, enormous, unending love, but they need more. They need a just and good world, a world beyond race and racism. The intense love of mothering, its tie to the future, gives you a place to stand. And a place to go.

Notes

Preface: A Word on Theory, Method, Language (and Source Notes)

1. Two conversations are going on in this book. One is between me and the reader—maybe another white mother of a black kid, maybe someone else who cares. The other conversation is between me and my colleagues. We tend to talk in obscure references, odd words. For my academic colleagues: check the notes. For the general reader: try doing what we do. Skim the notes first, and if something catches your attention, go back to it when it comes up. Academics are notorious for reading from the back.

2. In this I am following the language and logic of Sara Ruddick, *Maternal Thinking: Towards a Politics of Peace,* New York: Houghton Mifflin, 1989.

3. I thank Gail Letherby for drawing my attention to auto-ethnography as a body of literature, and for pointing out to me that I have been doing a form of it since before it actually had a name; see for example an article I did in *Qualitative Sociology* (Katz Rothman, "Reflections: On Hard

Work," Volume 9, number 1, 1986, pp. 48–53). For analysis and discussion of autoethnography as a method, see Ellis, Carolyn, and Arthur P. Bochner, *Composing Ethnography: Alternative Forms of Qualitative Writing*, Walnut Creek, CA: AltaMira Press, 1996; and Mykjalovskiy, E., "Reconstructing Table Talk: Critical Thoughts on the Relationship Between Sociology, Autobiography and Self-Indulgence," *Qualitative Sociology* 19, no. 1, 1996, pp. 131–151.

1. Family, Obviously

1. Garfinkel, Harold. 1967. *Studies in Ethnomethodology*. Englewood Cliffs, NJ: Prentice Hall.
2. Weitz, Rose. 2004. *Rapunzel's Daughters*. New York: Farrar, Straus and Giroux.

2. Our Story

1. Kennedy, Randall. 2003. *Interracial Intimacies: Sex, Marriage, Identity and Adoption*. New York: Pantheon, p. 475.
2. Ibid., p. 401.
3. Banks, cited in Kennedy, pp. 434–436.
4. Fogg-Davis, Hawley. 2002. *The Ethics of Transracial Adoption*. Ithaca: Cornell University Press.
5. Kennedy, p. 436, italics in original.
6. "Black children should be placed only with Black families whether in foster care or for adoption. Black children belong physically, psychologically and culturally in Black families in order that they receive the total sense of themselves and develop a sound projection of their future. Human beings are products of their environment and develop their sense of values, attitudes, and self concept within their own family structures. Black children in white homes are cut off from the healthy development of themselves as Black people." Day, Dawn. 1979. *The Adoption of Black Chil-*

dren: Counteracting Institutional Discrimination. Lexington, MA: Lexington Books, p. 98.

7. For a fuller discussion of this, see Roberts, Dorothy. 2002. *Shattered Bonds: The Color of Child Welfare*. New York: Basic Books.

8. Van Ausdale, Debra, and Joe R. Feagin. 2001. *The First R: How Children Learn Race and Racism*. Lanham, MD: Rowman and Littlefield, p. 15. The authors are citing D. Hughes, "Racist Thinking and Thinking About Race: What Children Know About but Don't Say," *Ethos: Journal of the Society for Psychological Anthropology* 25 (1997), pp. 117–125.

9. Rothman, Barbara Katz. 2001. *The Book of Life: A Personal and Ethical Guide to Race, Normality and the Human Genome Project*. Boston: Beacon Press. Originally published as *Genetic Maps and Human Imaginations*. New York: W. W. Norton & Co., 1998.

10. See for example Leslie Fiedler's *Freaks: Myths and Images of the Secret Self* (New York: Anchor Books, 1978), and fictional treatments such as Ursula Hegi's *Stones from the River* (New York: Simon and Schuster, 1997). I am also indebted to Jacki Ann Clipsham and Ruth Ricker for helpful conversations on dwarfism, community, and identity.

11. Dalmage, Heather M. 2000. *Tripping on the Color Line: Black-White Multiracial Families in a Racially Divided World*. New Brunswick, NJ: Rutgers University Press.

4. Motherhood in the Marketplace

1. Simonds, Wendy, and Barbara Katz Rothman. 1992. *Centuries of Solace: Expressions of Maternal Grief in Popular Literature*. Philadelphia: Temple University Press.

2. Ann Anagnost, "Maternal Labor in a Transnational Circuit," in Taylor, Janelle, Linda L. Layne, and Danielle F. Wozniak, eds. 2004. *Consuming Motherhood*. New Bruns-

wick, NJ: Rutgers University Press, p. 155; Mitchell, Lisa M. 2001. *Baby's First Picture: Ultrasound and the Politics of Fetal Subjects*. Toronto: University of Toronto Press.

3. Zelizer, Viviana A. 1985. *Pricing the Priceless Child: The Changing Social Value of Children*. New York: Basic Books.

4. Schabner, Dean. 2002. "Preacher Calls Adoption Fees Discriminatory." ABCNEWS.com, March 12.

5. Rothman, Barbara Katz. 1989. *Recreating Motherhood*. New York: W. W. Norton & Co. New edition, New Brunswick, NJ: Rutgers University Press, 2000.

6. Rothman, Barbara Katz. 1986. *The Tentative Pregnancy: Prenatal Diagnosis and the Future Of Motherhood*. New York: Viking/Penguin. New edition, New York: W. W. Norton & Co., 1993.

7. Taylor, Janelle, Linda L. Layne, and Danielle F. Wozniak, eds. 2004. *Consuming Motherhood*. New Brunswick, NJ: Rutgers University Press.

8. Simmel, Georg. 1957. "Fashion." *American Journal of Sociology* 62, no. 6: 61–76.

9. Bourdieu, Pierre. 1984. *Distinction: A Social Critique of the Judgement of Taste*. New York: Routledge.

10. McCracken, Grant. 1988. *Culture and Consumption: New Approaches to the Symbolic Character of Consumer Goods and Activities*. Bloomington, IN: Indiana University Press.

11. Zaretsky, Eli. 1976. *Capitalism, the Family and Personal Life*. New York: Harper Colophon.

12. Ibid.

13. For a fuller discussion, see for example the work of Arlie Hochschild's *The Second Shift: Working Parents and the Revolution at Home* (New York: Viking), 1989, and Ruth Schwartz Cowan's *More Work for Mother* (New York: Basic Books), 1985.

14. A German colleague, Ninette Rothmueller, has pointed out to me that: "To have and to get (thus also have had and got) translate into the SAME German word which is *bekommen.* Thus one could argue that there is not even the vocabulary in German to make the distinction, which is made in English. 'Have' also translates into *haben,* which does not describe a process but a fact (owning, inhabiting . . .) in the German language. Thus my idea is that saying (as a German speaker): 'She got a baby' pays attention to the fact that becoming a mother (here giving birth) is a process rather than a fact."

15. Annette Lareau has recently shown in detailed ethnographic work the ways that middle-class child rearing involves "concerted cultivation," rather than the "accomplishment of natural growth," which is the goal of working-class and poor families. Lareau, Annette. 2003. *Unequal Childhoods: Class, Race and Family Life*. Berkeley, CA: University of California Press.

16. Miller, Daniel. 1997. "How Infants Grow Mothers in North London." *Theory, Culture and Society* 14, no. 4: 67–88.

17. Miller describes this in painful, altogether too recognizable, detail.

18. Gaskin, Ina May. 1975. *Spiritual Midwifery*. Summertown, TN: The Farm Publishing Company.

19. See, for example, Brigitte Jordan's *Birth in Four Cultures: A Cross-Cultural Investigation of Birth in Yucatan, Holland, Sweden and the United States* (Montreal: Eden Press), 1983, and Sheila Kitzinger's *Birth at Home* (New York: Penguin Books), 1979, and *The Experience of Childbirth* (Baltimore: Penguin Books), 1972.

20. For example, Arthur and Libby Colman's *Pregnancy: The Psychological Experience* (New York: The Seabury Press),

1971, and Niles Newton's *Maternal Emotions: A Study of Women's Feelings Toward Menstruation, Pregnancy, Childbirth, Breastfeeding, Infant Care and Other Aspects of Their Femininity* (New York: Paul B. Hoeber, Inc.), 1977.

21. For example, Judith Walzer Leavitt's *Brought to Bed: Childbearing in America 1750–1950* (New York: Oxford University Press), 1986, and Dorothy Wertz and Richard Wertz's *Lying In: A History of Childbirth in America* (New York: Free Press), 1977.

22. Rothman, Barbara Katz. 1982. *In Labor: Women and Power in the Birthplace*. New York: W. W. Norton & Co. New edition, 1991.

23. Klassen, Pamela. 2001. *Blessed Events: Religion and Home Birth in America*. Princeton, NJ: Princeton University Press.

24. Robbie Davis-Floyd is the author of many important anthropological works on birth and midwifery, including *Birth As an American Rite of Passage* (Berkeley: University of California Press), 1992, and Davis-Floyd, Robbie, and Carolyn F. Sargent, eds., *Childbirth and Authoritative Knowledge: Cross-Cultural Perspectives* (Berkeley: University of California Press), 1997.

25. Klassen, *Blessed Events*.

26. For a fuller discussion, see Linda Blum's *At the Breast* (Boston, MA: Beacon Press), 1999.

27. Doulas are the most recent entrant into the birthplace: women with little training, hired to simply be present and supportive during a birth. See Bari Meltzer's unpublished dissertation. University of Pennsylvania, forthcoming.

28. Janelle Taylor, "A Fetish Is Born: Sonographers and the Making of the Public Fetus," in Taylor et al., *Consuming Motherhood*, pp. 187–210.

29. Scholl discusses the latest and fanciest developments in this

technology. Scholl, Sommers J. 2004. Unpublished paper. Eastern Sociological Society.

30. Taylor in Taylor et al.

31. Mitchell, *Baby's First Picture*, p. 125.

32. Anagnost in Taylor et al., p. 154.

33. Yngvesson, Barbara. "Going 'Home': Adoption, Exclusive Belongings, and the Mythology of Roots," in Taylor et al., pp. 168–186.

34. I thank Janelle Taylor for pointing out to me the particular vulnerability felt by lesbian mothers, who choose this route as a result.

35. Taylor, private communication.

36. Wozniak in Taylor et al., p. 77.

37. See chapter 6 in this book for a discussion of whiteness studies.

38. Anagnost in Taylor et al.

39. Kim, Hosu. Unpublished dissertation work. CUNY, forthcoming.

40. Landsman, Gail. "'Too Bad You Got a Lemon': Peter Singer, Mothers of Children with Disabilities, and the Critique of Consumer Culture," in Taylor et al., pp. 100–121.

41. Layne, Linda. 2003. *Motherhood Lost: A Feminist Account of Pregnancy Loss in America*. New York: Routledge.

42. Klassen, *Blessed Events*.

5. Adoption in the Age of Genetics

1. See the work of Katarina Wegar for a fuller discussion of the history of the sealed records controversy, including media events such as reunions on *Donahue, Geraldo, Oprah,* and *Sally Jessy Raphael*. Wegar, Katarina. 1997. *Adoption, Identity and Kinship: The Debate over Sealed Birth Records*. New Haven, CT: Yale University Press.

2. The popularization of ideas about "genealogical bewilder-

ment," being lost, not whole, unrooted, because of adoption, is best expressed in Betty Jean Lifton's work. See Betty Jean Lifton's *The Journey of the Adopted Self: A Quest for Wholeness* (New York: Basic Books, 1994) for what is probably the clearest statement.

3. Novy, Marianne, ed. 2001. *Imagining Adoption: Essays on Literature and Culture*. Ann Arbor, MI: University of Michigan Press, p. 1.

4. Kirk, H. David. 1964. *Shared Fate: A Theory and Method of Adoptive Relations*. New York: Free Press.

5. Johnson, Patricia Irwin, ed. 1985. *Perspectives on a Grafted Tree*. Fort Wayne, IN: Perspectives Press.

6. Solinger, Rickie. 2002. *Beggars and Choosers: How the Politics of Choice Shapes Adoption, Abortion, and Welfare in the United States*. New York: Hill and Wang.

7. Patton, Sandra. 2000. *Birth Marks: Transracial Adoption in Contemporary America*. New York: NYU Press, p. 172.

8. Keller, Evelyn Fox. 1995. *Refiguring Life: Metaphors of Twentieth-Century Biology*. New York: Columbia University Press.

9. See, for example, Wayne E. Carp's *Family Matters: Secrecy and Disclosure in the History of Adoption* (Cambridge, MA: Harvard University Press, 2000).

10. See William March's *The Bad Seed* (Sagebrush Publishing, 1997), the novel on which the movie was based.

11. For a rich discussion of adoption in literature, see Novy, *Imagining Adoption*.

12. Herrnstein, Richard J., and Charles Murray. 1996. *The Bell Curve: Intelligence and Class Structure in American Life*. New York: Free Press. But don't read this book unless armed with the rebuttals. I particularly recommend Fischer, Claude et al. 1996. *Inequality by Design: Cracking the Bell*

Curve Myth. Princeton, NJ: Princeton University Press; and Kincheloe, Joel L., Shirley R. Steinberg, and Aaron D. Gresson, eds. 1996. *Measured Lies: The Bell Curve Examined*. New York: St. Martin's Press.

13. I have discussed this in detail. Rothman, Barbara Katz. 1986. *The Tentative Pregnancy: Prenatal Diagnosis and the Future Of Motherhood*. New York: Viking/Penguin. New edition, W. W. Norton & Co., 1993.

14. Smith, Janet Farrell. 2002. "A Cautionary Tale on Genetic Testing: The Case of Foster and Pre-Adoptive Children," An Occasional Paper published by the John W. McCormack Institute for Public Affairs. University of Massachusetts, Boston; and *The Ethics of Genetic Testing in Adoption*. Transcript edited and with an introduction by Janet Farrell Smith. Colloquium March 10, 2000.

15. Kennedy, *Interracial Intimacies*, p. 388.

16. See, for example, Lori Andrew's powerful treatment of Johnny Spain's life story, *Black Power, White Blood: The Life and Times of Johnny Spain* (Philadelphia: Temple University Press), 2000.

17. Landsman in Taylor et al., *Consuming Motherhood*, pp. 100–121.

6. Talking About Race

1. I will be citing a number of the books I found most interesting and important in the growing field of whiteness studies, but it is by no means a comprehensive review of the literature.

2. Baldwin, 1984, in Roediger, David R. 1998. *Black on White: Black Writers on What It Means to Be White*. New York: Schocken Books.

3. Baldwin in Roediger, *Black on White*, p. 178.

4. Roediger, David R. 1991. *The Wages of Whiteness*. Verso.

5. Roediger, David R. 1994. *Towards the Abolition of Whiteness*. Verso.

6. Ignatiev, Noel. 1995. *How the Irish Became White*. New York: Routledge.

7. Allen, Theodore W. 1997. *The Invention of the White Race: The Origin of Racist Oppression in Anglo America*. Verso.

8. Jacobson, Mathew Frye. 1999. *Whiteness of a Different Color: European Immigrants and the Alchemy of Race*. Cambridge, MA: Harvard University Press.

9. Brodkin, Karen. 1999. *How Jews Became White Folks and What That Says About Race in America*. New Brunswick, NJ: Rutgers University Press.

10. Guglielmo, Jennifer, and Salvatore Salerno, eds. 2003. *Are Italians White?: How Race Is Made in America*. New York: Routledge.

11. Theodorson, George A., and Achilles G. Theodorson. 1969. *A Modern Dictionary of Sociology*. New York: Barnes and Noble Publishers.

12. For a fuller discussion, see Katz Rothman, Barbara. 2001. *The Book of Life: A Personal and Ethical Guide to Race, Normality, and the Human Genome Project*. Boston: Beacon Press. Originally published as *Genetic Maps and Human Imaginations*. New York: W. W. Norton & Co., 1998.

13. Duster, Troy. 1990. *Backdoor to Eugenics*. New York: Routledge.

14. For discussions of the biomedical reconstruction of race, see David Rothman's "Genes, Medicine, and the New Race Debate" in *MIT Technology Review*, June 2003. http://www.technologyreview.com/articles/rotman0603.asp.

15. My German friend, student, and colleague Ninette Rothmueller read this and said it "made her German soul shiver"

to think what that meant for Jews in Nazi medical experiments.

16. Moscou, Susan. Unpublished dissertation. Brandeis University, forthcoming.

7. Images

1. In Blum, Linda. 1999. *At the Breast*. Boston, MA: Beacon Press.

2. After reading so many times of this crucial, definitive moment in the life of the black child in the white family, I asked Victoria: "Have you ever heard a white person use the word 'nigger' in a bad way to a black person?" "No," she answered. And then quickly corrected herself: "Well, on television."

3. Ruddick, Sara. 1989. *Maternal Thinking: Toward a Politics of Peace*. New York: Houghton Mifflin.

8. Children of a Diaspora

1. Bird, Carmel. 1998. *The Stolen Children: Their Stories*. Australia: Random House.

2. George Yance, in *Who Is White?: Latinos, Asians and the New Black/Nonblack Divide* (Boulder, CO: Lynne Rienner Publishers, 2003), concludes that Asian Americans and Latinos will move into "whiteness," while there will be no assimilation of African Americans. He concludes—and I strongly agree—that the main racial issue in the U.S. has been and will continue to be the divide between blacks and whites. Thus a black/nonblack dichotomy is the best way to approach race in America, rather than the more typical white/nonwhite dichotomy.

3. Bussolini, Jeffrey. 2003. Unpublished doctoral dissertation. City University of New York.

4. McBride, James. 1996. *The Color of Water: A Black Man's Tribute to His White Mother*. New York: Riverhead Books.

5. Senna, Danzy. 1999. *Caucasia*. Madison, WI: Turtleback Books.

6. See, for example, Sandra Patton's *Birth Marks: Transracial Adoption in Contemporary America* (New York: NYU Press), 2000, and Jaiya John's *Black Baby, White Hands: A View from the Crib* (Silver Springs, MD: Soul Water Publishing), 2002.

7. Bartholet, Elizabeth. 1993. *Family Bonds: Adoption and the Politics of Parenting*. New York: Houghton Mifflin.

8. Ladner, Joyce. 1978. *Mixed Families: Adopting Across Racial Boundaries*. New York: Doubleday Anchor Books.

9. Day, Dawn. 1979. *The Adoption of Black Children: Counteracting Institutional Discrimination*. Lexington, MA: Lexington Books.

10. Simon, Rita James, and Howard Altstein. 2001. *Adoption, Race and Identity*. New York: Transaction Press; Simon, Rita James, Howard Altstein, and Marygold S. Melli. 1994. *The Case for Transracial Adoption*. Washington, DC: American University Press; Simon and Altstein. 1991. *Transracial Adoptees and Their Families: A Study of Identity and Commitment*. Westport, CT: Greenwood Press; Simon. 1981. *Transracial Adoption: A Follow Up*. Lexington, MA: Lexington Books; Simon and Altstein. 1977. *Transracial Adoption*. New York: Wiley Interscience.

11. Kennedy, Randall. 1994. "Orphans of Separatism: The Painful Politics of Transracial Adoption." *American Prospect* 5, no. 17 (March).

12. Dalmage, Heather M. 2000. *Tripping on the Color Line: Black-White Multiracial Families in a Racially Divided World*. New Brunswick, NJ: Rutgers University Press.

13. See, for example, Maria P. P. Root's *The Multiracial Experi-

ence: Racial Borders As the New Frontier (Thousand Oaks, CA: Sage), 1996, and Naomi Zack's *Race and Mixed Race* (Philadelphia: Temple University Press), 1993.

14. Compare the studies of Simon and Altstein.

15. See, for example, Lise Funderberg's work on the adult children of black/white parents, *Black, White, Other: Biracial Americans Talk About Race and Identity* (New York: William Morrow and Company), 1994.

16. Walker, Alice. 2000. *The Way Forward Is with a Broken Heart*. New York: Random House.

9. Protégés

1. In another time and place, in England when class functioned much like race, George Bernard Shaw described the *Pygmalion* experiment, the *My Fair Lady* story, with its unburdened joys of success for the experimenter/benefactor, and its very real costs of marginality for the protégée. By moving to the world of romantic rather than parental love, the story was able to have a happy ending.

2. Langston Hughes wrote about the problems inherent in the imbalance of power in the protégé relationship in his short story "The Blues I'm Playing," the story of a black woman pianist and her white woman benefactor. See "The Blues I'm Playing" in *The Ways of White Folks: Stories* (New York: Vintage), 1990, pp. 99–124.

3. I have written about this. Rothman, Barbara Katz. 2001. "Sometimes Being a Good Mentor Is a Personal Call." *The Chronicle of Higher Education*. April 5, p. B5.

4. Blockson, Charles L. 1989. *A Commented Bibliography of One Hundred and One Influential Books by and About People of African Descent (1556–1982)*. Amsterdam: A. A. Gerits and Sons, p. 16.

5. Sancho, Ignatius, and Vincent Caretta. 1998. *Sancho Letters:*

Letters of the Late Ignatius Sancho, an African. New York: Penguin Classics.

6. Olson, Richard. 2001. *The Gilded Cage: A Chamber Opera*. Unpublished libretto.

7. Gates, Henry Louis. 2003. *The Trials of Phillis Wheatley: America's First Black Poet and Her Encounters with the Founding Fathers*. New York: Basic Civitas Books.

8. When Susanna died, Phillis wrote to a friend who had come over with her on the same slave ship: "I was treated by her more like her child than her servant." See David Lander's article "The Prodigy," *American Legacy*, Summer, pp. 71–74. But the fact that she even had to say that calls it into question: What is the difference between being treated like her child and being her child?

9. Capitein, J. E. J. 2001. *The Agony of Asar: A Thesis on Slavery by the Former Slave, Jacobus Elisa Johannes Capitein, 1717–1747*. Grant Parker, translation and commentary. Princeton, NJ: Markus Wiener. And http://www.ghana300holland.nl/eng/gem_erf/capitein/content002.htm.

10. The Pet

1. Ladner, Joyce. 1978. *Mixed Families: Adopting Across Racial Boundaries*. New York: Doubleday Anchor Books, p. 32.

2. Kennedy, Randall. 2003. *Interracial Intimacies: Sex, Marriage, Identity and Adoption*. New York: Pantheon, p. 424.

3. Berlin, Ira, Marc Favreau, and Steven F. Miller, eds. 1998. *Remembering Slavery: African Americans Talk About Their Personal Experiences of Slavery and Emancipation*. New York: The New Press.

4. Ibid., p. xviii.

5. For a fuller history of the changing context of slavery, see Berlin et al, *Remembering Slavery*, Introduction.

6. Ibid., pp. xxxiv–xxxv.

7. Lorenzo Ezell interview, in Yetman, Norman R., ed. 1970. *Life Under the "Peculiar Institution": Selections from the Slave Narrative Collection*. New York: Holt, Rinehart and Winston, pp. 112–113.

8. Sterling, Doris, ed. 1984. *We Are Your Sisters: Black Women in the Nineteenth Century*. New York: W. W. Norton & Co., p. 12.

9. Ibid.

10. Robert Shepherd in Yetman, pp. 264–265.

11. Sterling, *We Are Your Sisters*, p. 5.

12. Mary Armstrong in Yetman, p. 20.

13. Novy in Novy, Marianne, ed. 2001. *Imagining Adoption: Essays on Literature and Culture*. Ann Arbor, MI: University of Michigan Press, p. 41.

14. Simpson, Eileen. 1987. *Orphans: Real and Imaginary*. New York: Weidenfeld and Nicolson, p. 68.

15. Marrone, Carmella. Unpublished doctoral research. City University of New York.

16. Boyce, Patricia Simino. 1998. *The Social Construction of Bereavement: An Application to Pet Loss*. Unpublished doctoral dissertation. City University of New York.

17. Thank you to Ananya Mukherjea for her phrasing here, and to Ananya and Gail Garfield for helping me verbalize and clarify the differences in these relationships.

11. The Trophy Child

1. Rose, Phyllis. 1998. *Jazz Cleopatra: Josephine Baker in Her Time*. New York: Doubleday; Wood, Ean. 2000. *The Josephine Baker Story*. London: Sanctuary Publishers.

2. Ananya Mukherjea pointed out the fascinating construction of "race groups" that Baker's collection represents, with its jumble of nationalities and religions standing in as "race" groups.

3. Rose, *Jazz Cleopatra,* p. 230.

4. Wood, *The Josephine Baker Story,* p. 272.

5. Rose, p. 232.

6. Ibid., p. 236.

7. Buck, Pearl S. 1964. *Children for Adoption.* New York: Random House.

8. Anagnost in Taylor, Janelle, Linda L. Layne, and Danielle F. Wozniak, eds. 2004. *Consuming Motherhood.* New Brunswick, NJ: Rutgers University Press.

9. Walker, Rebecca. 2001. *Black, White and Jewish: Autobiography of a Shifting Self.* New York: Riverhead Books, p. 24.

10. Walker, Alice. 2000. *The Way Forward Is with a Broken Heart.* New York: Random House, p. 51.

11. This photo was originally on the cover of *Time* magazine, a 1993 special issue on "The New Face of America." It was morphed from fourteen different racial-ethnic models, to construct a "new Eve." Marilyn Halter points out that the Betty Crocker ad for its seventy-fifth anniversary did a similar thing with seventy-five different women and produced a very close resemblance. (Halter, Marilyn. 2000. *Shopping for Identity: The Marketing of Ethnicity.* New York: Schocken Books, p. 180.)

12. Blockson, Charles L. 1989. *A Commented Bibliography of One Hundred and One Influential Books by and About People of African Descent (1556–1982).* Amsterdam: A. A. Gerits and Sons.

13. For one accessible version of this story, see www.museum of hoaxes.com.

14. Harris, Leon R. 1959. *Run, Zebra, Run.* New York: Exposition Press.

15. Ibid., p. 209.

16. Ibid., p. 260.

12. Imagine

1. Frank, Anne. 1991. *The Diary of a Young Girl* (The Definitive Edition). Otto Frank and Miriam Pressler, eds. Susan Massotty, trans. New York: Doubleday, p. 332.

2. Fox-Genovese, Elizabeth. 1988. *Within the Plantation Household: Black and White Women of the Old South*. Chapel Hill, NC: University of North Carolina Press.

3. For a discussion of white women who bore black children in the colonial South, see Kirsten Fischer's *Suspect Relations: Sex, Race and Resistance in Colonial North Carolina* (Ithaca, NY: Cornell University Press), 2002.

4. McBride's haunting book title. McBride, James. 1996. *The Color of Water: A Black Man's Tribute to His White Mother*. New York: Riverhead Books.

5. For a fictional treatment of white mothers of black children in the early twentieth century, see Cullen McCann's *This Side of Brightness* (New York: Metropolitan Books), 1998. In *Black, Jewish, and Interracial: It's Not the Color of Your Skin but the Race of Your Kin, and Other Myths of Identity,* author Katya Gibel Azoulay recounts that a colleague of hers, Andre Robinson, discovered that his aunt's maternal grandmother had been a Jewish woman who passed as a Negro in New Orleans in order to be the wife of a black minister (Durham, NC: Duke University Press, 1997), p. 184. These women *did* exist.

6. "Where the trail of evidence disappears, where intellect fails, one must rely on imagination, on possibilities that are technically unprovable." Hayden, Tom. 2001. *Irish on the Inside: In Search of the Soul of Irish America*. New York: Verso.

13. Home from the Schomburg

1. The authors of these memoirs—which really do stand as a powerful testimony not only to racism but to the liberal

white experience (or lack thereof) of racism in America—include: Maureen Reddy and Jane Lazarre, both white women who birthed their black children; Cheri Register, writing on the somewhat different experience of international adoptions in America; Sharon Rush, whose title practically defines the genre; and J. Douglas Bates, whose book is the only one I've found by a white adoptive father of black children. (Reddy, Maureen T. 1994. *Crossing the Color Line: Race, Parenting and Culture*. New Brunswick, NJ: Rutgers University Press; Lazarre, Jane. 1996. *Beyond the Whiteness of Whiteness: Memoir of a White Mother of Black Sons*. Durham, NC: Duke University Press; Register, Cheri. 1991. *"Are Those Kids Yours?": American Families with Children Adopted from Other Countries*. New York: Free Press; Rush, Sharon E. 2000. *Loving Across the Color Line: A White Adoptive Mother Learns About Race*. New York: Rowman and Littlefield; Bates, J. Douglas. 1993. *Gift Children: A Story of Race, Family, and Adoption in a Divided America*. New York: Ticknor and Fields.)

14. Going Places

1. Kingsley, Emily Perl. 1987. "Welcome to Holland." http://www.nas.com/downsyn/holland.html.

2. Goffman, Erving. 1963. *Stigma: Notes on the Management of Spoiled Identity*. Englewood, NJ: Prentice Hall.

3. Reddy, Maureen T. 1994. *Crossing the Color Line: Race, Parenting and Culture*. New Brunswick, NJ: Rutgers University Press, p. 22 (italics in original). Hettie Jones, in "Mama's White: Hettie Jones," (*Essence*, May 1994, p. 152), says, "I haven't forgotten, either, that walking down the street alone, I've got White all over my face . . . without my children I'm anonymously White. In all-White rooms, I'm part of the crowd."

4. Twine, France Winddance. 1999. "Transracial Mothering and Antiracism: The Case of White Birth Mothers of 'Black' Children in Britain." *Feminist Studies,* Fall.

5. Moosnick, Nora Rose. 2004. *Adopting Maternity: White Women Who Adopt Transracially or Transnationally.* Westport, CT: Praeger Publishers, p. 55.

6. Ibid., p. 40.

15. Culture: Celebrating Diversity

1. Buck, Pearl. 1954. *Johnny Jack and His Beginnings.* New York: The John Day Company, p. 22.

2. John, Jaiya. 2002. *Black Baby, White Hands: A View from the Crib.* Silver Springs, MD: Soul Water Publishing, p. 49.

3. Ibid., p. 148 (italics in original).

4. See, for example, Sandra Patton's *Birth Marks: Transracial Adoption in Contemporary America* (New York: New York University Press), 2000; Lisa Jones's *Bulletproof Diva: Tales Of Race, Sex, and Hair* (New York: Doubleday), 1994; Katya Gibel Azoulay's *Black, Jewish, and Interracial: It's Not the Color of Your Skin but the Race of Your Kin, and Other Myths of Identity* (Durham, NC: Duke University Press), 1997; Rebecca Walker's *Black, White and Jewish: Autobiography of a Shifting Self* (New York: Riverhead Books), 2001; and Rita James Simon and Rhonda M. Roorda's *In Their Own Voices: Transracial Adoptees Tell Their Stories* (New York: Columbia University Press), 2000.

5. Zola, Irving Kenneth. 1996. *Meaningful Relationships/Moments in Time.* Boston, MA: private publication, p. 36.

6. From Adam Pertman's 2000 book of that title, *Adoption Nation: How the Adoption Revolution Is Transforming America.* New York: Basic Books.

7. Halter, Marilyn. 2000. *Shopping for Identity: The Marketing of Ethnicity.* New York: Schocken Books, p. 5.

8. Quoted in Halter, ibid., p. 6.
9. Robert Wood in Halter, *Shopping for Identity,* p. 9.
10. Halter, *Shopping for Identity,* p. 23.
11. Pertman, *Adoption Nation,* p. 77.
12. Ibid., p. 68.
13. Ibid., p. 69.
14. Moosnick, Nora Rose. 2004. *Adopting Maternity: White Women Who Adopt Transracially or Transnationally.* Westport, CT: Praeger Publishers, p. 65.
15. Maryanne Novy called the work of Mary Waters to my attention on this issue. Waters studied white Catholic suburbanites in the late 1980s and found an almost contentless symbolic ethnicity, which "makes you both special and simultaneously part of a community. It is something that comes to you involuntarily through heredity and at the same time it is a personal choice. And it allows you to express your individuality in a way that does not make you stand out as in any way different from all kinds of other people." (Waters, Mary. 1990. *Ethnic Options.* Berkeley, CA: University of California Press, p. 150.)
16. I scan my collection of children's books, thirty years' worth of collecting children's books, looking for this one, Pete Seeger's *Abiyoyo* (New York: Aladdin Books, 1994), and am overwhelmed with the world we've created there: so diverse! Little brown babies with blonde grandmas, great black folks in history, Gloria goes to gay pride, great peace marches, free to be a family, the boys and their babies. If wishing made it so, if storytelling made the world, what a world we'd have! And yet, if we can't imagine it, we can't make it, and imagining it, sharing that dream with our children, is one of the places we have to start.
17. Senna, Danzy. 1999. *Caucasia.* Madison, WI: Turtleback Books.

18. Senna, in a book edited by someone whose name alone has to make you smile, thinking of multicultural America: Claudine Chiawei O'Hearn. 1998. *Half and Half: Writers on Growing Up Biracial and Bicultural*. New York: Pantheon Books, p. 12.

19. Senna in O'Hearn, *Half and Half,* p. 20.

16. Identity: Pride and Joy

1. Dalmage, Heather M. 2000. *Tripping on the Color Line: Black-White Multiracial Families in a Racially Divided World*. New Brunswick, NJ: Rutgers University Press.

2. I'd love to understand why the legacy of Bureau of Indian Affairs treaties that only counted "full or half-blooded Indians" remains in our language—the expression of "full-blood" is still routinely used in the United States only when discussing Native Americans.

3. Patton, Sandra. 2000. *Birth Marks: Transracial Adoption in Contemporary America*. New York: NYU Press, p. 173.

4. Intermix, www.intermix.org.uk.

5. Maria P. P. Root, "A Bill of Rights for Racially Mixed People," in Root, ed. 1996. *The Multiracial Experience: Racial Borders As the New Frontier*. Thousand Oaks, CA: Sage Publishing, pp. 3–14.

6. I realize that this is not unlike the more general critique of the black middle class; these are indeed very complex problems. My point is that they need to be addressed at a larger-than-psychological level.

7. Azoulay, Katya Gibel. 1997. *Black, Jewish, and Interracial: It's Not the Color of Your Skin but the Race of Your Kin, and Other Myths of Identity*. Durham, NC: Duke University Press, p. 128.

8. Ibid.

9. Ibid., p. 129.

10. Davis, Leon G., compiler. *Black-Jewish Relations in the United States, 1752–1984: A Selected Bibliography*. Westport, CT: Greenwood Press.

11. Ibid., p. x.

12. Ibid., p. xi.

13. For a study of that particular clash, see Maurice R. Berube and Marilyn Gittel's *Confrontation at Ocean Hill-Brownsville: The New York School Strikes of 1968* (New York: Praeger), 1969.

14. Walker, Rebecca. 2001. *Black, White and Jewish: Autobiography of a Shifting Self*. New York: Riverhead Books.

15. McBride, James. 1996. *The Color of Water: A Black Man's Tribute to His White Mother*. New York: Riverhead Books.

16. Jones, Hettie. 1990. *How I Became Hettie Jones*. New York: Dutton.

17. Zack, Naomi. 1993. *Race and Mixed Race*. Philadelphia: Temple University Press.

18. Lazarre, Jane. 1996. *Beyond the Whiteness of Whiteness: Memoir of a White Mother of Black Sons*. Durham, NC: Duke University Press.

19. See, for example, Lise Funderburg's *Black, White, Other: Biracial Americans Talk About Race and Identity* (New York: William Morrow and Co.), 1994; Kathleen Odell Korgen's *From Black to Biracial: Transforming Racial Identity Among Americans* (Westport, CT: Praeger), 1993; Maria P. P. Root's *The Multiracial Experience*; and of course Azoulay. In addition, Jewish families may be overrepresented among white families that adopt black and other nonwhite babies. In addition to all the same reasons for which they partner with black people, there is also the fact that many American adoption agencies are faith-based, and unwilling to place babies of Christian women with Jewish couples. There are

a number of support groups specifically for Jewish families made multiracial via adoption.

20. Azoulay, *Black, Jewish, and Interracial,* p. 187.
21. Ibid., p. 137.
22. Ibid., p. 138.
23. Ibid., p. 139.

17. Entitlement: That Can't Be Your Baby

1. Kelleher, Christa. 2003. *Postpartum Matters: Women's Experience of Medical Surveillance, Time and Support After Birth.* Unpublished doctoral dissertation. Brandeis.
2. Lorber, Judith. 1993. "Believing Is Seeing: Biology As Ideology." *Gender & Society* 7:568–81.
3. Dalmage, Heather M. 2000. *Tripping on the Color Line: Black-White Multiracial Families in a Racially Divided World.* New Brunswick, NJ: Rutgers University Press, p. 40.
4. Ibid., p. 85.
5. Register, Cheri. 1991. *"Are Those Kids Yours?": American Families with Children Adopted from Other Countries.* New York: Free Press.
6. Dalmage, *Tripping on the Color Line,* p. 48.
7. Moosnick, Nora Rose. 2004. *Adopting Maternity: White Women Who Adopt Transracially or Transnationally.* Westport, CT: Praeger Publishers, p. 93.
8. Ibid.
9. Ibid., p. 141.
10. Collins, Patricia Hill. 1990. *Black Feminist Thought.* Boston: Unwin Hyman.
11. Stack, Carol B. 1979. *All Our Kin: Strategies for Survival in Black Community.* New York: Peter Smith Publisher.
12. Twine, France Winddance. 1999. "Transracial Mothering

and Antiracism: The Case of White Birth Mothers of 'Black' Children in Britain." *Feminist Studies*, Fall, p. 4.

13. Ibid.
14. Ibid.
15. Dalmage, *Tripping on the Color Line*, p. 208.
16. Ibid.
17. Ibid., p. 216.

18. Hair: Braiding Together Culture, Identity, and Entitlement

1. See the lovely chapter "In the Kitchen," chapter 4 of Henry Louis Gates Jr.'s *Colored People: A Memoir* (New York: Vintage), 1994.

2. And a good version of that experience is found in Lisa Jones's *Bulletproof Diva: Tales of Race, Sex and Hair* (New York: Doubleday), pp. 11–16.

3. Heron, Carolivia. 1997. *Nappy Hair*. New York: Knopf. Ingrid Banks starts her wonderful book *Hair Matters: Beauty, Power, and Black Women's Consciousness* (New York: New York University Press, 2000) with the details of what happened when Ruth Sherman, a white teacher, read this to her Brooklyn class, and a thoughtful discussion of its significance. See pages 1–3.

4. Sinclair, Abiola. 1999. "Black Hair in a Cultural and Political Movement." Unpublished presentation to the Baruch College Women of Color Network, New York City, February 11, 1999.

5. Rose Weitz has done a wonderful book on the meaning of hair for women, black and white, in contemporary America: *Rapunzel's Daughters* (New York: Farrar, Straus and Giroux), 2004. That Rose and I were both working on hair as research projects at the same time meant that something

like one-third of all living sociologists who had studied midwifery were working on hair. Make of that what you will.

6. Byrd, Ayana D., and Lori L. Tharps. 2001. *Hair Story: Untangling the Roots of Black Hair in America*. New York: St. Martin's Press; Banks, Ingrid. 2000. *Hair Matters: Beauty, Power, and Black Women's Consciousness*. New York: New York University Press; Craig, Maxine Leeds. 2002. *Ain't I a Beauty Queen? Black Women, Beauty, and the Politics of Race*. New York: Oxford University Press; Rooks, Noliwe M. 1996. *Hair Raising: Beauty, Culture, and African American Women*. New Brunswick, NJ: Rutgers University Press; and one particularly wonderful collection that crosses all kinds of categories: Harris, Juliette, and Pamela Johnson, eds. 2001. *Tenderheaded: A Comb-Bending Collection of Hair Stories*. New York: Pocket Books.

7. Sieber, Roy, and Frank Herreman. 2000. *Hair in African Art and Culture*. New York: The Museum for African Art; Mastalia, Francesco, and Alfonse Patagno. 1999. *Dreads*. New York: Artisan. A traveling exhibit, *HairStories* is sponsored by MIZANI, a division of L'Oréal USA. The exhibition is organized by the Scottsdale Museum of Contemporary Art, and supported in part by an award from the National Endowment for the Arts. In Chicago, *HairStories* is sponsored by the Chicago Office of Tourism as part of the citywide summer initiative Embrace Art in Chicago: Summer 2004.

8. Cornwell, JoAnne. 1997. *That Hair Thing: And the Sisterlocks Approach*. San Diego, CA: Sisterlocks Publishing.

9. Due, Tananarive. 2000. *The Black Rose*. New York: Ballantine Books; and Bundles, A'Lelia. 2001. *On Her Own Ground: The Life and Times of Madame C. J. Walker*. New

York: Scribner. The major point of contention is about the meaning of straightening as applying a Eurocentric standard to African-descent people. The other issue is that of commercialization. Hair care has, since those early days of Madame C. J. Walker and her contemporaries, provided income and work-pride for countless African American women. Gail Garfield points out to me that undocumented African and Caribbean women continue to use hair as a form of off-the-books employment, setting up on street corners and peddling their skills. And at the other extreme of the market, large corporations like L'Oréal have been buying out black hair-care product companies.

10. Heron, *Nappy Hair*, unnumbered pages.
11. Gates, *Colored People*, p. 25.
12. Banks, *Hair Matters*, p. 72.
13. Morrow, Willie L. 1973. *400 Years Without a Comb: The Untold Story*. San Diego: Black Publishers of San Diego, quoted in Banks, *Hair Matters*, p. 7.
14. Patterson, Orlando. 1982. *Slavery and Social Death: A Comparative Study*. Cambridge, MA: Harvard University Press, quoted in Banks, *Hair Matters*, p. 8.
15. White, Shane, and Graham White. 1995. "Slave Hair and African American Culture in the Eighteenth and Nineteenth Centuries," *The Journal of Southern History* LXI, no. 1 (February), pp. 45–76.
16. Harris and Johnson, eds., *Tenderheaded*, pp. 21–22.
17. See a fuller discussion of this in Mark Higbee's "The Hairdresser and the Scholar," in Harris and Johnson, eds., *Tenderheaded*, pp. 11–14, and in Bundles, *On Her Own Ground*.
18. Davis, Angela Y. 1994. "Afro Images: Politics, Fashion, and Nostalgia. *Critical Inquiry* 21, no. 1, p. 37.
19. Rose Weitz, in *Rapunzel's Daughters*, reports a much higher percentage of black women wearing their hair straightened

than I was at first willing to believe. Partly it's being in academic settings, partly it's being in New York, but also partly I just wasn't willing to see. I listened to Rose Weitz, started to do some informal counts, and yes, a lot of black women are straightening their hair these days. Rebecca Carroll, interviewing approximately fifty girls for a book that was published in 1997, *Sugar in the Raw* (New York: Three Rivers Press, p. 142) found 90 percent had straightened and/or permed their hair, and compares that to eating disorders.

20. Craig, *Ain't I a Beauty Queen?*
21. Banks, *Hair Matters,* p. 73.
22. Discussed in Banks, *Hair Matters,* among others.
23. Russell, Paitra D. "On Short Nappy Hair and the Business of Blackness: From Ohio to South Africa." in Harris and Johnson, eds. *Tenderheaded,* p. 218.
24. Ibid., p. 220.
25. Brownmiller, Susan. 1984. *Femininity.* New York: Simon and Schuster.
26. See for example, Kathy Russell, Midge Wilson, and Ronald Hall's *The Color Complex: The Politics of Skin Color Among African Americans* (New York: Anchor), 1993.
27. Vance Gilbert, "Eliza Jane," http://www.vancegilbert.com/14lyrics.shtml.
28. John, Jaiya. 2002. *Black Baby, White Hands: A View from the Crib.* Silver Springs, MD: Soul Water Publishing, pp. 101–106 (quote, p. 106).
29. Rodriguez, Richard. 2003. "'Blaxicans' and Other Reinvented Americans." *The Chronicle of Higher Education.* September 12, 2003, pp. B10–11 (all quotes, p. B11).
30. Davis, Lennard J. *My Sense of Silence: Memoirs of a Childhood with Deafness.* 2000. Chicago: University of Illinois Press.

19. Weaving a Way Home

1. Anagnost, in Taylor, Janelle, Linda L. Layne, and Danielle F. Wozniak. 2004. *Consuming Motherhood*. New Brunswick, NJ: Rutgers University Press.

2. I thank Susan Frelich Appleton for sharing her thoughts and her forthcoming work on this distinction between public and private faces of adoption, and the inherent contradiction in the idea of a "baby shortage": "Adoption in the Age of Reproductive Technology," University of Chicago Legal Forum Symposium, *The Public and Private Faces of Family Law*.

3. For histories of adoption, see Elaine Tyler May's *Barren in the Promised Land: Childless Americans and the Pursuit of Happiness* (Cambridge, MA: Harvard University Press), 1997, and Wayne E. Carp's *Family Matters: Secrecy and Disclosure in the History of Adoption* (Cambridge, MA: Harvard University Press), 2000.

4. This line of thinking draws, of course, on the classic work of C. Wright Mills, *The Sociological Imagination* (New York: Oxford University Press), 1959.

5. Alison Berg, in *Mothering the Race: Women's Narratives of Reproduction, 1890–1939* (Chicago: University of Illinois Press, 2002, p. 17), says, "The issue of motherhood threatens to seduce the most vigilant anti-essentialist."

6. From *The Hedgehog Review* 5, no. 2, Summer 2003, special issue on "The Commodification of Everything," as cited in *The Chronicle of Higher Education*, December 19, 2003, online at http://chronicle.com.

7. See especially Arlie Russell Hochschild's *The Managed Heart: The Commercialization of Human Feeling* (Berkeley, CA: University of California Press), 1985, and her most recent work on this, *The Commercialization of Intimate Life* (Berkeley, CA: University of California Press), 2003.

8. Flanagan, Caitlin. 2003. "Housewife Confidential: A Tribute to the Old-Fashioned Housewife, and to Erma Bombeck, her Champion and Guide." *The Atlantic Monthly,* September, pp. 141–149, and Flanagan, Caitlin. 2004. "How Serfdom Saved the Women's Movement." *The Atlantic Monthly,* March 2004.

9. Rushdie, Salman. 1992. *Imaginary Homelands: Essays and Criticism, 1981–1991.* New York: Granta Books.

10. From Berg's title.

11. I thank Ananya Mukherjea for sharing conversations she and Craig Willse have had.

Acknowledgments

Many people were required to keep this book afloat. I owe much to Helene Atwan for suggesting it as a book in the first place.

Without the readers who carefully and oh-so-quickly responded chapter by chapter, I could never have done this. Thanks to my virtual study group; Heather Dalmage, Gail Garfield, and Eileen Moran read every chapter, often with overnight turnaround, and always with insightful, challenging comments.

Ananya Mukherjea entered the project as a research assistant and grew to be much more. Ninette Rothmueller provided a European point of contrast, and sent beams of sunshine my way. Daniel Colb Rothman and now Leah Colb Rothman have officially entered "study group" status, and I thank them for their help. Others who read selected chapters include Marianne Novy, Linda Katz Sanderson, Maren Lockwood Carden, Christine Hauskeller, and Wendy Simonds, each providing very special, very particular kinds of much-needed help. Janelle Taylor pushed my thinking and my work, and virtually guided me through a course in consumption studies.

I am deeply indebted to the Scholars Program of the Schomburg Library, and to Gail Garfield for helping me find my way there. Thanks especially to Colin Palmer, Miriam Jimenez, and fellow-Fellows Rhonda D. Frederick, Chouki El Hamel, Michele Mitchell, Samuel Kelton Roberts, and Jeffrey Thomas Sammons. I owe thanks as well to the Professional Staff Congress of the City University of New York and to two of my colleagues at Baruch College who were particularly helpful at an early stage of the project, Carolle Charles and Martia Goodson.

Among the many friends and family to whom I owe thanks are of course my husband, Hesch Rothman, and my mother, Marcia Katz Berken, each of whom helped keep the home fires burning. I owe a particular debt to Barbara Ellis, Alice Jackson, and her daughter Shirelle, and to Bettye Vann and her extended family.

This book absolutely would not have happened without Victoria Colb Rothman: I thank her with all my heart.

Index

Nishi, Setsuko Matsunaga (Suki), 32
Novy, Marianne: adoption myths by, 55–56; on *Daniel Deronda*, 126
nurturance: human connections formed from, 132; of infancy, 59; intimacy of, 133; of pets, 128–29; of pregnancy, 59–60; of trophy children, 134

objects: attachments to, 130–31; function of, 32; intrinsic beauty of, 32; replaceability of, 33; value of, 32–33
Olson, Richard, 115
"one drop" rule, 104
ordinariness, 6
othermothers, 202–3

parenthood, 7; defined by genetics, 65; as mentorship, 112; teaching compared to, 113; as value measure, 226
parenting, x; benefactor as role of, 112; ending years of, 13; journey compared to, 154; meaning of, 98; mothering compared to, 98–99. *See also* white parenting
Parents Without Partners (PWP), 97, 218
participant observation, 6
Passover, 162
Patterson, Orlando, 212
Patton, Sandra, 59, 181
Perspectives on a Grafted Tree (Johnson), 56
Pertman, Adam, 171
pet imagery, 127
pet model, 126
pets, 101–2, 149, 232; adoptees as, 120–21; children as, 127–33; loss of, 131; nurturance of, 128–29; slavery's ties to, 121; slaves as, 124; transracial adoptees as, 127–33; trophy children as, 134
phenotype, 64–65
phenylketonuria (PKU), 70
PKU. *See* phenylketonuria

PKU screening, 71–72
planned-for children, 189–91
political adoptions, 57
Political-Theological Dissertation Examining the Question: Is Slavery Compatible with Christian Freedom Or Not? (Capitein), 117
poverty, 18–19
pregnancy, nurturance of, 59–60
presenting: as family, 4–5, 198; as woman, 4–5
Pricing the Priceless Child (Zelizer), 34
protégé, 101–2, 149, 232; benefactors' roles with, 112; Capitein, Jocobus Elisa Johannes, as, 116–18; history of, 111; Sancho, Ignatius, as, 115; Wheatley, Phillis, as, 115–16
PWP. *See* Parents Without Partners

Quakers, 19

race, ix, x, xi, 28, 77, 79; of Aboriginal people, 89; American ideas about, 29; as biological category, 88, 89; biomedical construction of, 85; categories, 87; children's view of, 19–20; clarity of, 89; cost's ties to, 160; disvaluing of, 187; ethnicity versus, 81–82; experienced in family, 167–68; as fundamental cultural hierarchy, 97–98; groups, 82; hair's relation to, 206; overcoming of, 140; as physical characteristics, 90; relations, 81; sociology's acceptance of, 81; in soul, 90; as system of power, 179; as way of life, 92. *See also* transracial adoption
race matching, 14, 72
Race Traitor (journal), 80
raceless race, 138
racelessness of white, 78–79
racial essentialism, 82
racial identity, 183–84, 186; of African adoptees, 109; in Australia, 89